DURKHEIM

AND THE

JEWS OF FRANCE

CHICAGO STUDIES IN
THE HISTORY OF JUDAISM
A Series Edited by
William Scott Green

Durkheim

AND THE

Jews of France

Ivan Strenski

THE UNIVERSITY OF CHICAGO PRESS

CHICAGO & LONDON

IVAN STRENSKI is the Holstein Family Community Professor of Religious Studies at the University of California, Riverside. He is the author of *Four Theories of Myth in Twentieth Century History* and *Religion in Relation: Method, Application, and Moral Location,* and the editor of *Malinowski and the Work of Myth.*

The University of Chicago Press, Chicago 60637
The University of Chicago Press, Ltd., London
© 1997 by The University of Chicago
All rights reserved. Published 1997
Printed in the United States of America
06 05 04 03 02 01 00 99 98 97   1 2 3 4 5

ISBN: 0-226-77723-5 (cloth)
ISBN: 0-226-77724-3 (paper)

Library of Congress Cataloging-in-Publication Data

Strenski, Ivan.
    Durkheim and the Jews of France / Ivan Strenski.
        p.   cm. — (Chicago studies in the history of Judaism)
    Includes bibliographical references and index.
    ISBN 0-226-77723-5 (cloth : alk. paper). — ISBN 0-226-77724-3 (pbk. : alk.
        paper)
        1. Jews—France—Intellectual life. 2. Durkheim, Emile, 1858–1917.
    3. France—Intellectual life—19th century. 4. France—Intellectual life—
    20th century. 5. France—Ethnic relations.
    I. Title. II. Series.
    DS135.F83S841997
    305.892′4044—DC21   96-47904
                                                                        CIP

FOR MY DEAR BROTHER,

RICHARD PETER STRENSKI

31 October 1944–21 July 1995

◆

*I always expected to live a long life and
   to die at home in comfort.
I was like a tree whose roots always have water
   and whose branches are wet with dew.
Everyone was always praising me, and my
   strength never failed me.
When I gave advice, people were silent and
   listened carefully to what I said; they
   had nothing to add when I had finished.
My words sank in like drops of rain; everyone
   welcomed them just as farmers welcome
   rain in spring.
I smiled on them when they had lost confidence;
   my cheerful face encouraged them.
I took charge and made decisions; I led them
   as a king leads his troops, and gave
   them comfort in their despair.*

JOB 29: 18–25

CONTENTS

ACKNOWLEDGMENTS

I should like to thank the following colleagues and friends for the advice, useful or not, the kindnesses, deliberate or not, and the encouragement, intended or not, that benefited me greatly in the course of the research and writing of this book: Philippe Besnard, Mark Cladis, Chris Chapple, Michel Despland, Louis Dumont, Antoine Faivre, Clare Fischer, Ernest Frerichs, Armin Geertz, Etienne Halphen, Richard Hecht, Jeppe Jensen, Robert Alun Jones, Hans Kippenberg, Jennifer Lehman, Deborah Dash Moore, Jack Neusner, Jordan Paper, Bill Pickering, Sam Preus, David Rapoport, Robert Segal, Frits Staal, Jonathan Z. Smith, Charles Vernoff, Jerry Winter.

For generous use of library facilities, I should also like to thank in Paris the Bibliothèque de l'Alliance Israëlite Universelle, especially its Bibliothécaire, Madame Yvonne Levyne, the Bibliothèque de l'Histoire du Protestantisme Français, the Bibliothèque Nationale and Archives Nationales. In Los Angeles I salute the University Reference Library of the University of California, Los Angeles. Its magnificent collections and the efficiency of the people who work there make it a national treasure.

Thanks finally are due also to the Holstein Family Community Endowment in Religious Studies for much appreciated financial support and to the chair of the Department of Religious Studies, University of California, Riverside, June O'Connor, for her forbearance and understanding of the demands made on teacher-authors working to meet their publisher's deadlines.

1

ESSENTIAL JEWISHNESS

OR REAL JEWS?

In these days of sensitivity to ethnic and religious roots, gender difference, and the like, we often want to link membership in a particular group to the way people think. Many attempts of this kind have, accordingly, been made to fix Émile Durkheim's thought in what amounts to an 'essential' Jewishness.[1] By an 'essential' Jewishness, I mean the claim that Durkheim's thought is really a secularized form of Jewish thought, and necessarily so.[2] Thus, Durkheim's affection for justice, and justice over charity, or his tolerance of other religions is supposed to point to his deep Jewishness.[3] Durkheim's penchant for analysis is likewise felt to indicate an ineradicable and typically Talmudic sensibility;[4] his aversion to miraculous brands of messianism shows him to be in his heart a modern Maimonides;[5] his use of language indicates his continued employment of "the vocabulary of Jewish mysticism";[6] his dynamic direction of the *équipe* certifies his leadership as self-consciously 'prophetic' in the classic Jewish sense.[7] His orientation to the social domain, to ritual, to symbolism, to religion itself likewise reveals the indelible marks of "his Jewish intellectual heritage."[8] Thus, because Durkheim was born and raised a Jew, he remained 'essentially' and eternally Jewish in a significant sense; since Durkheim's thinking must have been Jewish from the start, it likewise forever continued to be Jewish, his own disaffiliation from things

Jewish or varying historical and social conditions notwithstanding. Such claims constitute what I mean when I speak of Durkheim and Durkheimian thought as 'essentially' Jewish.[9]

I take these declarations with utmost seriousness, not least of all because Durkheim occasionally spoke in the same vein. Michel de Montaigne's skepticism and practicality marked him of Jewish character, Durkheim himself offered.[10] But quicker still to turn essentialist talk of Jewishness against Durkheim himself were his anti-Semitic critics.[11] Durkheim's sociology was to them nothing more than a Jewish scheme to undermine authentic French thought. Thus, in 1912, the Bergsonian Gilbert Maire declared that sociology in the hands of Durkheim, "its 'grand priest,' was a Jewish science, a theory of the subordination of the individual to society . . . , a way in which to 'speak Hebrew into the social being.' "[12]

Against such approaches—anti-Semitic or not—I will argue that there is little to gain, in terms of *historical* knowledge about Jews or Durkheim, from attempts to attribute essentially Jewish traits either to Jews or to Durkheim. Here I take my cues from the eminent historian Yosef Hayim Yerushalmi, who some years ago drew a fundamental distinction between those who argued "that there must be an essential 'Idea' of Judaism behind the shifting forms that history casts up to our view" and the historian,[13] who will typically see the Jewish past as "multiplicity and relativity."[14] Similarly, discussing 'essential' German propensities toward anti-Semitism, the Israeli historian Omer Bartov judges such ethnic or religious essentialism even more harshly: "All essentialist views [are] . . . inimical to strictly historical analysis. People may well act as they do because of what they are; but tautology rarely makes for good history."[15] When the subject is Durkheim and the Jews of France, essentialists fail to live up to the responsibilities of the historian because they pass over the 'multiple' and 'relative' details of Durkheim's time and place and of the Jews of that same time and place as well. Among other things, essentialists ignore the possible non-Jewish sources of many of these supposedly 'essential' Jewish features of Durkheim's thought. Durkheim's 'Jewish' affinities for sociability and ritual, for instance, might just as plausibly have been formed by the 'essentials' of a French nationalist worldview as by his own Jewish upbringing.[16]

Equally useless from a historical point of view are attempts to speak of Jewishness in terms of a Judaism hypostatized as what Eugen Schoenfeld and Stjepan Meštrović call an "ideal construct."[17] Durkheim's passion for justice and his open tolerance of religious diversity supposedly form the substance of such a Jewish "ideal construct" trustworthy for understanding Durkheim.[18] Yet as familiar as such constructs of an ideal Judaism may be, Schoenfeld and Meštrović never think to ask the *historical* question of whether this ideal kind of Judaism actually (or even plausibly) influenced Durkheim in his own time and place. Schoenfeld and Meštrović seem oblivious of the historical question of whether Durkheim's actual Jewish world was typical of the "ideal" one they construct. Lacking evidence that Durkheim may actually have thought or lived the "ideally constructed" Judaism of Schoenfeld and Meštrović, we thus have no grounds for saying that this had anything to do with his work or that their "ideal" Judaism ever mattered at all to Durkheim. Thus, Schoenfeld and Meštrović write Durkheim's history "as a saga in which all the great deeds are done by entities which could not, in principle, *do* anything."[19] To begin an inquiry into the relation of Durkheim's thought and Judaism on the basis of such an ideal construct is therefore never to venture forth into Durkheim's world at all.[20] Historians, by contrast, take those very steps out into the world in which Durkheim lived by constructing the thought-world of Durkheim's time as best we can.

Essentialist treatments of Durkheim's relation to things Jewish or to Judaism simply fail to meet criteria of what would count as historical assertions *about* Durkheim. They fail to qualify as historical statements because, whether anti-Semitic or philo-Semitic, they are at best only assertions that a given feature of Durkheim's thinking *reminds* the reader of something one might connect with Jews in a particular time and place. But no historical status can be accorded the view that this or that feature of Durkheim's thought, in effect, reminds one of something Jewish, that it is analogous to some ideal feature someone chooses to isolate as essentially Jewish. As Robert Alun Jones has argued, such statements do not tell us about Durkheim because they do not tell us about Durkheim's "actions, intentions or meanings"; they do not "go beyond a more or less phenomenological rendering of the content of one's own imagination" but tell us only "about the subjective state of the 'historian's' mind."[21] Typically, attributions of an essential Jewishness to Durkheim suppress those supposedly 'essential' features of Jewish identity conspicuously absent from Durkheim's thought in favor of those 'reminding' essentialists of what Judaism is supposed to be. Thus, readers will search in vain for essentialist claims of Durkheim's devotion to otherwise long-regarded essential Jewish ideas and practices like the God of history, chosenness, the religious law or *halakhah,* or the dietary codes.[22] If, therefore, Durkheim was essentially Jewish, why does he lack so much of what has been considered essential to Judaism and Jewish life?[23]

As for Durkheim's own wishes in the matter of his Jewishness, whether 'essential' or not, we know that although he never denied his Jewish origins, Durkheim disavowed Judaism as irrelevant.[24] He never made an issue of representing himself in public as Jewish and, as I will show, began to move tentatively and inconclusively toward acting in ways that publicly affirmed his Jewishness only very late in his life. Throughout nearly all of his life, Durkheim seemed to have resisted identification of himself as Jewish, for example by resisting participation in some sort of collective Jewish memory. He was embarrassed—even among Jews in his own hometown—to be singled out as Jewish, especially if he was being singled out as some kind of paragon of Jewishness. Jean-Claude Filloux reports a story that Henri Durkheim tells about Émile, who attended a religious observance for his mother in the synagogue of Épinal. The rabbi in charge recognized Durkheim among the congregation and observed how the attendance of a distinguished Jewish Sorbonne professor showed that Judaism was alive and well. Durkheim reacted with extreme displeasure.[25] He did so because he had actively tried to dissolve his sense of ethnic and religious identity in French national identity. Steven Lukes, for instance, tells us Durkheim rejected his Jewish background largely as a result of conversations with Henri Bergson and Jean Jaurès while a student at École Normale Supérieure. To Durkheim, Judaism was not only " 'false,' but . . . a confused and distorted form of morality . . . expressed in theological and mythological, rather than positive or scientific idiom."[26] Durkheim also objected to the idea of the Jews as "a people apart."[27] Durkheim's daughter, Marie, raised her own children "completely without religion."[28] Three of his sons married non-Jews, and two subsequently converted to Roman Catholicism. Only the third son did not convert to Catholicism, despite marrying a Catholic woman after the death of his first wife, who had been Jewish.[29] Durkheim not only predicted the total assimilation of French Jews within a generation or two but also seemed to have welcomed it. So, we must ask why Durkheim's rejection of his own Jewishness should not be final and definitive—or at least why it should not weigh as much as the supposedly hidden Jewish features of his character. When it comes to Durkheim's identity, then, why not count Durkheim's passionate identification with the Third Republic, his reverence for the French revolution and the Declaration of the Rights of Man, as much as his supposed Jewishness? In this sense, he recalls other Jewish contemporaries such as Marc Bloch, the great historian. Bloch passed on a letter of testamentary instructions to his family just before undertaking the high-risk underground activities that eventually led to his death by a Nazi firing squad. Bloch says this about being Jewish and French:

> I am prepared . . . if necessary, to affirm here, in the face of death that I was born a Jew: that I have never denied it, nor ever been tempted to do so. . . . A stranger to all credal dogmas, as to all pretended community of life and spirit based on race, I have, through life, felt that I was above all, and quite simply, a Frenchman. A family tradition, already of long date, has bound me firmly to my country. I have found nourishment in her spiritual heritage and in her history. . . . I have never found that the fact of being a Jew has at all hindered these sentiments. Though I have fought in two wars, it has not fallen to my lot to die for France. But I can, at least, in all sincerity, declare that I die now, as I have lived, a good Frenchman.[30]

That, apparently, was the kind of Jewish Frenchman that Durkheim wanted to be.[31]

Given his sense of French identification, Durkheim's thought would have been also more like that of the Wilhelminian German Jewish artists and intellectuals discussed by Peter Gay: "When they wrote monographs, painted portraits, or conducted orchestras, they did so in ways which . . . were indistinguishable from the ways of other Germans."[32] If this was so for the Jews of Wilhelminian Germany, how much more so must it have been for a French Jew in the relatively open and accommodating republican France of Durkheim's day? Durkheim was not in effect a modern marrano, a kind of secret Jew hiding under the cloak of conversion to the values of Third Republic liberalism. He was not secretly trying to express his Jewish identity under the guise of his seemingly secular sociology of religion. Nor even, *pace* the estimable Deborah Dash Moore, was he negotiating his peace with modernity in a particularly Jewish way. What indeed is the difference between adopting a "Jewish perspective on modernity" and abandoning some particular Judaism and Jewishness altogether?[33]

The essentialists would have us believe, then, that despite Durkheim's abandoning his Jewish roots, despite his having avoided affiliation with major Jewish cultural, intellectual, political, and religious associations, despite his believing that Jewish ethnicity was disappearing in France, and despite even his renouncing his provincial Alsatian roots in favor of becoming a "Bordelais forever,"[34] Durkheim was nonetheless guided by some sense of original and essential ethnic and religious Jewish roots. But from a historical perspective, Jewishness is like other kinds of social identification: it is something learned, negotiated, and practiced over time. Thus, in response to those who argue for the ineluctable power of roots, Jewish or otherwise, I take my cues from Lucy S. Dawidowicz: those who don't use them may lose them.[35] In the light of 'routes' taken instead of 'roots,' Jewishness is something that can be altered and transformed, then maximized or minimized in response to circumstances and either brought out or obscured by other identifications. The extent to which Jewishness becomes a significant marker of identity for an individual depends, then, on the reading of historic and social circumstances both by the individual and by the surrounding society. I believe the time has come to put aside essentialist strategies and start instead to treat the Jewishness of Durkheim and Durkheimian thought as a historical question.[36]

In the Jewish case, one thinks of the kind of Jewish identity created by universalizing and spiritualizing movements such as the 'prophetic' reading of Jewish identity by the Reform or Franco-Judaism's identification of the ideals of 1789 with the 'true' message of Judaism. Essentialists might recall that these earlier movements confidently claimed to capture an 'essential' Judaism. One also thinks today of the relatively modern rise of Jewish collective cultural and political identity in the form of Zionism as a response to the anti-Semitic campaigns of the end of the last century. I am thus arguing that we have more to gain

by seeing Jewishness and Judaism as 'real' historical constructions relative to their own time and place than by considering
ethnic or religious essences.

And here, ironically, is where those insisting on an essentialist reading of Durkheim's Jewishness miss out the most.
Both Durkheim and his nephew, Marcel Mauss, were beginning to create for themselves, however incipiently and incom-
pletely, a sense of their own Jewish identity in response to the
anti-Semitism of their time.[37] It is this apparently new, budding
Jewish identity, called forth by the historical circumstances of
the day, that in turn might be said to have marked Durkheimian
thought. Dwelling on essences rooted in a past, however, will
likely cause readers to pass over emerging identities. Thus,
Durkheim's tentative and unresolved identification as Jewish
should be looked on relationally, or dialectically in terms of how
he strategized his own identity in a time and place where the
ineradicable accident of birth cut off all routes to escape definition by a hostile 'other.' I believe, therefore, that on the whole,
a 'Jewish' core of Durkheimian thought has not been found because it is not there. It is not there because Durkheim's Jewish
identity was not there until very late in his life—and then only
after its formative patterns had already been in place for decades. When Durkheim's Jewish identity was finally kindled in
him, it was expressed in his thought, but in ways bound up inextricably in history and far from where essentialists would
imagine.

Accordingly, the polemic strategy of this book divides into
two phases: first, I consider four major claims about the essential
Jewishness of Durkheim's thought and use them as foils; second,
I try to show how each of these foils provides an occasion for
revealing what a historical approach can tell us about the relation of Durkheim to things Jewish. In chapter 2, for example,
instead of arguing how some essential or ideal Jewish orientation accounted for the societist of Durkheim's thought, I will
discuss three historical solutions already proposed for the origins of the social orientation of Durkheim's thought. To these,
I will add a fourth, which links Durkheim's societism to the 'real'
Jews and Judaisms of his affinity. As a cultural reality of fin de
siècle French Jews, for example, being Jewish often drew from
novel sources and took on surprising forms. Thus, much of the
storied social orientation of 'essential' Jewishness as well as the

societism of Durkheim himself seems to have been a joint creation of French nationalism, anti-Semitism, and Jewish national
self-assertion rather than a survival of an essential ancient Jewish
piety.

In this way, shifting to a historical approach to the issue of
the Jewishness of Durkheim's thought not only disposes of problems afflicting essentialism but also inaugurates the beginning
of a historically fruitful inquiry into the relation of Durkheim's
thought to things Jewish. This book thus seeks to invert the order of essentialist assumptions about Durkheim's relation to
Jews, Jewishness, and Judaism. Instead of delving into the supposed Jewishness inside Durkheim, we should seek the Durkheim inside the world of real Jews. Instead of pursuing will-o'-
the-wisp essences, we should seek to reconstruct the historical
and social contexts in which Durkheim, the historical figure,
moved and in terms of which his thoughts and actions make
sense. This is to inquire about the relation of Durkheim to the
Jews of France rather than to varieties of mysterious religious or
ethnic essences. I believe we can bring to life the nature of the
relationship between Durkheim and things Jewish only by doing
an intense form of highly contextualized intellectual history
both of Durkheim and of the Jews of France. My models for this
sort of trenchant work are the "historicist" intellectual historians John Dunn, J. G. A. Pocock, and Quentin Skinner. In following the lead of these men, I am trying to place my own work into
a tradition best known in Durkheimian studies by the writings of
Robert Alun Jones, W. S. F. Pickering, Brian Turner, and W.
Paul Vogt.[38]

The lessons that these historicist intellectual historians
teach us are numerous. Skinner urges us, for instance, to "read"
texts in terms of the worlds of discourse in which they were historically situated. This means that texts should be surrounded
"with their appropriate ideological context"—with what gives
significance to the text and thus to the theory in the text.[39] Part
of the spirit of the times includes the books of the times dealing
with the same subject. For example, was Durkheim's interest in
'primitive' religion unique in our period of investigation? What
did Durkheim's Jewish contemporaries active in the same studies—such as Salomon Reinach, Israël Lévi, or Louis-Germain
Lévy—have to say about the issues that Durkheim addressed?
How does Durkheim's work match up with other works of Jewish

scholarship concerning key themes of *The Elementary Forms of the Religious Life,* such as Marcel Mauss's great teacher, Sylvain Lévi, and his *Doctrine du sacrifice dans les Brâhmanas.*[40]

To introduce context into the interpretive act is, therefore, not to claim that context determines the content of theory in the text. Following Skinner, Jones argues that the classic text "must be understood within the linguistic conventions which rendered it meaningful in the first place"—conventions such as would in part be embedded in the competing texts of the time.[41] Context should provide "the means to *understand*" texts," not to imagine that one could exhaustively explain them.[42] Context is nothing less than the "ultimate framework for helping decide what . . . it might in principle have been possible for someone to have intended to communicate" in a particular setting.[43] Thus, context cannot condescendingly be tossed out as peripheral to the issues raised in the text. What is 'outside' Durkheim's text should make a difference to what is 'inside.'

Context needs to be constructed so that it bears on the content and/or form of the text at hand. Context here is not just obligatory background data on the life of the author, data simply appended to a theoretical discussion, nor is it a list of typically inconsequential or supposed influences, nor is it a mass of details about any and all social and cultural facts surrounding the text in question. The contextual approach I pursue seeks, after the fashion of historian John Dunn, to treat the history of Durkheim's ideas as the history of an "activity."[44] Thus, we need to know what Durkheim was about when he made certain assertions. We need to know the overall research project in which Durkheim's writings were embedded and what others were doing relative to Durkheim's actions in the same period. As Dunn so well states, "Intellectual discussions will only be fully understood if they are seen as complicated instances of . . . social activities."[45] Rather than seeking hidden Jewish essences beneath Durkheim's utterances, I try to fathom the strategies that help us make sense of the things Durkheim does and says. In connection with things Jewish, quite often we will see that these show the Durkheimians active in battling their adversaries, some of the more prominent of whom were the leading anti-Semitic scholars of the day.[46] In this activity of combating anti-Semitism, they resembled none so much as Israël Lévi and Sylvain Lévi, their Jewish peers in the École Pratique des Hautes Études, Fifth Section.

More than that, focusing on context aids in "the recovery of intentions" of the authors in question.[47] Skinner argued that understanding texts in this way "presupposes the grasp both of what they were intended to mean, and how this meaning was intended to be taken."[48] As such, this at least provisional respect for human intentionality reflects what Jones says is a "fundamental postulate of sociology and history": the idea that "the understanding of any social action entails a grasp of the subjective, intended meaning of an action to the agent who performs it."[49] Thus, if we hope to understand Durkheim on, say, symbolism, we will need to know the context of conventions giving meaning to what he said *and* we will need to recover as much of his authorial intention as possible. Given a certain context or framework of significance, what were our theorists intending to accomplish? To paraphrase John Dunn, sometimes one cannot know what a person means unless one knows what that person is doing.[50] Why did the Durkheimians care about symbols? Why did they care as they did? Given an understanding of what they were doing and of the contextual conventions making sense of the discourse about symbolism at a crucial time in the lives of our theorists, *why* did they bother to engage the subject? Why did they intend to engage it as they did? Action, context, and intention must be considered together.[51] Therefore, long before deciding whether Durkheim's claims about symbolism were true or not, we need to try to understand why he would have written what he did as he did. Thus, it is not a question of the truth or falsity of Durkheim's claims about symbolism, not a question of why or why not Durkheim was *wrong* about symbolism. It is a question of what made Durkheim *think* he was right!

While agreeing with Skinner's appreciation of context and intention, Pocock brings to the task a sensibility for the ways that a "diversity of languages," a "polyvalent" character, typifies sophisticated texts such as Durkheim's.[52] In this regard, the historian becomes a kind of detective seeking the different discourses lurking beneath the surface—such as the theological discourse of symbolism to which, I argue, Durkheim addressed himself. Here Pocock forces me to query my claims that such a discourse would be the kind of language that Durkheim might speak. So, Pocock asks the historian whether "he can proceed from saying he has read a certain language in the texts of a past culture to saying that this language existed as a resource available to the performing actors in that culture." Is the Jewish context in which I imagine Durkheim to be writing one only of my own imagination? Or was "such and such a 'language'" available "as a cultural resource for actors in history" like Durkheim, as I have claimed?[53]

The only way to satisfy Pocock's stern requirements is to construct the context of discourse in the manner Skinner has suggested, which I accordingly try to do. Who were the great Jewish thinkers in the time of Durkheim? What was their way of talking about issues common to them and the Durkheimians? What particular 'Jewish worlds' did they, and perhaps also the Durkheimians, inhabit? What role did particular classes of Jews, Jewish institutions, and Jewish "argumentative contexts" play in the final shape of Durkheim's sociology?[54] In all these inquiries, although we will move through an almost unknown liberal Jewish world, we will seek in vain for an essential Jewishness. Instead, as Pocock himself promises, the historian "aims constantly to render the implicit explicit, to bring to light assumptions on which the language of others rested, to pursue and verbalize implications and intimations that in the original may have remained unspoken, to point out conventions and regularities that indicate what could and could not be spoken in the language in what ways the language qua paradigm encouraged, obliged, or forbade its users to speak and think."[55]

The truth about Durkheim's Jewishness will thus be found in more interesting, but out-of-the-way, places than in some essential and eternal Jewishness. Significantly, this truth is Durkheimian to a high degree. The fact that Durkheim was born and raised Jewish is of little significance when compared with his intellectual, thus social, relations with contemporaries—Jewish learning, Jewish scholars and community leaders—with his profound appreciation of unfashionable Jewish institutions, and indeed with his defense of entire dimensions of Jewish life held up to ridicule by both friendly and unfriendly critics of Judaism. These are the public Jewish discourses of the day, or the several Jewish "argumentative contexts" of Durkheim's time, or the readily accessible Jewish agendas of issues to which Durkheim might have been addressing himself.[56] They are all matters of the social and cultural context in which Durkheim's thought itself was immersed. All of these involvements of Durkheim's with Jews and Jewish ideas are matters of public record and thus are social to a high degree. We need only the eyes to see; we need only the will to conceive the problem of the relation of Durkheim to Jewishness or Judaism in an unconventional—as it happens, essentially Durkheimian—way. Jewishness in the Durkheimian sense is, then, not a category of 'nature' but rather a broader category of 'cultural' or 'social' reality relating more to those things we can realistically hope to know about Durkheim's mature affiliations, circles of dependencies, patronage, and participation in worlds of even higher order generality than to religious grouping itself. From a Durkheimian perspective, Jewishness is itself more a construction of the human social imagination than a feature of lineage or racial strain. That is, instead of seeking a terra incognita of Durkheim's essential Jewishness, or its supposedly eternal traces, we should turn to important relations between Durkheim and real Jews.

A Durkheimian approach also treats Judaism and Jewishness as robust historical realities whose nature may change in relation to historical location. In fact, the relativity of Judaism to its contexts is so strong that we should just get used to speaking in the plural of 'Judaisms.'[57]. Much of the burden of chapter 2, for example, will be to show how nationalist imperatives stimulated the formation of different Judaisms, much as they did with the Protestantisms and Roman Catholicisms formed in the same period. I want to free us from a sense of the fixed or idealized Judaism of our own imaginings and prepare us to see the several Judaisms that there were. These may at times look like quite 'other' Judaisms than the one or ones that pass for normal today. But I hope readers will welcome the appearances of these new worlds.

In a way it is easy to speculate why scholars may be more intrigued by the possibility of hidden or idealized Jewishness behind Durkheim than by Durkheim's relation to the Jews of his time. Putting together a picture of such other Judaisms of Durkheim's circle of acquaintance is very hard work. Furthermore, given our moment in history, there is relatively little incentive to do so. The Jews with whom Durkheim had the most contact are very much out of fashion. They are the liberal, French-born Jews of the fin de siècle, Jews who embodied what a recent historian has unkindly called "the torpor of the Judaism of France."[58] Conventional wisdom among intellectual historians teaches that the story of the Jews in France at the turn of the century rehearses a pathetic tale of rather shallow, ultraliberal assimilationism. What more, we might ask, is there to be learned from such foolish conformists to the spirit of the age, from their reputedly flaccid intellectual agendas, and from the possibility that the Durkheimians either might have written in association with such groups of Jews or might have addressed what they wrote to such Jews?

I believe much can be learned from looking more closely at these unfashionable French Jews and, in particular, at Durkheimian ideas in relation to theirs. This we will do in chapter 3. At the top of the list of such interesting lessons is their common absorption with the question of the nature of religion and its relation to the politics of patriotism. In this book I will dwell on how both Jewish and Durkheimian attitudes toward the social nature of religion seemed to have been shaped by this fin de siècle nationalism. I will then deal with how interests common to both Durkheimian and Jewish intellectuals made them part of the same "argumentative context" favoring a 'concrete' conception of religion, how they fashioned a program of symbolic interpretation of religion and encouraged critical study of the Jewish past. I do this to bring to life once again those other Judaisms. The quest, therefore, for Durkheim's hidden Jewishness is sterile compared with the vitality of the conversations—both in text and in subtext—in which the Durkheimians engaged, along with the different Judaisms of their own day.

Consequently, in chapter 4, we first need to establish historical and ideological links between Durkheimian scholarship and the approach to Judaism practiced by the French heirs to the Wissenschaft des Judentums. Thus, I will sketch out the program and origins of this French version of the Wissenschaft des Judentums, fittingly enough called the Science du Judaïsme. Why was there so remarkable a community of interest and approach between the French representatives of the Science du Judaïsme and the Durkheimians? After a review of these men and their institutions, we can then turn to the question of the religious and intellectual nurture these influential Jewish teachers offered the Durkheimians, in particular Henri Hubert and Marcel Mauss. In chapter 5, I will show how Hubert and Mauss were formed in the traditions of writing the history of religions as practiced by the French Jewish savants of their day—by the methods and doctrines of the Science du Judaïsme as practiced by Sylvain Lévi.

One final word is in order before launching into my story. Some readers may be wondering why a book ostensibly about Durkheim and the Jews of France seems to have so much to say about Durkheim's circle, especially Marcel Mauss. The plain fact is that of the many things learned about Durkheim and the Durkheimians, one stands out: their work was radically collaborative and collective. In some cases, we cannot assign specific single authorship to works generally recognized as authored by an individual member of the *équipe*. Thus, we can pass from Durkheim to Mauss and back again—without necessarily fearing that we have misrepresented the reality of authorship. Such was the 'team' Durkheim assembled round him and *L'Année sociologique* from 1896. There is, for instance, no question as to the collaboration of Mauss and Durkheim on *Primitive Classification;* the book is, after all, coauthored. But recent research has shown that their collaboration extended to a number of Durkheimian classics, even to works uncharacteristic of Mauss, such as *Suicide* (Mauss compiled all the massive statistics for this study). Most surprising of all, however, Durkheim's debt to Mauss likewise extended to Durkheim's magnum opus. French historian Georges Condominas shows that in *The Elementary Forms of the Religious Life,* Durkheim repeats "presque textuellement" Mauss's position first articulated in his inaugural lecture of 1901.[59] In particular, as we will see in chapter 5, Mauss's command over Indology and its attendant subspecialities—Sanskrit, Buddhist, and Vedic studies—informs the core of Durkheim's views on ritual, methodological atheism, and the new positive notion of the sacred emerging in *The Elementary Forms of the Religious Life.* At significant moments, when Durkheim wanted to clinch a critical argument, such as that the nature of religion is better expressed in terms of an impersonal 'sacred' than a personal god, he resorted to examples from Mauss's field of expertise—Indology. Thus, he cites Abel Bergaigne in *The Elementary Forms of the Religious Life* (p. 49f.). Therefore, when Durkheim made certain crucial points in his magnum opus, Mauss was actually the one speaking.

Further, in the whole matter of religion, we have every reason to suspect that Durkheim depended immensely on Hubert and Mauss, both for factual and for conceptual information. Hubert and Mauss played critical roles in Durkheimian scholarship on religion and were themselves well positioned within the networks of Jewish learning of the fin de siècle. Both Hubert and Mauss were equally as 'positive' about religion as Durkheim and seem to have been so before their association with Durkheim.[60] Neither Hubert nor Mauss learned the history of religions from Durkheim; both trained in history of religions independently of Durkheim's influence, as we will see, under some unambiguously observant Jewish scholars. Both also directed those sections of *L'Année sociologique* devoted to religion while Durkheim busied himself with the more 'sociological' topics of family, law, and morals. We therefore need to give much more credit to close collaborators such as Hubert and Mauss for what has long been assumed to be Durkheim's own personal contribution to the study of religion.

So, with these considerations of strategy behind us, let us begin by exploring the relation of Durkheim's Jewishness to his societist approach to human affairs: was this relation 'essentially' Jewish, somewhat Jewish, or something else altogether?

2

WHY SOCIETY?

FRENCH NATIONALISM AND

THE BODY OF JUDAISM

If any feature of Durkheim's thought can be called central, it surely must be what commentators have called its 'societism' or sociological nature.[1] As Durkheim himself tells us, "We believe fruitful the idea that social life must be explained, not by the conception that those who participate in it have of it, but by the deep causes which escape consciousness; and we also believe that these causes must be sought after principally in the manner in which associated individuals are grouped."[2]

Why was Durkheim a methodological holist? Why did he subsume individual thought and action to the forces of society? Why, furthermore, did he press the case for the reality of social things? Why, if not a socialist, was he at least a fellow traveler? Likewise, of all the features of Durkheim's thought believed to be determined by his Jewish birth and nurture, his 'societism' certainly ranks high. This at any rate seems to be implied in the comments of certain (typically anti-Semitic) contemporary critics of Durkheim. As we have seen, some of Durkheim's contemporaries, like the Bergsonian philosopher Gilbert Maire, maintained, "Sociology in the hands of Durkheim, its 'grand priest,' was a Jewish science, a theory of the subordination of the individual to society."[3] Others charged that sociology was "the Jewish science" or a "Jewish sect."[4]

André Durkheim, spring 1915. Photo courtesy of Étienne Halphen.

Such judgments betray a common enough anti-Semitic prejudice. They also have been the bases of friendly claims in behalf of the Jewish determination of Durkheim's thought.[5] In this view Jews, unlike individualistic Protestants, are essentially familial, tribal, and collectivist. Durkheimian societism or sociologism was therefore determined by, or at the very least resulted from, Durkheim's original Jewish identity and upbringing. Durkheim was determined by birth and nurture to imbibe this Jewish societist sensibility; thus, his general sociological approach emerged fully blown in adulthood.

Lending weight to this sort of thinking, Durkheim himself seemed ready to generalize about the collective ethnic characteristics of Jews.[6] In *Suicide*, for example, Durkheim reasoned that Jews are less prone to take their own lives than are, say,

Protestants, because of the tighter social bonds linking members of the Jewish communities of France.[7] Durkheim also felt that Michel de Montaigne's skepticism and his concern with the practical and concrete might be attributed to his being Jewish.[8] On closer inspection of Durkheim's position, however, we can see that it differs subtly from the confused ethnic or racial determinist views canvassed in the introductory chapter. On the question of the Jews as a biological designation, a 'race,' Durkheim followed Ernest Renan in denying the existence of a Jewish 'race' at all.[9] Like Renan again, Durkheim felt that whereas Jews may exhibit physical or collective characteristics, these were learned and acquired by repeated patterns of sociability. If these social conditions were to change, so also would Jewish behavior—and even physical appearance.[10] This position indeed became standard among the Durkheimians. Henri Hubert, for example, specialized in the study of race during the early part of the century and worked to undermine the logical status of the etiological pretensions of heredity promoted by the race theorists.[11] Can we, then, perhaps see something of Durkheim's taste for social explanations as founded—Durkheim-like—in the fundamentals of his Jewish nurture or socialization?

At least two main obstacles block this sort of polemic. First, even without knowing the numbers, we can clearly see that not all, most, or even many Jewish thinkers were similarly bitten with the societist bug. The Jewish philosophers of Durkheim's generation—those who opposed him in the name of the autonomy of reason, such as Léon Brunschvicg—seemed immune enough from some native Jewish tendency toward the social. What, then, can we say of Henri Bergson—hardly smitten with the sociological apperception? If the social was so essential to Jewishness and if this essential Jewishness was so irresistible, why did not all— or even more—Jewish thinkers of the time show the same commitment that Durkheim did, according to the claims of the essentialists?

Second, in Durkheim's time and place of fin de siècle France, there was no such thing as a monolithic national 'Jewish nurture.'[12] Even though, thanks to the Dreyfus Affair and the anti-Semitism of the late nineteenth and early twentieth centuries, such an identity was building, several different Jewish 'cultures' maintained their own identities in the fin de siècle. The Sephardic Jews of Bordeaux and Bayonne counted many generations born in France, stretching back to the Reconquista. The Ashkenazi Jews of eastern France had more in common with their coreligionists in the Rhineland than they did with the well-to-do Sephardim of the Southwest. Paris, as always, was exceptional. As a destination for cosmopolitan-minded Jews from the provinces, part of its Jewish community moved easily into the mainstream of French society. But other, more conservative immigrants, finding themselves adrift in the metropole, sought to re-create the familiarity of the small communities they had left in the provinces. Finally, beginning in the 1880s, a far different kind of Jew began to seek refuge in France, especially in Paris: the far more religiously radical Jews of eastern Europe. They were strangers both to France and to modernity; their arrival and the attempts to absorb them into the Jewish mainstream changed French Jewry forever.

Yet if we take such regional differences among French Jews into consideration, something of a case might be made for speaking of an Alsatian 'Jewishness' behind Durkheim's personal and professional interest in, say, that traditional collectivity, the family.[13] It would hardly be surprising that Durkheim's extraordinary devotion to his family owed something to his provincial Jewish upbringing. In *Suicide,* Durkheim even tells us of the way Jewish communities (especially from his own region, eastern France) tended to accentuate their close-knit internal relations, often falling back on the family unit in response to local anti-Semitism.[14] Therefore, this early Jewish social experience perhaps resulted in Durkheim's sociological interest in the family as a category of inquiry. Yet even when we give weight to Durkheim's origins in the Jewry of Alsace or Lorraine, it is hard to tell how much of his devotion to family was, for example, 'Jewish' and how much 'Alsatian' or provincial. Indeed, the French at large are likewise notoriously familial.

We therefore run into the gaps between the Judaism of Durkheim's time and that of our own. Are we right to assume—in light of Jewish nationalism, or in light of renascent Judaism in the West, or in light of the significant Jewish contributions made to socialist thinking since the turn of the century—that the varieties of Jewishness of Durkheim's time and place were particularly 'societist' at all? Israel's success as a vital nation-state, for instance, also makes it natural for us to think these days that the Jews of Durkheim's affinity were as nationalist about Israel as are many Jews of today.[15] Thus, it is easy to forget, amid the successes enjoyed by the present state of Israel, that societal (here, political) embodiment was won at great price and against stiff opposition from other Jews.[16] Likewise the American phenomenon of the lively assertion of Jewish 'ethnicity' and solidarity is also of more recent vintage and local (eastern European) origin than fully appreciated.[17] Thus, despite the vigorous and explicitly Durkheimian societist interpretation given the nature of Judaism by such modern thinkers as Mordecai Kaplan, we should not assume that Judaism was always and everywhere as social as Kaplan would have liked it or that Durkheim was therefore Jewish (not Kaplan's claim) because he was societist.[18] Kaplan is free to read Durkheimian societism into Judaism, but I do not think that we are therefore free to read Judaism or Jewishness into Durkheim's societism. Finally, as prominent Jewish membership in antisocialist movements like neoconservatism or as magazines like *Commentary* should remind us, Jewishness and socialism are by no means identical or mutually sustaining. Some writers, like Irving Kristol, have even argued the opposite.[19] Further, if the Jews of Durkheim's affinity achieved a societist sense, was it a uniquely Jewish one, or was it perhaps a solidarity common to certain larger trends of the age? Was the Jewish societist sense of the time, to the extent there was one, a feature of, say, the rise of socialist or solidarist movements, revolutionary class solidarity, a reinvigorated French patriotism in preparation for World War I, an anti-Semitic isolation of Jews as a targeted 'race,' or something else? Were there not therefore other sources of Durkheim's societism, sources even more powerful than anything identifiable as a single Jewish heritage active in forming the mind of Durkheim?

In this chapter I will first argue that the Jews of Durkheim's acquaintance, the overwhelmingly bourgeois Parisian majority, do *not* offer models of societism and certainly not of radical leftist collectivism. Like other members of the urban bourgeoisie, they tended instead toward individualism—as did Durkheim himself in his unique way.[20] To the extent that Durkheim's Jewish associates can be said to have been societist in their attitudes, they would have needed to *acquire* such attitudes. They would have had to *become* societist. Thus, secondly I want to dwell on how both the developing Jewish and the developing Durkheimian societal views of religion seemed part of larger trends toward societist thinking, among which I will emphasize fin de siècle French nationalism and its dialectical 'shadow'—Jewish nationalism. Finally I will deal with the way interests common to both Durkheimian and Jewish intellectuals made them part of the same "argumentative context" favoring a concrete and societist conception of religion.

Before I make any such arguments about Jewish sources of Durkheimian societism, we need to address current arguments in the literature about non-Jewish sources. Of these, two stand out. The first comes from W. Paul Vogt and, to a lesser extent, Brian J. Turner. They independently argue that largely socialist, preexisting trends inherent to progressive French thought induced Durkheim and many of his contemporaries into societism.[21] By the 1880s, such eminently French movements such as solidarism and socialism swept Durkheim along with them.[22] Durkheim's thought is societist, Vogt says, because Durkheim was deeply involved in these national movements of French social reconstruction. Durkheim could not really help being societist in his social thought because so much else in the French thought-world of his times was societist as well.[23]

The second argument about the origins of Durkheim's societism issues from Robert Alun Jones. He gives Durkheim's attraction to societism a somewhat antinationalist turn, and unlike Vogt and Turner, he argues that Durkheim's societism was imported from Germany rather than being homegrown. Durkheim became societist as a secondary consequence of his belief that social thought should focus on 'things.' He adopted this (social) realism from the Germans while touring their research centers in 1886.[24] Jones implicitly discounts the societist trends of the French social thought of the day and believes that French thought was overwhelmingly 'Cartesian' and individualist. Instead, Durkheim was attracted by the societism of the Germans, which at the same time was linked to their devotion to the study of 'things.' Let us look at each of these worthy efforts before offering an alternative.

For Vogt and Turner, the sources of Durkheim's societist thinking are to be found in his engagement in the social problems created by the economic conditions of social life of the 1880s. Because of its dominance of economic life and values in the late nineteenth century, classical liberal economics provoked its own antithesis in the form of a range of reactions, which Vogt calls "societist." These include the syndicalist and socialist movements, Durkheim's work on division of labor, his critique of utilitarianism, the concern of his collaborators with questions of social equality, Marxism and individualism (Célestin Bouglé), working-class life, price theory, or needs (Maurice Halbwáchs), or working-class salaries, poverty, and monetary theory (François Simiand).

Each societist grouping believed, in its own way, that the ills of individual and social life could be addressed only by seeing these problems from a social point of view. National well-being was not the function of individual self-improvement or goodwill. Society is more than just the sum of its individuals. Society thus had to be approached from a more profound perspective. Progress would come only by attacking the underlying societal causes of the present unhappy condition of French humanity. Included in this loosely related societist grouping was the socialism of someone like Jean Jaurès, the solidarism of Alfred Fouillée or Léon Bourgeois, and the academic sociology of the Durkheimians.[25] Socialism saw the evils of the day as completely economic in nature. In place of the mythical 'hidden hand' of the market, the socialists substituted the *dirigiste* hand of central planning and a command economy. The solidarists, in contrast, felt that transformation of the system of economic ownership and management would not suffice to stem conflict. Mere economic change would not eliminate greed, for example. Greed would remain because it knew no natural bounds, and social conflict would begin anew. Conflict between the economic classes or between individualist economic values and collectivist ones could be bridged only by reconciling individual greed and socialism. Mutuality should be encouraged among all people, as should social harmony and a sense of conscience about what one owed in terms of the personal social debt to others.[26]

The Durkheimians shared many of the values of both their solidarist and their socialist brethren. But they distinguished a separate and original position for themselves on the spectrum of societist thought. The "incessant irenism" of the solidarists was, to them, "muddleheaded." Although Durkheim himself had tried to reconcile oppositions such as individualism and societism,[27] the solidarists' hoped-for harmony between utilitarianism and societist approaches was not possible.[28] As for the socialists, although the Durkheimians shared the socialist contempt for utilitarianism, they felt that the socialist emphasis on economic need was equally economistic. "Moral activity and institutions," rather than satisfaction of brute economic needs (socialists), lay at the basis of the Durkheimian solution of the social crisis.[29] For Durkheim, sociology strove "to discover through science the moral restraint which can regulate economic life, and by this regulation control selfishness and thus gratify needs."[30]

What makes Turner's treatment of Durkheim distinctive is his appreciation of the sociologist's love-hate relationship with the French socialist movement. Durkheim was both drawn to the humanist ideals of socialism and repelled by its collectivist threats to human liberty.[31] Turner believes Durkheim was trying to rethink socialism by developing his "corporative scheme"— Durkheim's novel way of dealing with the pathology of social atomization induced by economic liberalism. Instead of some socialist *étatisme* or Marxist dictatorship of the proletariat, Durkheim wanted to revive a scheme of occupational groupings or guilds separate from state power.[32] These would organize individuals into meaningful social units. Otherwise, individuals were atomized by conditions of mass society and were thus subject to control by the larger forces of capitalist production or state power. Durkheim's guilds would interpose themselves between the state and the individual and, in doing so, would replace traditional religious associations and families. These new guilds would form social bases for enhancing human liberty and individual power.[33] Now how does this account of Durkheim's involvement in the societist movements of his day bear on the question of the Jewishness of Durkheimian thought?

If one argues that Durkheim's Jewishness explains his societism, one will have to show at least that the evidence for this exists, which might be put up against the very substantial evidence of Durkheim's participation in the societist discourse, evidence ably brought out by Jones, Turner, and Vogt. I do not think the prospects of finding the first type of evidence are promising. At best, the Jewish contribution to a societal sense is diffuse, such as the contribution of the group to identity and personal life. What Durkheim shares with the likes of Albert Schäffle, the socialists, and the solidarists, on the other hand, is specific, ramified, and well documented by Turner and Vogt.

But there is another dimension to Durkheimian societism, one that might be traced to his Jewish roots—a certain taste for concreteness and down-to-earth realism. Throughout his study, Turner acknowledges Durkheim's intellectual debt to the German economists. From Schäffle in particular, Durkheim is supposed to have acquired a model of method: society should be treated as an organism that functions and evolves and, moreover, as an organism whose 'soul' is morality. Further, Schäffle believed in a 'corporative socialism,' which may well have been the prototype for Durkheim's.[34] Yet, on the whole, Turner, like Vogt, emphasizes the domestic French political context of Durkheim's moral and methodological societism. Durkheim's thought about socialism developed in response to the vicissitudes of the domestic French political scene. Jones, on the other hand, wants to underscore the Germanness of Durkheim's societism. Like Turner, he believes that Durkheim discovered (and subsequently imported) societism while on a study tour of German universities and research institutes in 1886.[35] Yet Jones wants to make rather more of this than Turner. For Jones, Durkheim's attraction to German thinkers holds vital lessons for us about his critical view of French intellectual life and education. Durkheim's links with the German social scientists account not only for his societism but for a special dimension of it—his devotion to the concrete and empirical, Durkheimian scientific realism.

In 1887, Durkheim reported on his information-gathering trip to observe the conditions of the scientific work of the German universities. Durkheim especially admired the Germans' epistemological ethic of scientific realism, their sense of the importance of getting into contact with 'things.' By contrast the French, Durkheim felt, were bogged down in "the interpretation of legal texts, of speculation, for example, about the intentions of some legislator of the *ancien régime*."[36] Important to note in this context is that Durkheim immediately goes on in the same report to link this German taste for the concrete with the societist spirit of the German school of moral philosophers, a spirit that so thoroughly distinguished their thought from the individualism of the 'Cartesian' French.[37] Unlike the Germans, the Cartesian French, says Durkheim had "no idea of the nature of law, customs, morals and religions, what is the role and the relation of the diverse functions of the *social* organism."[38] By contrast with the French again, this German school of moral philosophy had developed, to a high degree, the sociological apperception.

> [It] has pointed out that this claimed autonomy [of the individual] is only apparent; that there is no abyss between each of us and other men; that heredity reduces us to being only the continuation of our ancestors; that the existence of common feelings erases at every moment the alleged line of demarcation which separates our consciousnesses and confounds them. The individual is an integrated part of the society where he is born. That society penetrates him in every part. To isolate himself and abstract himself from it is to diminish himself. Such a pronounced feeling for the collective life, for its reality and its advantages, seemed destined to be, until recently, the essential characteristic of German ethics.[39]

Jones believes that in thus linking scientific realism to societism, Durkheim addressed a set of questions about the future of French science and pedagogy, occasioned by his firsthand encounter with German university life and research programs. Durkheim's societism on this account stems from dissatisfaction with the French intellectual scene. Armed with the lessons of his German sojourn, Durkheim was eager to overturn the dominance of Cartesian classicism, individualist epistemology, and social theory. In Jones's view, Durkheim was looking for an alternative to the "utterly inadequate" vocabulary of French philosophy, and he found it in Germany. France could progress in the education of its elites by adapting methods of empirical moral and social inquiry perfected in Germany. If Jones is right, Durkheim was thus not affirming, with Vogt, his own already formed societism of French origin, much less acquiring some sort of essential Jewish social sensibility: he was importing German notions.

Jones, Turner, and Vogt make a tremendous contribution to our grasp of the historical origins of Durkheim's societism and in effect seem to crowd out anything that might be called an essentially Jewish source of Durkheim's orientation to societism and concreteness. But I should to come round to a Jewish "argumentative context" through the 'back door,' so to speak. To his credit, Vogt names names and shows that a real societist trend existed in the last decades of the nineteenth century in the intellectual circles Durkheim frequented. But he does not account for this trend itself. Nor, outside citing Durkheim's progressivism, does he tell us why Durkheim should have joined it as he did. Why is Durkheim *not* a socialist or even a Marxist but rather a bourgeois societist, someone eager to defend public policies of economic and political individualism while holding out for methodological holism in the social sciences? Similarly Jones speaks as if Durkheim were somehow alone in his societism, in the conclusions that he drew about the need to query the Cartesian heritage. Further, in Jones's scheme, societism, as antireductionist *social* realism, was only a secondary consequence of Durkheim's scientific realism. For this reason, I feel that Jones's thesis needs amplification by locating Durkheim within the context of larger societist trends in politics and economics of the day, common to both socialism and solidarism, as Vogt has so well done. Further, we need to explain why a focus on things entails that one of those things is society. Durkheim might, for example, have been a psychologist, a methodological individualist, and focused instead on the 'concrete'—even biological—human person, as other admirers of Wundt had done. Bronisław Malinowski here is a fine case in point.[40]

Let me first consider a wider context into which to place Durkheim in this regard. The trends rightly isolated by Jones—realism and societism—were also linked by Durkheim's moral philosopher contemporaries, but in ways rather different from what he himself did. A figure close to Durkheim with analogous tendencies toward concreteness and societism was Durkheim's great friend and colleague at Bordeaux, the Protestant philosopher Octave Hamelin.[41] Here, *pace* Jones, is someone whom Durkheim knew and loved all his life but who does not seem to have drawn his societist and concrete conclusions from the Germans mentioned in connection with Durkheim.[42] For example, one contemporary critic said Hamelin's idealism "pursues the concrete everywhere."[43] For Hamelin, as for Durkheim, the matter of concreteness, of getting in touch with 'things,' bore on the nature of moral philosophy. Hamelin wanted to locate ethical inquiry in a comparative societal context. In his various lecture courses on morals, Hamelin, for example, showed an acquaintance with cross-cultural comparison from ethnography and history of religions, something we usually associate only with ethnologists, historians of religions, or the Durkheimians. In his lectures on Armand de Quatrefages's *Universality of Moral and Religious Sentiments,* for example, Hamelin shows sophistication about the societal relativity and diversity of moral systems, ranging from the American Indians, fetishism, and Hottentots to the Buddhists. With a familiarity we might associate with Durkheim, Hamelin discusses Sir John Lubbock's *Origins of Civilization* but judges it deficient in its treatment of tribal cultures.[44]

Like Durkheim as well, Hamelin featured the social and collective nature of morality. In Hamelin's view, Charles Renouvier was on firm ground to attempt to bring moral philosophy into relation with concrete social realities. But Renouvier did not go far enough in his quest for concreteness. Using words that might well be Durkheim's, Hamelin argued that Renouvier's *morale* remains a "pure *morale.*"[45] Renouvier's moral philosophy implies an "isolated moral agent," even though no such thing exists in reality.[46] The social nature of human life, including moral life, must be given more status, says Hamelin. "Man is—he cannot be other than a social being . . . man has always been social [since] the social is not . . . a mere accessory and efflorescence of individual [but] a milieu and necessary cradle as well. It is a prolonging of the external world on which the individual depends, as he depends on the world in general. [Therefore] part of moral fact seems social."[47] On the other hand, Hamelin drew short of Durkheim's fully concrete societism, saying, "Moral facts are not simple social facts."[48] For Hamelin, morality has no "empirical foundation";[49] he also rejected moral relativism.[50] Hamelin thus rejects Durkheim's German program of a science of morals.

Thus, Hamelin emerged with a position much like the one that Jones outlined for Durkheim, even if they differ considerably as to what concreteness and societism finally meant. However, what needs to be recalled in terms of Jones's attribution of German influences to Durkheim is their absence (except for Georg Hegel) in Hamelin's societism and concreteness. Instead, Hamelin seems to have developed these orientations as part of a particularly French neo-Hegelian evolution in his thinking. In doing so, he seemed to follow the lead charted out in Vogt's discussion of the French political and economic societists. Hamelin was, for example, personally acquainted with such key players in the socialist camp as Lucien Herr (likewise a key figure in French neo-Hegelian socialism).[51] In the early 1880s, while a young colleague of Durkheim's on the faculty of the university at Bordeaux, Hamelin advocated a "socialist morality."[52]

It could therefore be that Durkheim participated in a broader French intellectual project of seeking concreteness and society than that restricted to what he found in German scientific and economic thinking. Jones's analysis has made it possible for us to ask further questions. Who besides Hamelin were the other French societist and realist contemporaries of Durkheim? Given that German intellectual achievements were impressive to certain French thinkers, like Charles Andler, Durkheim, Herr, and Hamelin, what was it about the conditions of the time that caused these leading French intellectuals to be so impressed by the Germans? Why were the ideals of concreteness and scientific realism and the specifically German appreciation of the societal so powerfully attractive—not only to Durkheim but to his generational and professional peers?

Could perhaps Durkheim's Jewishness come into play here? In the introduction to the first edition of Durkheim's *Socialism* (1928), Marcel Mauss suggests that Durkheim's early socialization shaped his orientation to social things. This interest was due in part to the master's "personal inclination," Mauss says. "As early as his [Durkheim's] years at normal school, through personal inclination and in an atmosphere animated by political and moral interests, and together with Jaurès and his other friend Hommay, . . . he dedicated himself to the study of society."[53] We know what these "political and moral interests" were from Vogt's discussions. But what is this "personal inclination" of which Mauss speaks? It could well have been some part of Durkheim's youthful character that formed before his early twenties at the École Normale Supérieure. It might also have been some remnant of his Jewish rearing, leaving ajar the 'door' for the Durkheimian essentialist.

I doubt the latter is the case, at least not quite as the essentialists would have us imagine. Instead, nationalism—and the Jewish relation to the French national revival of the late nineteenth and early twentieth centuries—may speak directly to these questions. Since Jewish identity has so often in Jewish history had to contend with political identity—its own or others'— dwelling on the political context of Durkheim's life and times might shed some light on the central questions of Durkheim's

Jewish identity. Yes, Durkheim and some of his generation were, of course, caught up in a societist wave of thinking, inspired by the social conditions and economy of the day. But in this chiefly economic understanding of the word, Durkheim's societism had just as much to do with national and international politics, with his patriotic devotion to the nation. After all, he undertook his journey to Germany in order to stock himself with knowledge that would explicitly strengthen French national education and thus the resources of the French nation as a whole.[54] To Durkheim, nothing was more important for the national interest than education: were education to be slighted, Durkheim tells us, the "great soul of the fatherland would break up and dissolve into an incoherent multitude of small fragmentary souls in conflict with each other."[55]

If, with Vogt and Turner, we then restrict our search for the roots of Durkheim's societism to the *internal* French economic and partisan political realms, we will miss the role such powerful trends as nationalism played in Durkheim's life and in the life of the Jews of France. Or if, with Vogt, we further restrict our scope to economics, being Jewish would have no part to play in socialist inclinations because Jews were by and large not socialists but were instead the butt of socialist attacks as paradigms of the individualist, utilitarian, capitalist exploiting class. Yet if we depart from Vogt's predominantly economic viewpoint and, *pace* Turner, shift to the larger international political context of the fin de siècle, I think we can at least open territory where Jewish identity—either as it was in its various regional forms or as it was in the making of a national Franco-Jewish or Zionist identity—may have had some role to play. The peculiar political status of Jews in France seems to come into play here—both as the old, variously integrated, regionally based minorities and as a newly emergent, national entity becoming aware of itself in the wake of the Dreyfus Affair and the anti-Semitism of the late nineteenth and early twentieth centuries. Consistent with my earlier statements, I am not, of course, claiming that an exclusive or innatist sense of Jewishness caused Durkheim's attraction for concreteness and sociability. Rather I am saying that one could argue that the social conditions impinging on the traditional Jewish communities such as the one in which Durkheim was raised, and those new national ones emerging in response to anti-Semitism and to which his critics assigned him, may well have contributed to the formation of what Mauss referred to as Durkheim's "personal inclination" to the social. In the language of historian John Dunn, both Durkheim and many Jews of his milieu "reacted" to the anti-Semitism of their day by developing societist ways of thinking.[56] Consider the folowing scenario.

From his earliest years, Durkheim along with others of his generation moved vigorously in the flow of French nationalism, which crested in the decade just before World War I. He was in fact an excited and exaggerated patriot long before the late 1890s, when being a patriot became popular.[57] Being a Jew in France at this time had a strong correlation with one's patriotic fervor. Although a nationalist mood affected the entire nation, Jews like Durkheim, especially Jews from Alsace or Lorraine, seem to have felt the special need vigorously to assert their patriotic devotion.[58] In this exaggerated patriotism, both Durkheim and, in particular, the French Jews of the lost eastern *départements* seem in predictable harmony with each other. We might, then, want to consider the dynamic of membership in this Jewish community as at least one of the contributing factors to Durkheim's societism.

As we will see, however, although we *may* link Durkheim's affinity for societism with his Jewish rearing and youthful identity, this Jewishness was different from what one might imagine in these days of ethnic politics. This was a Jewishness variously animated by—even produced by—French nationalism and its shadow, the anti-Semitism of the era, rather than anything independent of it. As Salomon Reinach attested in 1908, "Anti-Semitism . . . remained a political religion of an imposing minority of French people."[59] It was a kind of Jewishness that came into being because of the peculiar character of the French Judaism of Durkheim's time—a Judaism being challenged by the demands laid upon it by the crisis of French nationalism following the debacle of defeat in the Franco-Prussian War. We need to look on Durkheim's attraction to societism as a feature of the reaction of an ambitiously careerist but provincial figure, who was responding to threats posed to the nation that had succeeded in winning his complete loyalty and who at the same time was a member, however marginally, of an occasionally marginalized former nation within a nation.[60] We should, then, look more closely for patriotism behind both the "societism" of

Durkheim and whatever group-mindedness existed among the Jews of France in the fin de siècle. As we will see, this theme of Franco-Jewish patriotism also accounts for the way the French Jews of Durkheim's acquaintance also articulated their views about the nature and study of religion.

Having stated my claim, I should enter a second caveat: while French nationalism shaped fin de siècle French Judaism, it equally well shaped each of the other religious communities of France. Durkheim's societism was like the similar "societism" developing within all the other religions in France of Durkheim's day. In fact, none was as much affected by the nationalist tide as the Catholics, who had been marginalized by a chronically anticlerical France. Like the Jews, the Catholics stemmed from an ancient tradition of religious societism. And the Catholics made a special point of asserting and developing this precisely at the same time and for the same nationalist reasons as the French Jews and Durkheim.[61] So, let us look into the role played by fin de siècle French nationalism in shaping the way members of different religious communities felt and thought.

The first thing we need to do, however, is revise our Anglophone image of the French as natural-born collectivists or socialists. In many ways, societism runs very much against the grain of anything one might call French national character; individualism is far more deeply entrenched.[62] Here, we should recall Jones's account of Durkheim's rebellion against the prevailing individualism of the French scientific and educational establishment. Individualism here assumed the form of Cartesianism, which Theodore Zeldin has argued functioned in the fin de siècle as an unofficial national ideology. For Zeldin, as for Jones, Cartesianism amounts to the "triumph of individual reason, . . . the rejection of authority, the questioning of all dogmas, . . . the assertion that man is above all a thinking being, who is not dependent on sensations or experience for his ideas or for the discovery of truth."[63] In this light, the societism of the socialists, the solidarists, and the Durkheimians should be seen as exceptions proving the rule of a national individualism. I will argue that the national crisis of the fin de siècle, culminating in what Eugen Weber has termed the "nationalist revival," for a short while challenged the reign of French individualism, thus for a short while making Durkheimian (and other societisms) viable.[64]

Equally important in the makeup of the French individualism has been the spell cast by the Revolution's assertion of *liberté*,
spectacularly evident in the anarchist explosions of Durkheim's
day. This tendency to rank the fissiparous ideal of liberty (along
with equality) over the equally revolutionary, but social, value
of fraternity is for Steven Lukes one of the peculiar defining
marks of French individualism.[65] I am arguing that the special
circumstances of the nationalist revival of Durkheim's time,
however, dictated that French individualism would be treated
to a withering critique from within. For example, just this sort
of French individualism, made up of Cartesianism plus the ideal
of unbridled *liberté*, was what Durkheim rejected when he took
up with the German thinkers.

In his skepticism about this sort of French individualism,
Durkheim was not alone, even if his remedies for it were unique.
While affirming Cartesian intellectual styles as distinctively
French, fin de siècle right-wing nationalist thinkers also felt that
undisciplined individualism topped the list of the nation's sick-
nesses. Selfishness among the common citizenry appalled them;
and the intellectuals were little better. They not only were full
of "egoism" but also were languishing in "lazy melancholy."[66]
Inconsistent Cartesians, right-wing thinkers further associated
selfishness with the critical attitudes of dissenting intellectuals.
The individualism of 'the intellectuals' was destroying the nation, as witnessed by the national furor resulting from the agitation of Émile Zola and others during the Dreyfus Affair. Intellectuals should have been setting examples of loyalty for the nation.
Instead, they were guilty of sowing seeds of skepticism and disaffection with key national institutions such as the army. Ironically, to right-wingers, Durkheim's defense of Alfred Dreyfus was
the very epitome of "individualism," as is well-known from his
public quarrels with the Catholic integralist philosopher Ferdinand Brunetière. And in some sense, Durkheim's statement is
indeed a powerful brief in behalf of individualism, even if it is
one of a highly polemical and subtle sort. So, across the ideological spectrum, the feeling prevailed that to counter the dissipat-
ing forces of individualism, France needed a counter-force
equipped to "heal society and intellectual nihilism."[67] Concerned thinkers, the Durkheimians included, felt that religion,
or something at least called 'religion,' would provide that
'force.' As it had done for centuries past, this 'religion' would

bind citizens into common service to the nation, providing national unity and morale.[68]

While engaged in this effort to define a national morale, Durkheim took great pains throughout his career to distance his views from those of extreme societists or collectivists: he was never a socialist or Marxist; he always deplored those he felt were mystical pantheists, such as communists, 'religious' socialists, Saint Simonians, and the like.[69] Yet Durkheim published his passionate essay "Individualism and the Intellectuals" to affirm his own brand of societism.[70] To counter charges of the Catholic nationalist Brunetière, he argued that the defenders of Dreyfus were the sorts of individualists who would actually strengthen national solidarity. For Durkheim, individualism, properly reconceived along his new societist lines, was an entirely French, patriotic conception. Indeed, it was perhaps the only collective value capable of binding all French citizens together.

I suggest that we now go one step further—that we link Durkheim's assertion of individualism as a French social value to the societal values embodied in Durkheim's science of society. Both were part of a patriotic attempt to reform individualist Cartesianism along societist (and thus, for Jones, 'German') lines—one in the domain of a national morale, the other in the realm of science. In his embrace of individualist values, Durkheim likewise was a lot like the Parisian Jews of his own day—that is, a lot like the typical bourgeois.

Being Jewish in the France of Durkheim's day was not to be particularly societist— at least in matters of national politics or political ideology. In fact, late into the nineteenth century, Jews were as individualist as members of any other French religious community, that is, they were not particularly societist at all. French Jews, particularly the Parisian majority, were on the whole not socialists, or even conspicuous in asserting any sort of collective Jewish identity—much less a national Jewish or Zionist one. The Reinach family was, for example, politically and socially close to the opportunist bourgeois politics of Léon Gambetta.[71] Socialists (Fourierists) targeted Jews for attack, partly because of the prominence of the highly visible Baron de Rothschild. Even though over 60 percent of all Jews died as paupers in the last decades of the nineteenth century, socialist propaganda often posed French Jews as epitomizing rapacious capitalism and its economic individualist creed of selfishness.[72] Even in terms of the communal self-defense of Jewry, French Jews did not typically form a common front. For example, there was no national French Jewish refutation of Edouard Drumont's anti-Semitic classic of 1886, *La France juive*. Even when the Dreyfus Affair hit, French Jews were not—except for the exceptional Bernard Lazare—conspicuous in the leadership of those defending the accused as a matter of Jewish collective interest.[73] The Catholic intellectual Charles Péguy in fact claimed that Jewish indifference to Dreyfus's plight was simple selfish apathy or worse. "They would only ask to sacrifice Dreyfus in order to ward off the storm," says Péguy.[74] Thus, far from expressing a native and essential societism the various bodies of French Jewry fit pretty well the bourgeois profile of most other French citizens of the period. If anything, and this perhaps became one of the causes of a developing sense of Jewish nationhood, both the socialist Left and the intransigent Right conveniently lumped together the Jews of France, all the better to target them for attacks as being altogether too individualist.

In part, the individualism of French Jews reflected their success at having become French and bourgeois. Like the French Gentile bourgeoisie, bourgeois French Jews were thoroughly informed with the ideals of Cartesian individualist cultural mythology and liberal nationalist political ideology[75]—so much so that even Jewish solidarity came late to French Jews. Zionism arrived in France, as Yosef Hayim Yerushalmi observed in quoting Haim Hazaz, not as a "continuity, but a break, the opposite of what was before, a new beginning."[76] And when Zionism began to take hold, it never replaced the liberal nationalist individualism and the sense of having been born French, ideas that are still alive and well among French Jews today.[77] Only toward the end of the last decades of the century, perhaps in response to the rise of right-wing integral nationalism and its attendant anti-Semitism, did French Jews offer their own version of pan-Franco Jewish nationalism, culminating in Zionism, a Jewish "societist" politics.[78] In this sense, Durkheim's often puzzling lack of solidarity with his Jewish ethnic and religious kin was more the rule for Jewish behavior than the exception.

Aside from Durkheim's own unwillingness to affiliate with Jews, why and how were French Jews in general reluctant to identify collectively as Jewish? To proceed at this point, we need to sketch the pertinent history of the Jewish community in France up to the time when Durkheim appeared on the Parisian intellectual scene, beginning with the causes of Jewish individualism. In political and demographic terms, by the mid–nineteenth century, French Jews were rather few in number (80,000) and were Parisian (65 percent). Parisian Jews were highly acculturated, some would say 'assimilated,' to metropolitan styles of French culture. Outside the metropole, the main provincial Jewish communities were divided into either that of Alsace-Lorraine (Ashkenazi) or Bordeaux and Bayonne (Sephardi).[79] Although Jews had been effectively banished from France from 1394 until 1790, the great purge of Jews in the Iberian Peninsula following the Reconquista sent Portuguese and Spanish marranos fleeing to French coastal towns such as Bordeaux or Bayonne, where they maintained their secret identities for generations.[80] The emancipation of the Jews, begun in the Revolution and completed in Napoléon's reign, likewise drew more Jews, primarily from the numerous 'German' domains to the east. After the loss of Alsace and Lorraine in the Franco-Prussian War, numerous Alsatian Jews, mostly representing more conservative religious traditions, moved either to the French side of the new border or directly to the capital. Durkheim's family and many of the Jewish members of the *équipe* hailed from eastern France. Much as Peter Gay bluntly characterized the German Jews of the Wilhelminian period—"German Jews thought and acted like Germans"—how much more so, given French liberalism, could the equivalent also be said of French-born Parisian Jews?[81]

By the 1880s, native French Jewish individualism would be tested by the most important Jewish immigration into France up to that point—the massive flight of Jewish victims of the pogroms and persecutions of czarist Russia. They came in unprecedented numbers, and by 1914, they nearly outnumbered the Paris population of French-born Jews.[82] Their arrival—and in effect the anti-Semitic reaction to them—eventually changed the character of French Jewish identity and spirituality. The arrival of the eastern European Jews sparked two struggles: one, of (non-Jewish) anti-Semites against the new immigrants; the other, between the liberal, modernist French-born, individualist Jews of Paris and the ritualistic, particularist, and collectively identified eastern European Jews.

What was the character and flavor of the bourgeois French Jews and Judaism dominating the 'Jewish' thought-world of

Durkheim's day, the so-called 'French Judaism'? In France, Napoléon's emancipation of the Jews was not simply a matter of relief from certain odious restrictions. Emancipation in effect, if not in theory, meant at least two things. First, the political status of Jews changed from one in which Jews claimed a distinct ancient national identity to one in which they were exclusively French nationals. In the words of the Sanhedrin's declaration of 1807: "Israel no longer forms a nation."[83] Correspondingly, in renouncing its own national and political aspirations, the Sanhedrin accepted France as its "primary sociopolitical loyalty" and laid the conceptual foundations for the French Jewish identity of Durkheim's day.[84]

Second, the surrender of Jewish national political identity entailed that the domains of religion and politics would henceforth be separated as distinct spheres. Once again the words of the Sanhedrin statement of 1807 are clear: "We therefore declare that the divine Law . . . contains within itself dispositions which are political and dispositions which are religious: that the religious dispositions are, by their nature, absolute and independent of circumstances and of age; that this does not hold true of the political dispositions which are taken for the government of the people of Israel in Palestine when it possessed its own kings, pontiffs and magistrates."[85] Thus, in addition to their French political identity, Jews now also acquired a new identifying characteristic—religious identity, French Judaism. The Jews of France thus became French Jews. No less a figure than the great French Jewish scholar James Darmesteter even marked the precise date of this transformation: "From the 28th of September, 1791, there is no longer a history of Jews in France. There is only a history of French Judaism, as there is a history of French Calvinism or Lutheranism, and nothing more."[86] To this extent, then, Napoléon may be said to have created the French Judaism of his time and for some succeeding generations.

A fundamental paradox, however, afflicted the process of the Jews of France becoming a religion called French Judaism.[87] Although much in terms of political rights was gained within France, in reconceiving French Jewish identity in such a fashion, the Jews lost other things. In effect, French Jews officially renounced concrete Jewish societal status as well as their own national status. As we will see shortly, the creation of this 'religion' of Judaism meant that the French Jews had, in theory, like all other citizens of whatever religious denomination, "become individual Frenchman of the Jewish faith." 'Becoming a religion' in the new sense meant that the French Jews came to be identified with a movable venue of worship like the synagogue, a system of explicit beliefs and (to a much lesser extent) practices, rooted in the *individual* conscience and concerning sacred things, but not with a separate Jewish nation-state.

In this individualized sense, both the Protestant and the Roman Catholic communities, in theory at any rate, became individualized 'religions' too. Catholicism resisted these trends longer than Judaism and Protestantism. But, in principle, it too was no longer the 'religion' it once had been. It could no longer claim to be the bearer of the encompassing values defining and dominating the nation, much as it had in the age of Christendom. The same role had also been played for those respective bearers of the values of Buddhist, Confucian, Hindu, and Muslim civilizations—'Buddhism,' 'Confucianism,' and so on.[88] In their modern forms the religions no longer played—at least without competition from other religious traditions or from 'secularism'—the encompassing roles they had in their heyday; they emerged as individual 'religions,' standing against other major subsystems of the nation such as the political and economic domains. They have become 'denominations,' defined by their adherence to distinctive dogmas or beliefs held by individual believers in the privacy of their own consciences. Thus, French Jews, like members of every other 'religion' in the modern dispensation, lived privatized or individualized spiritual lives. Judaism became one of many possible ideologies individuals might hold in the privacy of their own hearts, differing from other French citizens in that they worshiped in a synagogue and held different beliefs.[89]

But at the very moment our story of the Durkheimians begins, the 'religions' too began to stir against the constraints of having 'become religions.' Like the intransigent Catholics of the day, Jews eventually faced certain theological dilemmas of their new (reduced) identity as individual members of the Jewish 'religion.' French Jewish scholars of today speak of Judaism's need for the "acquisition of a proper physiognomy" in the wake of emancipation.[90] But there is also divine logic guiding such thinking: had not the God of all creation spoken to the patriarchs and prophets, to Israel as a people and nation with a message meant for all humanity? How could such cosmic prospects be satisfied by a cozy domesticated compromise with or submission to political powers? Were the borders of Israel to be pushed back to the inner recesses of the individual human heart? Countless French-born Jews certainly thought so.

But their voice was just then, at the turn of the century, beginning to be challenged by two forces. One was the arrival of the assertive, ritualistic, enthusiastic, and unembarrassedly religious Jewishness of the eastern European Jews;[91] the other was the rise of anti-Semitism linked with renewed French nationalism. With the rising anti-Semitism of the 1880s, the Dreyfus Affair, and the arrival of the new Jews from eastern Europe, French Jews of the fin de siècle found themselves caught in the crosscurrents of religious identity. Although they embraced the norms of official France, at the same time significant numbers were becoming more aware of the unavoidability of their own (at least perceived) differences and less agreeable to the official French doctrine of the liberal individualist values of the secular state.[92] Thus, the highly individualized, spiritualized ('disembodied') form of Judaism that had developed as a result of the Napoléonic emancipation proved, for at least a time and for certain segments of French Jewry, to be historically unstable.[93] This in turn, I believe, led Jews to embrace a greater sense of Jewish social embodiment, culminating for some eventually in the rise of political Zionism. As a result, Jewish religious identity was beginning to express itself in a kind of theological analogy to Durkheim's epistemological ideal of devotion to society and to the 'things' of scientific realism discussed by Jones.

Significantly, even important members of the liberal wing of French Jewish opinion, such as Hyppolite Prague, the editor of the *Archives israélites,* or the Jewish theologian Maurice Liber, of the Société des Études Juives, argued the case for Jewish reembodiment, Jewish realism. In a two-part article "L'Esprit du Christianisme et du Judaisme" (1906), Liber stated that Judaism is not a mere list of beliefs, a kind of mysticism "without priests, without sacrifices . . . and ceremonies."[94] Liber argued that Judaism was practical and worldly: it was an "ethic."[95]

Liber's article explicitly countered the chief representative of German theological thought of the time, Adolf von Harnack, and his famous masterpiece, tellingly entitled *The Essence of Chris-*

tianity. Liber felt that Harnack and other German theologians had committed "malicious and unjust" slanders against Judaism.[96] For them, Judaism was reduced to a familiar set of essentials diametrically opposed to Harnack's essential Christianity. Judaism had been superseded by Christianity; Jesus was original and owed little or nothing to Judaism; Talmudic Judaism was desiccated and decadent. Liber's article asserted that Judaism was not just "great ideas"; it was also a social and ritual entity and undigestible Jewish essence, a socially embodied view of the nature of Judaism. This he called a Judaism of practical morals and ritual practices, of "culture . . . work . . . art." Liber was not alone in these views; Prague, *Archives israélites* editor, claimed as early as 1900 that French Jews had just as much right to concrete group identity as their Christian fellow citizens. In a most un-Cartesian way, Prague went on to assert Judaism as "our laws and practices."[97] For Prague, this meant that Judaism is distinct and, in particular, not "hyperspiritual" like Christianity.[98] It links matter and soul and achieves thereby "the perfect harmony of the human and divine in us."[99] For Prague at least, such concerns for group identity and social embodiment had practical religious and political roots. In an editorial five years later, Prague reported that both the Catholics and the Protestants were working to build up their communities in reaction to the Law of Separation. Should not Jews put similar efforts into supporting their community as well?[100] Thus, by the end of the nineteenth century, Judaism was being regarded by significant representatives of the Jewish community in Paris as a religion fully social and concrete.

Eventually, this uneasiness about societal disembodiment gave way to deliberate practical attempts to resocialize Judaism. Reembodying Judaism took at least three forms. First and most radical was the attempt to reembody Judaism by way of political or Herzlian Zionism. Second was the equally particularist, but apolitical, attempt to embody Judaism culturally in the form of the so-called Jewish Renaissance of "Les Amis du Judaïsme" in Paris. Finally, alongside and often opposed both to political Zionism and less so to Les Amis du Judaïsme was a renewed movement asserting the collective nature of Judaism among so-called Franco-Jews.[101] As we will see, French Judaism still represented the most powerful Jewish societist trend of Durkheim's generation. Franco-Jews felt that Judaism should culminate in a veritable religion of French nationalism; indeed that 'Jewishness' gained its highest form of social corporeal existence in 'Frenchness.'

Let us first consider the Zionist polemic against Judaism as a 'religion.' Zionism claimed a very small minority of French Jews until some years after the turn of the century. Yet it would later become a significant solution to the disembodied, individualized status of Judaism in France. Zionists held that reconciling Judaism with their status as a religion in modern France was neither possible nor desirable. As such, Zionism was a rejection of the idea of the individualized 'religion' codified by Napoléon. The contradictions of modernity led some Jewish thinkers to reconsider the ideal of Judaism as a 'people'—in effect to reject the assumptions of the political modus vivendi worked out with the French state by which the Jews of France became French Jews. If Judaism could not be socially embodied in France, it might reclaim its political and ethnic identity in a Zionist entity such as the state of Israel. The leading Jewish intellectuals of the period came to the Zionist solution with the greatest reluctance, as we will see. The fact, however, that Sylvain Lévi, a leading representative of the French Jewish community and the most important Jewish thinker of this study, seemed headed in this direction is a fact of some significance.

On the other hand, Jewish intellectuals like Salomon Reinach (and Sylvain Lévi, as we will see) preferred a cultural rather than political way of realizing a distinctive Jewish societal identity. Offering an alternate path to Jewish cultural revival, they felt that Jews should find a third way, between indifference to Jewish identity and adoption of Zionist religious politics. Judaism was to be celebrated as a source of moral and intellectual wisdom of universal import. This entailed that Jews should not only cultivate their own rich cultural heritage for themselves but also foster the study of Judaism according to universal scientific principles of detachment, such as promoted by the Science du Judaïsme.[102] Their movement, in many ways reminiscent of the Polish "Bund," took the positive form of French Jewish cultural assertion, the so-called Jewish Renaissance of 1906–18.[103] A new association, Les Amis du Judaïsme, led the way to a virtual boom of self-conscious Jewish cultural activity early in the century. Prominent in the membership of Les Amis du Judaïsme were major figures of French culture such as Léon Blum and the composer Darius Milhaud. Figures important to the present study were Israël Lévi and Salomon Reinach, one of its founders.[104] The Amis said that French Jews should assert their uniqueness and, in so doing, enrich all forms of *cultural* activity in behalf of a renascent Judaism.[105]

At the same time that French Jews were becoming more convinced that their Judaism should become more concrete—either politically or culturally—they were also becoming even more devoted to France. Patriotic mobilization of spirit, if not of matériel, in distant preparation for World War I was under way. Ironically, such deeper identification with the nation served the movement of French Judaism toward further social embodiment, neither with the Zionist project nor with Jewish culture but with France itself. So, whether to move toward a distinct Jewish national or cultural identity or to claim identification with France, French Jews had become more conscious of the need to embody their religion in suitable societal forms. Thus, at the religious level, in seeking social embodiment, French Jewish thought developed analogously to the German and Durkheimian scientific orientation toward society and 'things,' as discussed by Jones.

In light of these Jewish societist movements, we might imagine that during Durkheim's time, French Jews, and the Durkheimians along with them, were moving in directions that would favor at least the two major features taken for granted by Durkheimian thought: religion is both social and concrete. In this view, Durkheim's 'Jewishness' is not about his secret religious or ethnic identity but about how Durkheimian thought seems to mimic the movement to social concreteness typical of prominent Jewish religious thought of the period. I do not know exactly what we should make of the fact that these like-minded movements toward concreteness and sociability came from such different sources. Neither I nor, surely, Jones believes that these theological trends within the Jewish community had anything directly to do with Durkheim's orientation toward society and 'things.' Although Durkheim's integration of individualism and nationalism seemed to mirror the Franco-Jewish values, I do not imagine that Liber and Prague developed the conviction that Judaism needed to be social and concrete *because* of German social science and moral philosophy. This Jewish theological movement for a concrete social embodiment of Judaism expresses an inherently politico-religious dynamic—rather than anything one can identify as a debt to German thought.[106] The embrace of social concreteness by Durkheim and his *équipe* was likewise not the play of modern-day marranos, analogies with Jewish theology notwithstanding. Yet however unlikely the possibility that Durkheimian concreteness and societism sprang from the same Jewish religious and political ground as Liber's and Prague's quests for Jewish social concreteness, they might both nonetheless spring in part from a—third—common source. Durkheimian thought is notorious for straddling the boundary between science and 'religion,' between the scientific study of society and social reconstruction. I merely note that at the same time that Franco-Jewish intellectuals had elevated the concrete social domain in their appreciation of Judaism, the Durkheimians were doing the same. Other societist movements—in addition to those economic and scientific trends isolated by Jones, Turner, and Vogt—may have stirred the Durkheimians. So, the question remains whether developments on the Jewish theological plane can be squared with principles discussed by Jones, Turner, and Vogt on the level of socialist economic and scientific thought coming mainly from German authors. What possibly could account for the convergence of a French Jewish theology of social embodiment with Durkheim's scientific societist convictions of the same period? How can we explain why the social realism discovered by Durkheim in Germany found such an analogy on the Jewish religious plane in this way?

One factor alone could have been influential enough to shape intellectual developments across frontiers as broad as that dividing Jewish theology and Durkheimian science. This was nationalism, in particular the transcendent or religious French nationalism of the fin de siècle. No one disputes that the Durkheimians were not deeply energized by the nationalist fervor of the day.[107] The same is true, and in equal measure, of Durkheim's Jewish contemporaries. Furthermore, both Durkheimians and Franco-Jews sought to maximize the values of individualism together with nationalism against the right wing's attempts to suppress individualism under the force of nationalism. To reach a solution to the puzzle of the broad movement toward societism that linked the scientific and moral beliefs of Durkheim with the religious and moral pursuits of French Jews, let us now explore how nationalism figured in Jewish life and thought.

James Darmesteter, the genie of Franco-Jewish theory, typifies the nationalist feelings of Franco-Jews from as early as 1870. Taking leave of his spiritualist tendencies, Darmesteter gradually came round to the view that Judaism required a more particular and concrete social embodiment than some sort of abstract 'humanity.' Without such concrete social embodiment, Judaism would result only in "deracinating Christianity and deracinating itself."[108] Therefore, Judaism had to be incarnated in France itself.[109] Paris would replace Jerusalem, and Jewishness would "dissolve" in "the catholic union of the future," which would be the "moral equivalent of the ancient Hebrew faith."[110] The strength and durability of French nationalist loyalties among Jewish citizens was furthermore so considerable that even despite the Dreyfus Affair, Zionism never succeeded in ruling the loyalties of the French Jewish community in Durkheim's day. Even when Zionism became a considerable force in the late nineteenth and early twentieth centuries, as Vicki Caron notes, it was the newly arrived eastern European and North African Jews who led the movement.[111] More typical of Durkheim's day were the words of Franco-Jewish liberals such as Salomon Reinach. He labeled the nascent Zionist national movement as superstitious—just "a new religion founded on the idea of a native land."[112] To the extent that Reinach voiced feelings shared by the largely French-born Jewish population, we can understand why Zionism did not compel the loyalty of French Jews in Durkheim's France. Although the Dreyfus Affair gave many of them pause to question their loyalty to the republic, Franco-Jews remained substantially unshaken in their patriotism.

But the patriotism of every day would not be enough to match the crisis of nationalism that occurred after the debacle of defeat in the Franco-Prussian War. Beginning in 1870 and reinforced in 1895 and then again in 1905, French national feeling reached a fever pitch. So potent was this sentiment that, as Eugen Weber observed, by 1914 all French political parties were nationalist in the sense of supporting drastic military preparations against Germany.[113] Although the language differed, the message was always the same: France risked national safety in the face of German power; the losses of 1870 had to be avenged.[114]

The revival of national feeling was felt especially in the theology and practice of the traditional religions. From 1870, the

new nationalist spirit dominated the internal life of the traditions, so much so that it set the agenda of religious life. In Catholic circles, well-known right-wing revanchist groups like the Action Française arose. The feast of the warrior saint Joan of Arc
became a national holiday.[115] Attempts were even made to can-
onize Napoléon, an action that, its supporters promised, "would
achieve absolutely that union of patriotic and religious senti-
mentality to which the Church in France" was directing "its activities."[116] The cult of the martyrs and Christian heroes was already strong in the Church; in the years following the defeat to
the Prussians, the Church intensified this cult.[117] In 1886, Abbé
Profillet published *Les Saints militaires,* a book of accounts of the
lives of six hundred saints. Within a few years, this work had
expanded to six volumes and counted three thousand hero
saints.[118]

At first, partly because of a mixture of their bourgeois social
location, their own theological doubts, and their aversion to the
strident nationalist propaganda emanating from the intransigent Roman Catholic community, some prominent Jews resisted
the more extreme forms of nationalist rhetoric.[119] The rise of
chauvinism attending the war greatly distressed neo-Jewish inter-
nationalist and religious liberals, such as Reinach, much as it
had Jaurès. Resurgent nationalism coincided, observed Reinach,
with outbreaks of the occult and "superstitions" such as the belief in guardian angels and diviners. With perfect consistency,
Reinach likewise deplored Zionism because he felt that all forms
of nationalism increased intolerance, whether they be French
or Jewish.[120] Zionism was to him just "a new religion founded on
the idea of a native land."[121] Yet however astute and influential
Reinach may have been, and however mightily his case was
made, he was reduced to a minority voice within both France
and the Jewish community as French nationalists took charge
of the agendas of the religious traditions.

Thus, each of France's religious communities tried eagerly
to demonstrate its Frenchness, all the while developing theologies of social 'embodiment.' French Jews, Roman Catholics, and
Protestants sought not only to establish the depth of their
French 'roots' but also to gain greater identification with the
political apparatus of the nation-state. Catholics pursued the
double policy of insisting on the Frenchness of Catholicism as
well as on the Catholicism of France. In trying to reestablish

itself as *the* official religion of France, Roman Catholicism identified with the whole French nation rather than simply with the
consciences of the faithful.[122] Protestant gains in the public domain during the Third Republic were substantial, and these
gains were accordingly dubbed the "revenge of the Reformation." In some sense, the officially democratic ideals, the bourgeois market economics, and the emphasis on education all
counted as 'Protestant' values in France. No less a public philosopher than Charles Renouvier even called for mass conversion
to Protestantism as the surest guarantee of steady progress toward national modernization.[123] On the religious side, once the
Protestants had held their first legal synod (1871), they recov-
ered some of their own embodied nature in launching Protestant social institutions such as Tommy Fallot's Société d'Aide
Fraternelle et d'Études Sociales (1882) and the Association Pro-
testante pour l'Étude Pratique des Questions Sociales (1887).[124]
Some commentators even declare Solidarisme, for example, to
be an embodiment of rediscovered Protestant social values.[125]

Yet no members of a religious community felt as much pres-
sure to locate and celebrate their French 'roots,' to identify
themselves with the nation, as did the Jews.[126] Jews were routinely
accused of a lack of patriotism for being either too 'cosmopolitan' or too *deracinée*.[127] Jews, after all, had both a history of religious difference (as did the Protestants) and a history of separate nationhood. Further, with the recent influx of eastern
European Jews, the expanded French Jewish community was especially easy to target by anti-Semites as a subversive force, a
foreign 'body' within the French 'body' politic.[128] Similarly, the
Protestants had often been libeled by associating them with predominantly Protestant Germany or Britain. Ironically, so likewise were Jews tagged with the German label, since many of
them hailed from Alsace. There, Jews had retained the German
and Yiddish language even after 1789, and few, except the urban elites, learned to speak French until years later.[129] We should
also remember that Durkheimian thought and the Alsatian
Durkheim himself had been attacked in print for being 'German' as well.[130] In response to this attempt to cast Jews as strangers, the Jewish learned journal *Revue des études juives* featured
regular article-length historical accounts of France's many long-
lived Jewish communities, some of which even dated to Roman
times. French Jews emphatically asserted that they belonged in

France as much as members of any other religious community, since they had been a living part of French history from its beginnings.

Accordingly, French Jews lived up to their image of themselves by conspicuous displays of patriotism. Whether because of external pressures to conform or a natural attraction for republican values, French Jews happily adapted themselves to the conditions of French citizenship, especially to the approaching war. They did so as straightforward patriotism, by claiming, for example, that as good French citizens, they were "electrified" by the "cause."[131] But they also did so in large degree by trading on the imagery of the vigorous warrior and the ritual sacrificial traditions of ancient Israel. In bringing these metaphors from Jewish antiquity to bear on their situation in France, French Jews in effect merged their own history with the present course of French history—a perfect expression of the Franco-Jewish doctrine of a Judaism embodied in France itself. Thus, in 1916, the influential liberal Jewish newspaper *Archives israélites* called the victory in the Battle of the Marne as much a providential act as was the deliverance of the Israelites as narrated in the book of Esther.[132] A 1915 editorial, "Le Soldat Juif," was also published in the *Archives israélites*.[133] "Le Soldat Juif" said that by taking an active role in the army, French Jews would defend France in the same way that their ancestors had defended Jerusalem.[134] The same editor of the *Archives* took pride in pointing out how Jewish soldiers displayed the "spirit of the Macchabees" in elite fighting units such as the Zouaves, in which Jews numbered some 60 percent of the total.[135] Similarly, Jewish exhortations to patriotism were justified by citing Jewish equivalents for symbols of French national identity. Even nearly a generation before the war, in 1890, Rabbi Armand Bloch had recommended that Jews devote themselves to Joan of Arc. At the installation ceremony for a statue of the future national saint erected on the property of a Nancy synagogue, Bloch urged Jews to be comfortable with her presence among them. After all, the saint's residence there showed Jewish dedication to the nation; in addition, she was essentially the same as heroic Jewish biblical women such as Esther and Judith. A Jew honoring her honors them as well.[136]

Much as in the Catholic tradition, the religious metaphors of ritual sacrifice were keenly sharpened for service in the coming war. In a prewar Rosh Hashanah sermon, "L'esprit de sacrifice," Grand Rabbi Jacques Henri Dreyfuss argued that the sacrifice of Isaac proved something about Jewish character: it was "doubtless a deed which is most edifying and moving—the most renown[ed] manifestation of the piety which personifies the founder of our race."[137] When Grand Rabbi Dreyfuss then inquired about the essence of this piety, he answered by naming a series of civic virtues including service to "others," which had only the "commonweal" in mind. This piety consisted in the patriotic virtues of "heroism," "devotion," even "devotion pushed to its extreme limits."[138] On Yom Kippur 1916, in the war's midst, the message was the same. Hyppolite Prague editorialized in the *Archives israélites* that the "spirit of sacrifice is an innate virtue *chez* Israel."[139] Going further, Prague added: "It is because we love God that we consent to the sacrifices which make up the prescriptions of his cult, [because we love God that we submit ourselves] to his laws. . . . It is because we are French, [because] we love our *patrie,* that we consent to all these painful sacrifices of blood and self-interest, in the long run order to safeguard the existence of France and to assure her triumph."[140]

But despite their declared ardor and readiness to serve from the very outbreak of the war, French Jews still felt that they had to prove their patriotism to their fellow citizens, many of whom had fallen under the spell of the anti-Semitic propaganda of the decades before. Defending against these anti-Semitic slurs were many artists and intellectuals. Poet André Spire declared that Jews "went to battle with the pure spirit of sacrifice."[141] But tellingly, they fought for France with such "ardor and daring" in order to defend "the honor of the name 'Jew.' "[142] Consider as well the remarkable case of the great liberal Jewish intellectual Grand Rabbi Zadok Kahn, who addressed a class of Jewish seminarians being readied for induction into the army.[143] The conscription of Jewish seminarians was a controversial consequence of a recently promulgated (1892) law. Kahn reminded his audience that although Jewish clerics were traditionally supposed to represent Judaism's universalist and pacifist devotion to "unity, tolerance and charity,"[144] their service in the army had its "compensations."[145] In addition to being the "great school of rectitude, loyalty, devotion and abnegation,"[146] the army also taught "love of country, and what is called the *culte du drapeau . . .* the sacred symbol of our *patrie.*"[147] In serving patriotically, Jews would show that they were good Frenchmen, thus debunking their old stereotype and "inaugurating a new phase of our history."[148] This need to defend Jewish honor before their fellow citizens in a time of systematic anti-Semitism was felt right down to the grass roots of Jewish consciousness. Identified only as "Litwack," a descendant of recent Russian-Jewish immigrants to France penned this final letter before dying in a fatal assault: "So that the whole world might see that the Jews know how to die for liberty . . . we will demonstrate to France that the Jews know how to die for a country that makes no difference between its children. I am happy to die for a noble republican France, which is worthy of every sacrifice, because she will not forsake my wife, my child. . . . In an hour, we will march, and we will die for France, for Jews, for the emancipation of all Jews."[149]

So potent was the force of French patriotism that Jews routinely preferred loyalty to France even when this meant abandoning fellow Jews to the ravages of persecution and loss of life. Renewed pogroms by their Russian allies, for example, created an especially painful situation for French Jews, many of whom had themselves only recently fled Russia to escape the anti-Semitic campaigns of the 1880s. Normally, French Jews would have been vocal about these egregious Russian anti-Semitic policies. But with the Franco-Russian alliance serving as a linchpin of national foreign policy, French Jews felt constrained to keep silent in the face of renewed Russian pogroms.[150]

The transcendent power of French nationalism so overwhelmed religious loyalties that each of the traditions fell into line with the national will. The religions adapted their theologies and preaching to promote the patriotic message, such as by developing theologies of sacrifice, heroism, and martyrdom and in some cases even by reconceiving their identities in light of the national imperative. "After 1870, patriotism became the religion of France," said a sympathetic chronicler of these times, the Protestant *ecrivain* and theologian Paul Sabatier.[151] Even liberal Catholics like Alfred Loisy felt that despite avowing his belief in that "divine spirit in humanity [that] does not die," in "the unique God [who] is our human ideal,"[152] the religion of the "native land"[153] took precedence and that the "feeling for French humanity" was the "common religion."[154] In a 1917 correspondence with Maude Petre, Loisy noted that "to put the idea of humanity in the first place" was a "false humanitarianism" that had "done us some harm." Therefore, he concluded,

"It seems to me better to give a concrete form to our French ideal of humanity by starting from France."[155]

In a similar vein, Prague, editor of the Jewish newspaper *Archives israëlites,* declared in his 1914 leader "Religion et Patrie": "What patriotism has in common with religious sentiment is the exaltation of the soul, the transport to the sublime, and the tendency in a human effort toward an ideal end. Like religion, love of country is a sacred *foyer,* the crucible in which our noblest sensibility is elaborated and crystallized, and which pushes us on to heroic action, and make[s] the most obscure citizen a paladin of the national ideal."[156] Indeed, said Prague further, civic virtues seemed to update the ancient ritual devotion of Israel itself: "All the sacrifices on the altar of the *Patrie* which France offers at this very moment . . . bear a striking resemblance to those that true religious souls are ready to make to their God. . . . There is a strict correlation—an intimate kinship—between religion and patriotism—those most noble and pure sentiments of humanity."[157]

In conclusion, although the prevailing individualized condition of French Jews in being both bourgeois and individual members of a 'religion' made them unlikely sources of anything resembling Durkheimian societism, later developments in the history of the Jews in France, driven as they were by nationalism, might well have done so. Indeed, because of the patriotic fervor of the time, in addition to the internal French concerns about such issues as social reconstruction and societism, patriotism was, for a significant number of thoughtful intellectuals, all the rage. Along with the 'boats' of Protestants and Catholics raised by the patriotic 'tide,' Jewish patriotic and societist feelings were raised as well. We know, accordingly, that Durkheim exhibited these powerful patriotic sentiments, expressing them not only in a variety of writings but also in the nature of his work of social reconstruction and national educational and scientific reforms. We further know that his embrace of the societism and the study of 'things' which he declared on his return from his first study tour in Germany sprouted directly out of patriotic soil. Now, although Jewish tendencies toward religious societism and concreteness had their own causes internal to the religious dynamic of the Jewish community, Jews also reacted to the religious individualism dictated by the politics of 'religion' set into motion by Napoléon. Judaism for them needed to become more social and concrete than the new dispensation allowed. This future conception of Judaism, like that of each great religious tradition of France, was a reaction to the strictures placed on them by Napoléonic reforms. Perception of national need inspired each tradition to imagine that it might possibly be the salvation and soul of the French body politic. For Jews, identification with the national French body politic or with the distant pursuit of a Jewish national political embodiment pressed them toward a more societist and concrete conception of their own essential nature.

Was Durkheim completely immune to such national pressures weighing on the Jews of his time? We have no direct evidence either way, although we know that a close Jewish confederate of Durkheim's—Robert Hertz—went to war partly in order to show that as a Jew, he was as totally devoted to France as any non-Jew. "Jewish by origin and French by all the thoughts of his mind and strivings of his moral being, he reckoned that the blood of the men of his race and of his own conscience would be usefully shed to liberate their children from all reproaches of egoism, particularist interest and indifference in the eyes of a suspicious France." [158] If this is what someone as close to Durkheim as Hertz had felt, is it possible that nothing of the same motives drove so conscientious a patriot as Durkheim? The question cannot be answered given our present lack of evidence. I have tried simply to construct a scenario in which such evidence as might arise would make sense.

What I have argued is, then, that although we *may* link Durkheim's affinity for societism with his Jewish rearing, this affinity is for a Jewish identity called forth by French nationalism and its 'shadow'—the anti-Semitism of the fin de siècle—rather than for something springing from a preexistent 'essence.' This French, nationalistically driven sense of being Jewish had much to do with the peculiar character of the life of Jews in Durkheim's part of France in the midst of the national crisis leading up to World War I. One needs, however, immediately to add that if the regional and the religious conditions of Durkheim's birth predisposed him for active nationalism, it seems impossible at this time to separate these conditions cleanly. Was it 'region' or 'religion' that made more of a difference to Durkheim? Durkheim's attraction for societism may, then, in part have been a feature of the vigorous patriotism typical— *but not exclusive to*—the Jews of his time and region, sincerely answering what he and they took to be the call of the country.[159] Whether Durkheim felt as he did about France because he had been born and raised Jewish or because he hailed from Alsace is impossible to decide. But the possibility remains that Jewish identity was a factor in Durkheim's attitudes. Remarkable none-theless is the analogy between Durkheim's turn to societism and concreteness and the similar turn articulated by some of the most influential Jewish theologians of his day. In putting this analogy into place before my readers, I wanted to make the case that economic and scientific interests on their own do not seem to account for such remarkable correspondences across intellec-tual disciplines and forms of life. If there is any domain of life that might encompass the broad range of human endeavors in-volved in the politics of identification, the French (and to a lesser extent, the Jewish) nationalism of the epoch must surely head a list of candidates for such cultural work. That is where the eidence I have amassed has directed my thinking.

Thus, whereas national peril mobilized the religions of France to mine their traditions for ways to express societal loy-alty, we must not forget Vogt's and Turner's efforts to articulate the nature of social movements that sought to heal the alien-ating effects of modern society. Durkheim was part of these movements. One of the aims was to seek a common 'religion' for the nation. French opinion-makers of the era sometimes thought that "these religious and political aspirations" wit-nessed, "each in its own way, to this truth: humanity cannot be organized without a religion."[160] In traditional form or as a 'religion,' however, no single traditional religion could any longer legally or realistically claim hegemony over the others in modern France. None could hope to encompass the others— although the revanchist Catholics had not yet finished trying.[161] In response to this constitutional dead end, humanist and reli-gious or theological liberals began to innovate. They interpreted their own traditions in what, as we will see, might be called a symbolic way. Interpreted at such a 'higher' level, the religions might graduate to a universal encompassing status that was tell-ingly called in its day "la religion" (*the* religion) of the nation. The liberals of each of the traditions took on the theological task of defining just what the nature of "*the* religion" might be and showing, moreover, how "*the* religion" grew more naturally out of their particular 'religion' than out of others.

Given the Christian heritage of France, Protestants and Roman Catholics easily argued that the new religion of France would be an organic all-French extrapolation of themselves. Protestant and Roman Catholic liberal theologians thus felt that some greatly expanded version of Christianity could provide the needed moral glue to keep the nation in one piece. *The* religion of France ought to be some version—however expanded and universal—of Christianity, an 'ultra-Christianity' as it was termed by contemporary observers of the religious scene.[162]

Jews were somewhat divided about what to do. Unlike the revanchist Catholics, French Jews never believed that traditional Judaism could become *the* basis for *the* religion of France. But Jewish liberals joined in a common effort with their Christian fellows and argued that such a national religion might arise out of a radical reinterpretation of Judaism along the lines that Darmesteter had promised in articulating his vision of 'Franco-Judaism.' Thus, commentators of the day spoke of a 'neo-Judaism' to put alongside the 'ultra-Christianity' of the day.[163]

But this broad agreement among liberals did not mean there were no differences worth quarreling about. When the Durkheimians compared their definition of *the* religion with those offered by religious modernists or liberals, Jewish or otherwise, they inevitably opposed the latter. The national debate then became one to establish a normative, a priori definition of what the *real* religion should be for France. Let us now see just how the ideas of the Jewish modernists compared with those of the Durkheimians on the nature and future of religion.

3

REINACH'S MODERNISM,
DURKHEIM'S SYMBOLISM, AND
THE BIRTH OF THE *SACRÉ*

Every student of Durkheim knows that he simply assumed a bifurcated social world of 'symbols' concealing profound realities. Such a perspective became the conceptual basis for his claim that religion can be explained in terms of an underlying social basis.[1] As early as his second publication, the 1887 review essay on Jean-Marie Guyau's *L'Irreligion de l'avenir*, Durkheim thus said: "Christ and the miracles now merely represent the deity. Why should God not himself be a symbol?"[2] In his classic *The Elementary Forms of the Religious Life*, Durkheim again characteristically tells us that in the study of religion, we "must know how to go underneath the symbol to the reality which it represents and which gives it its meaning."[3] Thus, from the beginning of his intellectual career to the very end, Durkheim's approach to social reality remains constantly symbolist.

Why did Durkheim choose to characterize reality and explanation in this bifurcated and symbolist way? What is the "argumentative context" of his appeal to the metaphor of symbol?[4] Certainly part of the reason behind Durkheim's choice was his rationalist desire to seek the 'real' historical substratum *beneath* traditional or mythological religious representations.[5] Guided by the practice of demythologizing historians like Ernest Renan, Durkheim was hospitable to these rationalist assumptions about dealing with religious materials and merely argued about religion as they did. Others, however, have suggested that Durkheim's 'symbolism' points to his hidden or 'essential' Jewishness. In their view, it reflects perhaps the intricacies of symbol-rich Cabalistic thought or the ingenuity of Talmudic interpretive strategies inherited from Durkheim's youth. Jean-Claude Filloux, for example, tries to link Durkheim's "hymn to society" and other rhapsodic passages of *The Elementary Forms of the Religious Life* to Durkheim's early religious experience. From this observant youth, Filloux suggests, Durkheim was in some way loyal to Jewish notions of a God hidden from ordinary purview behind the screen of creation yet a God ever-agent in creation.[6] In Durkheim's social thought, these theological styles of discourse supposedly percolated to the surface.

Two points about Durkheim's audience need to be immediately made in response to these suggestions. In deference to his scientific audience (and his own deepest 'scientistic' beliefs), Durkheim merely assumed that scientific explanation consisted in showing what lay beneath surface realities—in showing what deeper things were symbolized by more obvious things. But he also sought to win over religious people to his sociology. Since his target audiences were often drawn from a special population of religious believers, these religious folk in turn would have had to find Durkheim's symbolist claims both plausible and agreeable to their religious faith. Thus, beyond needing to be agreeable to the scientific community, Durkheim's symbolic approach to religion needed to resonate with the trends of theological thinking and religious belief current in the France of Durkheim's time. And if it did, French Jews might well have been part of that audience.

If, then, part of Durkheim's symbolist way of talking about religion was directed at Jews, did it mark the beginnings of some kind of return to the religious observance of his youth? Rather than a survival of childhood religiosity, the symbolic approach to religion that Durkheim practiced was instead a contemporary phenomenon, one diffused across the spectrum of 'advanced' religious thought. Rather than nostalgia for a lost world of piety, Durkheim's symbolism was another of those ways in which he boldly engaged modernity from the inside. Symbolism preoccupied the avant-garde Jewish (and Christian) theology of Durkheim's maturity, connected with the Jews, such as Louis-Germain Lévy or Salomon Reinach, the Catholics, such as Alfred

Loisy, Edouard Le Roy, or Marcel Hébert, and perhaps most important of all, the Protestants, such as Auguste Sabatier. Dominique Parodi, the humanist philosopher and sometimes fellow traveler of the *équipe,* observed that the compulsion to extract the "symbolic value" of the old religious questions characterized the advanced religious thinkers of the times.[7] Catholic modernism was, for example, immortalized in novels of the day like Romain Rolland's *Jean-Christophe,* where one reads of the "clerical symbolists."[8] Likewise in a chapter entitled "The Symbolist Compromise" in Roger Martin du Gard's novel of the period, *Jean Barois,* Abbé Schertz, the *"prêtre symboliste,"* holds forth in typical fashion.[9] "True religion," says Schertz, "knows that these [anthropomorphic] representations are only finally symbols."[10] Thus, as Schertz echoes the Durkheim who announced that God should be seen as a symbol, he tries to win the heart of Barois for the symbolist cause. Durkheim's own atheistic theological liberalism, in this sense, either was derived from and/or adapted to his audience among the religious modernists or simply was generated by the Durkheimians as a common feature of a shared hermeneutic persective. Whatever the precise origins, Durkheim's symbolic reading of religion was, then, only a dialect of the common language of advanced religious discourse of his day. Religious symbolism needs to be apprehended within the context of the mature 'routes' Durkheim perforce took, rather than in terms of the 'roots' nurturing him secretly from his childhood.

We are thus face to face with those I will call religious or clerical 'modernists.'[11] They knew Durkheim; he knew them. Durkheim's right-hand man, Henri Hubert, could therefore toss off a reference to Philo's symbolic interpretation of sacrifice as a "fine example of what Jewish modernists seek to make of sacrifice,"[12] and in doing so, he showed how routinely the Durkheimians took the existence of Jewish and non-Jewish symbolic modes of interpretation as part of the intellectual scene. It seems plausible that the "argumentative context" of the Durkheimian symbolic approach to religion was made up in part of liberal or modernist Jewish thinkers who brought their particular Jewish theological agendas to bear on issues common to Durkheimian concerns. Far from falling into totally distinct intellectual communities, the Durkheimians and the Jewish religious modernists or liberals ought to be seen as different species within a common genus. I argue that the Durkheimians took for granted these Jewish religious modernist interpretive agendas, which they saw as normal parts of the religious scene of their own time and thus as normal vehicles for engaging religious modernists in polemic.[13]

Until now, however, attempts to locate the "argumentative context" of the Durkheimian symbolic approach to religion have almost universally passed over religion and consequently have not taken note of the modernist religious context.[14] Strategies to uncover the historical genesis of Durkheim's symbolism have focused on the more fashionable realm of the cultural avant-garde.[15] Thus, Edward Tiryakian has linked Durkheimian symbolism with the revolutions in the arts of the fin de siècle. The new cultural trends that swept through the Parisian scene after the death of Victor Hugo in 1885 presumably caught the Durkheimians in their surge.[16] In September 1886, Jean Moréas published his symbolist manifesto in *Le Figaro;* Charles-Pierre Baudelaire, Paul Verlaine, Stéphane Mallarmé, Arthur Rimbaud, and Maurice Maeterlinck thrived; impressionism, postimpressionism, and expressionism, Vincent Van Gogh and Paul Gauguin, followed later by Pablo Picasso, Georges Braque, and Juan Gris, all flourished exactly when Durkheimian thought was taking shape.[17] Tiryakian would have us believe that the Durkheimians participated in the radical symbolism of this Parisian avant-garde.[18] Durkheim's 'going beyond the letter' thus reflected the symbolist view that reality was no longer quite as solid as it had once seemed. Hidden forces determined the shape of the seemingly sturdy surface of things.[19] These radical artistic departures correspond exactly to the new paradigm for looking at reality introduced by the Durkheimians; they too sought to plunge beneath the surface of mundane social appearances.[20]

Stimulating though Tiryakian's vision may be, it fails to fit the facts, since Tiryakian fixes the Durkheimians on the wrong cultural coordinates. The mysticism and occultism of symbolism puts it well beyond the Durkheimian pale. The Durkheimians never saw themselves as part of an avant-garde, artistic or irrationalist or otherwise. Moreover, none of the major contemporary observers of the age saw the Durkheimians as Tiryakian chose to see them. One of the most prominent barometers of the mood of these times, *L'Ésprit de la nouvelle Sorbonne* by "Agathon,"[21] attacked the representatives of French positivistic thought, among whom Durkheim featured prominently[22]—hardly an advertisement for the supposedly radical avant-garde pedigree of the Durkheimians.[23] If Tiryakian's thesis fits anywhere, it fits more naturally with someone like Henri Bergson and his followers than with Durkheim. As Mark Antliff has shown, it was the Bergsonians who were close, or at least were presumed to be close, to the very avant-garde and symbolist movements that Tiryakian fancies.[24] As early as 1897, Durkheim clearly revealed his distaste for these and other radical cultural trends. "The anarchist, the aesthete, the mystic, the socialist revolutionary, even if they do not despair of the future, have in common with the pessimist a single sentiment of hatred and disgust for the existing order, a single craving to destroy or to escape from reality."[25]

As champions of the rationalist spirit of the Sorbonne over the then reigning Bergsonianism of the Collège de France, the Durkheimians saw themselves as scientists above all (even though, as we will see, their *moraliste* ambitions threw them into the same orbit with the religious modernists). They sought to *explain* religion rather than give expression to it.[26] Thus, in terms of symbolic notions of explanation, Durkheim was especially disturbed that people commonly believed that science saw only the "surface of things" whereas religion reputedly got to the "depths." Durkheim intended sociology instead to usurp religion in getting to these "depths": "We must closely examine these hidden sides of things, those supposedly mysterious realms that religion reserves for itself."[27] Accordingly, Durkheim attacked the very symbolists that Tiryakian wants to link with him. Durkheim accused them of mistakenly attributing the epistemological power of science to religion: "Neo-mystics and litterateurs have strongly contributed to making this apparent contradiction fashionable."[28]

Putting further distance between the Durkheimians and the artistic community was the fact that Durkheim himself was at best indifferent to the arts.[29] Likewise, his entire *équipe* was indifferent as well.[30] The *équipe*'s only practicing artist and professional art historian was Henri Hubert, who was apparently completely unmoved by the artistic fashions of his day—and this when Hubert lived in the same Paris suburb, St. Germain-en-Laye, in which some of the leading symbolists lived, gathered, and showed their work. A review of Hubert's original sketches and watercolors reveals nothing of an attempt to ape the fashions of the avant-garde but instead shows the work of a talented amateur engaged in an essentially private pastime, works rendered in the easy style of a weekend artist at leisure.[31] As a reviewer of the arts in *L'Année sociologique,* Hubert likewise seemed remote from the avant-garde and its sensibilities. His review of a work on aboriginal African art in 1913 did not, for instance, celebrate the aesthetic of pure 'primitive' form or its liberated abstract design. In vain further do we seek evidence of an artistic sensitivity that might be called 'modern'—one that treats art for art's sake, as an autonomous mode of representation. Hubert observed that a rich mythological tradition, and thus a world of Durkheimian 'collective representations,' must lurk behind such painting and make it possible.[32]

In this vein, something of Durkheim's Jewish nurture may be relevant in his suspicion of the arts, even if such feelings might just as easily have resulted, say, from Durkheim's class suspicions of the rarefied world of the aesthete. At any rate, Louis M. Greenberg has argued that the tendencies of Durkheim's rationalist Talmudic father discouraged indulgence in the arts, mysticism, or poetry—an attitude that certainly typifies Durkheim's adult opinions. By contrast, the mystical character of Bergson's Polish Jewish Hasidic rearing may have pushed intuition to the center of the philosopher's thought.[33] Greenberg argues that Moïse Durkheim's devotion to the puritanical and rationalist bent of Rashi's Talmudic school of Troyes derailed such attractions. Instead, the emphasis on biblical exegesis and Talmudic jurisprudence suppressed interest in such "frivolities" as the arts. Thus, Durkheim simply did not feel that the arts mattered much. If Greenberg is correct about Durkheim's special regional and class-specific Jewish nurture, then Tiryakian's thesis suffers.

To secure the tie between Durkheimian symbolism and the symbolism of the religious modernists, we should probably dwell for a moment on the most conspicuous occasions of Durkheim's use of the language of symbolic interpretation of religion. Durkheim's second publication, the 1887 review of Guyau's *L'Irreligion de l'avenir,* already reads like a veteran's 'symbolist' interpretation of religion. "To be sure, it has been said that dogma is untenable if taken literally, but why should we be confined to its literal expression? Words have no meaning in themselves; the mind has to seek the idea, and even the most sacred texts need interpretation. Unfortunately, once Luther had given the believer the authority to be an interpreter, he was instantly persuaded to put his own ideas in place of divine thought; and soon there were everywhere nothing but symbols, even in the most essential dogmas, including that of revelation."[34]

If the most advanced religious communities have thus already moved in the direction of radical symbolism, Durkheim is telling us that it is nothing special for him simply to follow the "religious 'common-sense'" of these theological liberals.[35] Furthermore, Durkheim's symbolist view of religion persisted undiminished through his life, culminating in perhaps his heartiest embrace of this view on 18 January 1914. Before an association of humanist and religious (Gentile and Jewish) liberals or modernists, the Union of Free Thinkers and Free Believers,[36] Durkheim reaffirmed his original position of nearly thirty years earlier. Religious doctrines were revisable and thus (only) symbolic. "If . . . [the believer] considers that formulae are only provisional expressions which last and can only last a certain time, if he thinks that they are all imperfect, that the essential thing is not the letter of these formulae but rather the reality they hide and which they all express inexactly to a greater or lesser degree, if he thinks that it is necessary as a consequence to look beneath the surface to grasp the underlying principle of things, I believe that up to a certain point there is an enterprise we can embark upon by common consent." With fundamentalists, however, no such fruitful conversation is possible: "If he [the believer] values a denominational formula in an exclusive and uncompromising way, if he believes that he holds the truth of religion in its definitive form, then agreement is impossible and my presence here has no meaning."[37] Durkheim thus identified himself as part of the larger "enterprise" of the symbolic reading of religion, which we know to be characteristic of the liberal or modernist theologians whom he addressed.

We likewise know that the Durkheimians read and reviewed all the major theological works of their time. They understood well the major trends and issues of contemporary Christian theology, such as the symbolist Protestant theology of the Fifth Section's Auguste Sabatier[38] or the so-called modernist crisis in Roman Catholic circles centering around the biblical critic Alfred Loisy. From the side of the religious liberals, Loisy wrote a long and thoughtful review of *The Elementary Forms of the Religious Life* and generously cited Durkheim as an important influence in forming the sociological dimension of his own thought.[39] These interactions meant that beyond the religious modernists' prominence in the national culture of the day and besides the attention given to them by *L'Année sociologique,* we should take seriously the relation of these modernists to the Durkheimians. Interestingly, Loisy and Hébert reciprocated the Durkheimians' interest by considering them to be peers—but as *theologians.*[40] In his long review of *The Elementary Forms of the Religious Life,* Loisy relishes the irony of catching the antitheological Durkheim doing pretty much with the Scriptures what Loisy himself would. "The procedure of [Durkheim's] consisting in imputing this moral and social meaning to the origins of rituals is no more legitimate than that of the Christian exegetes who retrieve from the animal sacrifices described in Leviticus the prophetic symbol of the saving death of Christ."[41] The Catholics similarly attacked the scientific pretensions of Henri Hubert and Marcel Mauss's *Sacrifice: Its Nature and Functions.* Although the work pretended to offer only "*a* theory of sacrifice," it dogmatically decreed "*the* theory of sacrifice."[42] Catholic modernist Paul Legay similarly charged that Hubert and Mauss's work was "a kind of *philosophy* of sacrificial ritual—considered in itself."[43] Thus, the modernist theologians of the time saw through the quasi-religious polemic of Durkheim and his *équipe.* That we can now also 'see through' Durkheimian polemic strategies, thanks to what we know of the clerical modernists, will help us recapture and reintegrate Durkheim's quasi-religious symbolism into his overall intellectual vision.[44]

A final, speculative consideration might reinforce this link between the Durkheimians and the hermeneutic of religious liberalism, if not outright modernist religious symbolism. I refer to Durkheim's father, Rabbi Moïse Durkheim (1805–96). He seems to have been something of a liberal exception to the traditionalist rule of his own community. From a photograph that has survived to this day, we know that, contrary to expectations one might have of such a distinguished leader of a conservative and provincial Jewish community, Moïse Durkheim shed his traditional beard and wore modern secular garments in public. He seems to have been something of a reforming or modernizing Jew. Greenberg tells us as well that Moise Durkheim wanted to cultivate his already somewhat developed interests in secular learning, especially both in the "sciences and in philosophy."[45]

Such analogies and relations thus force the discussion to return to addressing the essentials, such as religion itself, and thus away from dallying in the world of the avant-garde. At a minimum, if we take the contemporary theological context of Durkheimian work seriously, Durkheim's talk of symbols would seem to be part of a context of attempts to interpret or explain religious discourse, under the conditions of reform and revision, rather than, say, radical anticlerical abolition of religion. By this logic, we should pay special attention to Durkheim and his *équipe* as men of these modernist religious times.

But who exactly were these free-thinking theologians, these practitioners of a symbolic interpretation of religion? What did they believe? Who, besides Durkheim and Guyau, was concerned about the future of religion or its lack thereof? And why were they concerned? Were there Jews among them? If so, did they and the Durkheimians have anything to do with each other? First, what did modernists believe, and how, in particular, did this bear on the whole matter of Durkheim's symbolic reading of religion?

Although Jews did not dominate the clerical modernist scene in Catholic France, some played major roles in shaping the life of the movement and, I will argue, in forming Durkheimian religious thought. Here, the main figure in our period is Salomon Reinach. I will argue, in fact, that the Durkheimian confrontation with Reinach over the nature of *what was ultimately symbolized* in traditional religion helped shape the Durkheimian notion of the *sacré*. To understand the relation of modernists like Reinach to French Jewry and the Durkheimians, we therefore need to understand something of the situation from which someone like Reinach and other Jewish liberals arose and thus how the Durkheimians were situated with respect to these phenomena.[46]

Modernists or liberals, whether religious or secular, Gentile, Jewish, or Durkheimian, generally stood for certain closely related fundamentals: the primacy of science, the belief in social evolution and the possibilities of progressive reform, opposition to religious literalism and ritualism, the adoption of symbolist modes of interpreting religious doctrines and scriptures, and the development of nontheistic, impersonal conceptions of the focus of religious life. Two features of the modernist outlook on knowledge and social processes link Durkheim immediately to the religious liberals. Both shared a faith in *science* and in the related belief in the possibility of social and religious *evolution, progress, and reform.*

Religious modernists were committed to the epistemological primacy of science. Thus, although religious dogmas are to be read symbolically (not literally), as we will see, scientific claims are to be taken literally. Religious doctrines need to be measured against what we know from the sciences. They should, then, be read so as to be 'inoffensive' to science.[47] In 1924, Loisy noted that when doctrines conflicted with "reality . . . a new and broader interpretation of these formulas . . . was indispensable."[48] Biblical literalism or absolute ecclesiastical authority was out; symbolic interpretation of religion was accordingly the stuff of their religious liberalism, inoculating it from contradiction with the sciences.

An upshot of this attitude was the prominence of modernists in the application of the methods of scientific historiography (as then understood) to the study of religious traditions. They were great demythologizers of religious traditions; indeed in their own ways, they were historical positivists, seeking the 'real' historical substratum *beneath* traditional or mythological religious representations.[49] Guided by the example of the German biblical criticism of Renan, they were by and large products of German 'scientific' history or 'historicism.' Hubert and Mauss's historicism was, for instance, learned in part from the Jewish modernist historian of religions Sylvain Lévi. In part, at any rate, Durkheimian sociology continued the trajectory of modernist critical approaches to religious materials.[50]

Prominent among members of the modernist Jewish community known to Durkheim[51] and his group was, for example, philosopher and rabbi Louis-Germain Lévy (1860–1937).[52] As the founder of the leading society of reform-minded Jews in France, the Union Libérale Israëlite, Lévy vigorously promoted a version of modernist neo-Judaism. In a way, he also epitomized the scientific spirit of the Jewish critical exegetic study of Judaism itself, which inspired the reform. Thus, although fully ordained into the rabbinate, he broke with the conservative tendencies of that body after his studies in the science of religion section of the École Pratique des Hautes Études. His doctoral dissertation, published in 1905 as *La Famille dans l'antiquité Israë-lite,* argued for a spiritualized version of ancient Hebrew mono-theism. But true to the lingering conservatism of French Juda-ism, it raised objections to the existence of totemism in the Jewish Bible.[53]

As for their belief in evolution, progress, and the possibili-ties of reform, the modernists saw the world of human affairs—religion included—as constantly changing, typically in adaptive or progressive ways, thus making a belief in the gradual reform of religion or society more plausible. In temperament, the reli-gious modernists represented a spirit of the internal reform of religious traditions, approximating as well much of the Durk-heimian program for a humanist morality based on Christianity to succeed traditional Christian religion. As gradualist reform-ers, the modernists were content to retain appearances, so long as their inner meaning changed. For the most famous French religious modernist of the period, Roman Catholic biblical scholar Alfred Loisy, modernism was an effort to seek accommo-dation and reform within the Church, not violent revolution. Loisy wanted only to "relax" the Church's "intransigent atti-tude, to allow discussion of problems being posed in the present day, [and] in doing so, to seek a good faith solution."[54] On the Jewish side, Salomon Reinach wanted to relieve his coreligion-ists of dietary regulations and in other ways to minimize their separation from non-Jews, such as by celebrating the Shabbat on Sunday.[55] Like the Durkheimians, the religious modernists felt that revision of the old faiths could spur change, say, in terms of providing a moral basis for national revival. Such a na-tional neo-religion would become for France the "soul of its democracy,"[56] a *"religion de la patrie."*[57] In their shared gradual-ism, the modernists were also like Durkheim in social matters. He was never a socialist and certainly neither a Syndicalist nor a Marxist. They and the Durkheimians marched alongside each other some way as fellow liberals—something that Syndicalist radical Georges Sorel tried to expose in a notable series of at-tacks on his common liberal enemy.[58] Thus, instead of the revo-lutionary ambitions of which Tiryakian peaks, the religious mod-ernists and the liberal Durkheimians pressed a plan for revising and adapting traditional religious beliefs in light of 'modern' life, rather than overthrowing them.

Modernists also opposed religious literalism (or 'fundamentalism') as well as ritualism. Opposition to scriptural and doctrinal literalism is in effect to assert the religious primacy of interpreting traditional doctrines and biblical literature *symbolically*. In the eyes of religious modernists, religious dogmas and scriptures are not to be interpreted literally; doctrines in particular have no precise meaning. Rather they are to be read loosely as indicating certain states internal or external to human consciousness as "symbolic constructions."[59] Thus, modernism, as Loisy tells us, "was a more or less diffuse effort, intent upon softening the rigor of Roman absolutism and theological dogmatism."[60] In Roger Martin du Gard's novel of the period, *Jean Barois*, Abbé Schertz, the *"prêtre symboliste,"* explains that the doctrine of the "real Presence" of Christ in the Eucharist is not, for example, a literal piece of magic but is "a symbol, a symbol of the continuous felt action of God on my soul."[61] When Barois objects that Schertz has left out what ordinary Catholics take to be real, Schertz replies that he has instead found what is really "essential. . . . In terms of practice, our reason cannot accept the dogmas, it is true. But on the contrary, the symbol that we reveal is clear and satisfying to our reason, contributing to our betterment."[62]

For Jews, modernism in this domain amounted to a rejection of biblical literalism but also, because of the orthodox hegemony over French Judaism, of antiritualism. In general, we may speak of Jewish liberalism thus as a movement chiefly of legal, ritual, and social reform; Jewish modernism arose from "historico-exegetical" revolutions in textual criticism and from philosophical innovations such as pragmatism and Bergsonianism.[63] But for all practical purposes, in France during the fin de siècle, the two movements merged. Critical treatments of the sacred traditions of Judaism became in turn a tool of practical religious reform. Thus, when we speak of Jewish liberalism and modernism in the fin de siècle, we can use the terms interchangeably.

Unlike the vigorous rise of German liberal Judaism, no separate reform movement developed in France until 1907.[64] In fact, until then, Jewish denominationalism was virtually absent in France altogether. Conservatives made up the vast majority of the French rabbinate in the fin de siècle, but their preeminence was new. Indeed, from 1870, the French rabbinical leadership had been effectively and firmly 'reorthodoxed.'[65] As we will see, even among relatively liberal Jews, such as the great Indologist and teacher of Mauss, Sylvain Lévi, significant aspects of conservative Jewish teaching and practice continued to exert their power. Although liberalizing tendencies of the Enlightenment had touched French Jewry just as they had affected all of European Jewry, the rabbinate's theological positions had hardened. Attempts to reform traditional religious practice were rejected wholesale. As the fin de siècle approached, the newly reorthodoxed conservatives resisted incipient symbolic or modernist modes of biblical interpretation and reimposed biblical literalism. At the same time, the conservatives stifled standard liberal or reform attempts to modify law and liturgy. Dietary restrictions stayed in place.[66] The Shabbat would not be celebrated on Sunday, nor would mixed marriages enjoy liturgical blessing. The French language would not replace Hebrew in the liturgy. The authority of the Talmud and *minhagim* remained firm and unshaken.[67]

In reaction to this hardening of orthodoxy, French liberal Judaism was initiated by laypeople determined to 'modernize' what they took to be burdensome legal and liturgical practice, as well as untenable beliefs. Liberals traced their lineage back at least to the early-nineteenth-century thinker Joseph Salvador. His major works appeared between 1822 and 1859.[68] During the 1840s, sparked by critical approaches to sacred texts and traditions, liberal Jews sought a freer way of interpreting the Bible, which in turn was realized by the adoption of a symbolic style of interpretation. Thus, in the name of what he called a new Judaism, modernist Reinach urged that although Leviticus and the Torah should stay, they needed to be interpreted symbolically—"in the light of the conscience and intelligence which men have received from God."[69] Antiritualist as well, Reinach thus felt that "true religion" goes beyond the externals of religious life; real religion "is a matter of feeling, not of practices."[70] Reinach accordingly wanted Jews to abandon ritualistic "externals" wholesale and to replace them with loosely held beliefs in monotheism, progress, and justice.[71]

Even before Reinach, James Darmesteter (1849–94), the great Avestan scholar at the École Pratique des Hautes Études and later at the Collège de France (1885), carved out much of what would become the Jewish modernist position in Durkheim's time. Darmesteter circulated in a world populated by like-minded liberal Jewish and Gentile contemporaries who, if not personally known to the Durkheimians, were certainly well-known to them by reputation. These included historians of religion, such as Reinach, and liberal Protestants, such as Albert and Jean Réville.[72] Darmesteter also maintained relations with an international community of scholars, such as an American student of Durkheim's, Morris Jastrow, and Oxford Indologist Friedrich Max Müller, whose work became the object of Durkheimian arguments against a mythophilic naturism.[73] Darmesteter's conception of Judaism dominated the thought of generations of liberal Jewish intellectuals from the 1880s through the years of the First World War.[74]

In France, Darmesteter was virtually responsible for formulating and popularizing a view of a modern Judaism similar to that of Moses Mendelssohn's "prophetic Judaism."[75] Like Renan, his teacher, Darmesteter feared that with the clerical party discredited in the cultural wars attending the foundation of the Third Republic, the French populace would dismiss religion totally.[76] Even though religion, and especially Judaism, needed to change, Darmesteter felt that religion itself was still necessary for the health of the nation. Traditional Judaism contained the seeds of a true universal religion and could be mined for this universal content. Darmesteter called this universal Judaism the "prophetic faith." In doing so, he traded on the reputation of the prophets as idealist ethical reformers and iconoclasts, opposed to the priestly, 'materialist,' and ritualistic tendencies of ancient Hebrew religion. To a rationalist such as Darmesteter, this prophetic faith fit well with what he took to be the best of the modern spirit. This faith favored the irreverent and critical spirit of science; it opposed 'superstition' and 'magic.'[77] Darmesteter saw in the prophets the religious modernists of their time, since they opposed the ritualizing tendencies of the priesthood, tendencies that led people far from the inner ethical core of real religion.[78] They opposed magic too; for Darmesteter, magic was the preoccupation of "charlatans and fools."[79] Thus, trading implicitly on the critical, libertarian, and iconoclastic heritage of the Revolution, Darmesteter held up the iconoclastic reforming religion of the ancient prophets as an ideal of what 'modern' Judaism, and thus the modern religion of France, might be.[80] By appealing to the ideal of prophetic religion, Darmesteter prepared the way conceptually for further generations of Jewish liberals, perhaps with Durkheim among them.

Darmesteter was, then, an 'essentialist' regarding Judaism— but notably one whose claims about the Jewish essence may be out of favor today. Judaism's essential nature was thus concealed *beneath* its present appearances. The reformer needed to go beyond appearances and, like Durkheim, beyond the explicit formulations of traditional faith, to grasp and assert the hidden essence of Jewish religious life. Moreover, Darmesteter's prophetic Judaism—not all that different from Durkheim's humanist societism—was equivalent in content to the spirit of the Enlightenment and Revolution. Republican France in a way fulfilled the promise of the prophets of Israel. This identification permitted Darmesteter to see the eternal message of the Jewish prophets symbolized in the republican political language of his own time, much as Durkheim could see his societism lurking beneath the theistic symbols of traditional religious faith.

Although a good deal less poetic than the gifted Darmesteter, Louis-Germain Lévy felt that traditional Judaism needed to do much the same job of inner reinterpretation that Darmesteter wanted. It "only needs to cast off the practices, institutions and customs which have their *raison d'etre* in other times and places, but which today are fossilized to the point of being an encumbrances. Once relieved of all this dead weight, Judaism will present the necessary characteristics of religion in general and modern religion in particular. It will be a religion fitted out with all the positive and historical essentials, and at the same time be a rational and secular religion."[81]

Lévy does more than just recapitulate the spirit and letter of Jewish modernist symbolic approaches to religion: he gives it a simultaneously nationalist and Jewish spin, which echoes what we observed about Jewish trends toward concreteness and societism in the previous chapter. In being interpreted symbolically, Judaism qualifies for being "the religion" of France. It replaces the *religions concrets* and lays a unifying moral floor under French national feeling. Although a 'religion,' Judaism, as Lévy reads it, is not a 'faith': its nature is not fixed by doctrines, as the official Napoleonic conventions insisted that 'religions' must be. Further, whereas the rites and doctrines of these so-called religions offend reason, Lévy's neo-Judaism does not.[82] Neo-Judaism is "perfectly compatible with the affirmations of modern thought" and science.[83] Thus, Lévy rejected any idea of religion as "passé." Religion (especially Judaism) can be modernized. Like Darmesteter, Lévy believed first and foremost that Judaism could develop and evolve from what it had been traditionally: "Judaism was not a fixed and immutable religion, but a progressive and ever-changing one."[84] In Lévy's view, the course of this evolution would carry Judaism onto a 'higher,' more universal plane—that of his own neo-Judaism.

Since Judaism could transcend its own particularity, Lévy felt that Judaism was thus not even a 'religion' in the sense Judaism had become with emancipation. Following the lead of Renan and, after him, Darmesteter, Lévy said instead that this new Judaism was a version of the universal religion, a natural religion. "In the last analysis," says Lévy, "Judaism is not *a* religion among many others, but *the* religion."[85] As a result, far from being empty and ritualistic, this religion-as-such provides dynamogenic energy and idealistic direction to life. The religion contributes "force, peace, serenity [which] develops qualities of idealism. . . . It establishes a fixed pole in the midst of our life, conveys a sense of seriousness to our tiniest acts, disciplines our desires, concentrates our capacities into something both singular and strong, and directs them towards altruistic ends."[86] Lévy held that, as a kind of system of universal morals, his "religion of the twentieth century will be born of the fusion of prophetism and science."[87] For Lévy, Judaism "is a religion, because it establishes the strictest of relationship[s] between God and man . . . it isn't a faith in the sense where the word implies an ensemble of revealed *truths* . . . *Judaism is essentially the moral practice of life.*"[88]

A final feature of modernist approaches to religion brings us to perhaps the most consequential theological outcome of modernism. After all is said and done about symbolic readings of traditional religion, questions about the ultimate *signification* of religious language must be faced. Here, the modernists differed among themselves as to what was symbolized in speaking of 'God.' Although answers varied, personal divinity was generally seen as only a symbol of the ultimate reality. In place of personal divinity, the modernists spoke of divinity typically in more or less pantheist, impersonal, or undetermined ways.[89]

This applies to the Catholic modernist Loisy, who referred not to the personal God of the Bible but to an indefinable "mysterious *entity*," to the "*sacré*,"[90] or to "a Being *above* all beings, a Power above all powers, a Spirit above all spirits."[91] But it also applies, as we will see, to the Jewish Reinach's rationalist notion of the sacred as negative prohibition or scruples and, of course, to the rather different, but recognizably related, Durkheimian idea of the sacred as the social. There is perhaps no better way of bringing together these several points about the nature of Jewish clerical modernism than to focus on Reinach, and especially on how the Durkheimians forged their latter-day notion of the sacred apparently to oppose Reinach. Although Reinach and the Durkheimians were united in their wish to displace the personal God from the center of religion, they disagreed so sharply about how this should be managed conceptually that their differences outweighed the similarities that had put them together against traditional believers.

The key Jewish modernist with the greatest affinities for, and actual relationships with, the Durkheimians was Salomon Reinach (1858–1932). More than just a Jewish modernist, Reinach commanded a focal point right in the midst of the entire modernist debate involving a broad spectrum of the leading intellectuals of the day, including the Durkheimians.[92] Reinach was, for example, Loisy's most loyal and vocal champion, publicly speaking out in his behalf on numerous occasions. Of Loisy's book *Autour d'un petit livre* (1903), Reinach said that it "marks a remarkable date in the evolution of religious ideas and recommends itself, by its substance and form, to the sympathetic meditations of all thinkers."[93] In this sense, he saw Loisy's fight against Roman authority as part of his own fight against the Jewish conservatives—almost as if modernism itself forged such a solid bond between them that it overcame the profound differences of their origins and their memberships in different religious traditions.

Reinach's work was, for the Durkheimians, a frequent source both of admiration and of competition and irritation.[94] Oddly enough, although the Durkheimians maintained a certain neutrality about Loisy, they fought Reinach on many issues. The nature of this relationship between the Durkheimians and the leading Jewish modernist of the day was thus ambivalent at best. And it therefore captured something of the essence of the nature of the relationship between Jewish modernists as a whole and the Durkheim school.

The reasons for the sharpness of difference between the Durkheimians and Reinach are not immediately clear. Contrast with Durkheim's generous attitude to the new refugees is telling. Class differences as well cannot be discounted. Unlike Durkheim and Mauss, who hailed from humble origins in the more conservative Jewish communities of eastern France, Reinach was a member of a long-emancipated family of Jewish notables, the epitome of 'gentry Jewry.' Durkheim's father remained essentially poor throughout his life, drawing only his meager state salary as chief rabbi of the Hautes Vosges. He even struggled to help finance Durkheim's studies in Paris. The Reinachs, on the other hand, were a family of commercial investors and governmental professionals with ample resources to satisfy their material needs.[95] Salomon Reinach's two brothers, Joseph and Theodore, were famous in their own right. The elder, Joseph (1856– 1921), was the author of a seven-volume history of the Dreyfus Affair (1901-8), *Histoire sommaire de l'affaire Dreyfus*. All the Reinachs opposed Zionism. Joseph Reinach even joined Cardinal Mercier in forming a group, Les Amis de la Terre Sainte, officially to oppose a " 'confessionally' Jewish state in Palestine."[96] Because of Joseph's abilities as a journalist and political analyst, Léon Gambetta appointed him *chef-du-cabinet* in 1881. He also served in the Chamber of Deputies for several terms, where he was an outspoken critic of the condemnation of Dreyfus. In 1886, he was awarded the Légion d'Honneur. Hardly less distinguished was Salomon Reinach's younger brother, Theodore (1860–1928). Mixing scholarly and political roles as easily as his brother Joseph, Theodore was a classics scholar at the École Pratique des Hautes Études, Fifth Section. He wrote his *Histoire des Israëlites* (1884) with the intention of using it to present his version of the liberal position on the nature of Judaism. He opposed Zionism, arguing the standard line of a Judaism 'become a religion,' namely that ever since the French Revolution, French Jews were not a nation but a religious community. For a time, he edited the *Revue des études grecques,* and later he won election to the Académie Française. Like his brother Joseph, he was also active in national politics, serving in the Chamber of Deputies from 1906 to 1914.

Salomon Reinach was thus a quintessential, if complex, iconoclast Jewish modernist. A remarkable virtuoso intellectual, unlike his two more conventional brothers, the younger Salomon became perhaps France's greatest popularizer of the history of religions since Renan. His exposé of the world religions, *Orpheus* (1909), became an enormous literary success in anticlerical France. By the end of its first year of publication, it was already in its sixth edition. By the time Durkheim published *The Elementary Forms of the Religious Life* in 1912, *Orpheus* had passed into the sixteenth of its thirty-eight editions and had already been translated into five languages. Most important for this discussion, it became the envy of the Durkheimians.[97] Salomon circulated easily in the social world of arts and letters and fell naturally into the company of the fashionable artists and intellectuals of the day. Like others of the avant-garde milieu, his views on morality were what might be called progressive—even libertine for his opposition to social 'taboos.' At the same time, unlike the more straitlaced and conventional Durkheimians, he made his way along the edges of the avant-garde world of the arts. Reinach and Max Jacob, for example, shared the favors of the demimondaine Liane de Pougy.[98] A Dreyfusard, Reinach championed many left-wing causes of the day. As a talented journalist and self-interested chronicler of the religious history of his times, he paid particular and sympathetic attention to the reform movements in the Roman tradition, such as Loisy's modernism. In addition, Loisy and Reinach exchanged more than one hundred letters over their years of correspondence.

Like the Durkheimians, Reinach was absorbed in the then-new cross-cultural comparativist anthropological writings of British scholars such as William Robertson Smith and Sir James Frazer. In fact, at the time, Reinach—not Durkheim—was recognized as the French *porte-parole* of these two great representatives of the *école anglaise*.[99] Thus, Reinach proudly wrote, "When I began, in 1900, under Smith's and Frazer's influence, to lecture in France on taboos and totemism, I had to explain these terms, which nobody understood at that time."[100] It is small wonder that the Durkheimians, who were at least as early as Reinach in publishing on these matters, were irritated by Reinach's intrusions into what perhaps to them seemed like their private preserve.[101]

Despite the common modernist and symbolist commitment

to getting behind the 'appearances' of traditional religions, Reinach's ultimate aims for using the new ethnography were rather different from those of the Durkheimians. Frazer and Robertson Smith had already begun this task of exposing 'obsolete' or 'barbaric' and 'primitive' features of religion, features surviving unwittingly "beneath the surface" of contemporary religions, as Durkheim tells us.[102] But whereas the Durkheimians sought to address religions in general, Reinach was primarily concerned to apply the new ethnography to the in-house modernist task of reforming Judaism. Taking his cues from Frazer and Robertson Smith, Reinach felt that Jewish dietary laws and other practices were nothing more than primitive 'taboos' or 'scruples' in hiding.[103] Reinach's goal was to eliminate these and all other taboos that had survived so long into the modern day and, in doing so, to liberate Judaism from the dead hand of the past.

As a pious 'neo-Jew,' Reinach believed such a strategy of exposing the primitive lurking beneath the contemporary only showed Judaism in its best light. Reinach believed that a survey of the prehistory of religions would reveal how each religion had evolved and changed. Jewish religion was no exception. Ethnography then showed how much *better* Judaism had become over the years in gradually eliminating its own 'barbaric' elements. If, then, Jewish religion had continually evolved over the years, why not encourage further development today? In this respect Reinach could not have agreed more with Durkheim's speech before the Union of Free Thinkers and Free Believers in 1914.[104] Both men wanted the religions of the day to reconsider their identities in light of the new ethnography.

Yet there were differences. Despite his iconoclastic Voltairean reputation, Reinach was a sincere if undeviatingly liberal Jew, typical of his class and Parisian origins. He could wax eloquent about being so in ways we cannot imagine the 'Jewish' Durkheimians being. Thus, using the standard modernist image of reform and regeneration, he said, "The old tree of Judah will let fall its dead leaves and in doing so, its powerful roots will not grow the less—a witness to its inexhaustible vitality."[105] His neo-Jewish reformist zeal thus turned the work of the British comparativists toward his sincere modernist 'iconoclast' critique of the conservative religiosity of his own community first and then, by extension, to the dominant Catholic religiosity of his own country.

Unlike Durkheim and his confederates, Reinach was accordingly active in the leadership of Jewish affairs and proudly identified himself as Jewish. He was part of the prewar 'Jewish Renaissance' and was joint founder, along with Israël Lévi, Darius Milhaud, and others, of Les Amis du Judaïsme in 1913.[106] On the other side, he was not an ethnic patriot. Jewish advancement meant progress along the critical, Enlightenment, and universalist axis. Like Salomon Munk and the other leaders of the French version of the Wissenschaft des Judentums, he viewed Judaism as an integral episode in the "moral and social history of humanity" rather than as an objective end point of history itself. He cared more about what made Jews similar to other people and about how Judaism contributed to the march of humanity than about what set Jews apart.[107]

Reinach thus consistently opposed anything that would, in his eyes, exaggerate Jewish exclusiveness. Typical was his distaste for North African and eastern European Jews as 'unwashed masses.'[108] Of the Hassidim, Reinach said, "They constitute communities hostile to the modern spirit; their noisy and disorderly form of worship has all the appearances of a religious frenzy."[109] By the time of Reinach's maturity, the presence of these new Jews, with their foreign customs and habits, was seen as disturbing the hard-won modern and 'French' identity of Franco-Jewry. Against these models of Jewish particularity and ethnicity becoming daily more prominent in Reinach's Franco-Jewish world, Reinach opposed Zionism and denied the existence of a Jewish 'race.'[110] He was, in short, a model 'iconoclast' modernizer of Judaism: if the "tree of Judaism was half-dead," as Reinach asserted, he assigned himself the task of reviving it with a severe pruning.

In his dislike for the newly arrived eastern European Jews, Reinach fit right in with other bourgeois French-born Jews.[111] These Jews had always been sensitive to the image of the Jew as outsider. Now the flood of new immigrants threatened to overwhelm their small and largely Parisian population. By 1914, the immigrants nearly equaled in numbers the native-born Paris population of Jews,[112] threatening to make Jews in general look alien once again.[113] By simple force of their numbers and enthusiasm, these new arrivals thus threatened to transform the liberal Judaism of Reinach's peers into something altogether alien. Reinach was deeply troubled by this prospect and fought throughout his life to combat the antimodern spirit of the newly arrived Jews. All this transpired while Reinach remained an active member of the Alliance Israëlite Universelle, which was devoted to the welfare of these same Jews (albeit in order to inform them with French cultural values).

We have no evidence that the Durkheimians sympathized with this passion to revive traditional Judaism. They were certainly not active in the effort. If anything, because of Christianity's larger role in determining the shape of French and indeed Western society, the Durkheimians might even have leaned toward the Christian modernist program. Thus, although the Durkheimians in some sense sympathized with the reform of the traditions, they did so as *spectators,* not as participants. Insofar as free inquiry would lift the cloud of ecclesiastical oppression from Catholic thinkers—and thus from France as a whole— their democratic and humanist aspirations would be furthered. Yet on the whole, the Durkheimians remained silent in the midst of the modernist crises assailing the traditions. They were so reluctant to draw the practical conclusions of their discoveries that they said nothing. Whether this silence was discretion or indifference is hard to tell. Suffice it to say that the Durkheimians were ready to profit intellectually and professionally from whatever happened to the traditional religions of France.

Even though Reinach and the Durkheimians could agree that the traditions needed to be interpreted symbolically, this did not mean that they agreed on what lay behind the appearances of traditional religion. Surprisingly, the observant Jewish Reinach practiced a rationalism that was Voltairean and iconoclastic, whereas the apostate Durkheimians were much more tolerant and positive about traditional religion. What accounts for this difference among modernists about the results of symbolic readings of religion? Did intellectual opposition between the provincial, conservatively reared Durkheim and the highborn Reinach reflect class resentments? Ambitious to find a place for himself on the crowded ladder of academic advancement, perhaps Durkheim found no common intellectual ground with the metropolitan, socially established, and hyperliberal Reinach? This scenario gains plausibility when we attend to the way in which Durkheim played 'fox' to Reinach's 'lion.' Durkheim seemed to target the neo-Jewish elites for certain circulation, and eventual replacement by a Durkheimian ascendancy, in the study of religion and society. I will thus argue that their estrangement related to the Durkheimians' attempts to create hegemony for themselves in the then-new efforts in the study of religion and thus ultimately to achieve dominance in defining the nature of religion itself. Despite many shared values, neo-Jewish liberals like Reinach simply stood in the way. So the prospect of Durkheimian dominance of the scientific approach to religion required the elimination of Reinach's competing program.

Eliminating Reinach as a competitor was not easy, however. For one thing, he enjoyed great professional and social prestige. Especially galling to the science-minded Durkheimians, early on Reinach outshone them as the chief representative of Robertson Smith and Frazer in France—the same great figures the Durkheimians sought to represent in their milieu. Qualms aside, the Durkheimians were envious of the success of Reinach's outrageously popular rationalist handbook of the history of religions, *Orpheus,* printed and reprinted some thirty times in Durkheim's lifetime. Despite Reinach's reputation as a popularizer (and worse),[114] the Durkheimians felt that in the domain of religion, Reinach's opinions mattered to them.[115] The Durkheimians respected Reinach's anthropological angle on contemporary social phenomena, as worked out in *Orpheus.*[116] Henri Hubert admitted, "We have no equivalent to it." Yet Hubert referred to Reinach's *Orpheus* as a "pamphlet," written for "women and young girls."[117] Reinach's celebrity left the Durkheimians no recourse but to oppose him with steadily increasing determination.

One particular tactic for undercutting Reinach seemed to find favor with the Durkheimians. Whenever Reinach insinuated or claimed affinity with the Durkheimians, they would immediately deny it—regardless of the merits.[118] Typical of this systematic distancing of Reinach was a conflict with the Durkheimians over the content of the symbolic interpretation of religion. Reinach believed that if one sought what lay behind traditional religion, one would find 'scruples.' To the libertine freethinker Reinach, religion was simply a scheme of taboos and prohibitions. How could the Durkheimians plausibly deny this, since Reinach's 'scruples' and Durkheim's early definition of religion in terms of 'interdictions' hardly seemed different?[119] Accordingly, Reinach noted that his 'scruples' and Durkheim's 'interdictions' were really "two different aspects of the same thing." An 'interdiction' was simply a prohibition decreed, whereas a 'scruple' was more informal—a "subtle prohibition."[120] In fact, one recognized Durkheim's revised sacred, Reinach replied, only in *reacting against* what is sacred. Thus, between Reinach's 'scruples' and Durkheim's 'interdictions' little or no difference in nature seems to exist.

The Durkheimian reaction was telling. Although Reinach tried magnanimously to agree with Durkheim on what lay behind religious symbols, the Durkheimians simply refused to admit common ground. Every claim to affinity by Reinach was matched by an equal and opposite effort by the Durkheimians to fend off his comradely embrace.[121] Perplexed no doubt by what seemed (and was) bad faith, Reinach ironically noted in his review of *The Elementary Forms of the Religious Life,* "In expressing my satisfaction in agreeing on such serious questions with a thinker as profound as Monsieur Durkheim, I suppose that if he has not noted these agreements himself, it is because he believes all his readers agree as well with me."[122]

Given this unwelcome embrace from Reinach, the Durkheimians seem to have become even more determined to sharpen differences with Reinach by articulating new—and undigestible—theoretical views. One such new view was the Durkheimian resolution of the problem of the definition of religion in terms of a positive sacred. In a 1913 review, Hubert replied to Reinach's review of *The Elementary Forms of the Religious Life* by stating the new positive definition of the sacred, a definition for some time normative for the Durkheimians. Hubert accused Reinach's definition of religion of being "sterile" and at best "minimal." Worst of all, in thus defining religion negatively, Reinach could not account for the noble achievements of religion.[123] Granted, said Hubert, although Reinach might be right about the horrors of the Inquisition, what of the glories of the Sistine Chapel?[124] Furthermore, Hubert declared that in *The Elementary Forms of the Religious Life,* "everything positive about religion is given in its fundamentals, in its elementary forms."[125]

By 1912, the Durkheimians had taken up with a new, positive notion of 'sacred' to replace the earlier idea of 'interdiction' as the defining characteristic of religion.[126] In 1906, Hubert and Mauss articulated a position that, in 1912, would become the position of *The Elementary Forms of the Religious Life*. They noted that "behind ideas of separation, purity"—the old negative sacred and so on—there are "respect, love, and strong feelings . . . which translate themselves into gesture and thoughts."[127] A richer notion than earlier thought, the new sacred was as well something palpable, an *"idée force"* around which the whole paraphernalia of religion forms.[128] It would become for the Durkheimians their normative position on what ultimately lay behind the surface phenomena of religion. As a result, taboo was for the Durkheimians not part of the essential definition of religion. At most, taboo in *The Elementary Forms of the Religious Life* played a secondary and negative role in the definition of religion. Reinach, on the other hand, started and ended his understanding of religion with taboo, signaling in this way his unwavering mistrust of religion.[129] In place of taboo and scruple, Hubert and Mauss added: "Sacred things are social things. In our opinion, everything is conceived as sacred for the group and its members which characterizes a society." The Durkheimians meant to emphasize that there is something worth cherishing *beyond* and inside of our interdictions, taboos, and scruples. These are the ideals and fundamental values that "characterize a society." Here, Reinach's negative definition of the "sacred" would prove "insufficient."[130]

So instead of joining forces with Reinach, the Durkheimians took off on their own course.[131] Reinach's image as popularizer may have driven the Durkheimians to articulate a definition of the sacred that he could never adopt.[132] Further, identification with Reinach the popularizer did nothing for the scientific reputation of the Durkheimians. So strong was this aversion that the Durkheimians did not even have the good grace, as we have seen, to acknowledge common ground where it patently existed. I am thus suggesting that at least some Durkheimian opposition to Reinach was motivated by considerations external to the logical merits of the case. Some of Reinach's positions were actually *too* much like those of the Durkheimians. They simply needed to put semiotic distance between themselves and Reinach in order to be heard above the din of the religious liberal approaches of their day. Durkheimian academic imperialism was notorious, and their treatment of Reinach, liberal Jew notwithstanding, was typical.[133]

Durkheimian scientific aspirations cannot likewise be totally divorced from politics. Reinach embodied much of the engagé reformist zeal of religious modernism; the Durkheimians tried to maintain the image of a scientific 'remoteness' from public events, especially those involving the tense relations between the official Roman church and the modernist movement. As a rule, the Durkheimians therefore almost never identified with their respective religious traditions (even with the modernizers), or Hubert with the Catholic modernists or liberals close to him, or Mauss and Durkheim with the Jewish liberals of their circle of acquaintance. Rather, they appropriated the *école anglaise* for purposes neutral both to traditional theological hermeneutic and polemic and to its neo-Jewish modernist reformers. Paradoxically, however, the very irreligion of the Durkheimians allowed them to be more tolerant of the *religions concrets*—the religious traditions—than of the religiously interested neo-Jewish theologians like Reinach. As we will see in the next chapter, they defended the very Talmudic Judaism and its institutions that Jewish liberals, as much as scholarly anti-Semites, scorned. The Durkheimians had no stake in the reform of French Judaism along neo-Jewish lines or in the internal politics of any of France's religious communities. To the Durkheimians, both conservative Judaism and reformed Judaism remained religions and therefore subject to their symbolic sociological rereading. If the Durkheimians could be tolerant and culturally relative about tribal Australian religions, they would surely not be troubled by the existence of Judaism, whatever kind it might be.

In light of this difference of ultimate aim, the Durkheimians apparently did not want to be confused with their competition—especially not with someone whose scientific credentials were as dubious in key areas as Reinach's. Despite Durkheimian sympathy with elements of the religious modernism, their deviations were even more significant. The simple fact that Durkheimian symbolic approaches to religion were like neo-Jewish ones bred competition for attention, even if this was competition for attention 'within the same league,' so to speak. In a way, the 'affinity' of the Jewish liberals and the Durkheimians seems responsible for breeding this kind of contempt.

The main framework erected around Durkheimian symbolic interpretation was not reformed Judaism or indeed any sort of reformed 'religion' in the traditional sense of the term. Durkheim sought instead to build up a civic morale by way of symbolic reinterpretation of religion as a social reality. For all their liberality of thought, the neo-Jews were still Jews and pious, albeit radical, ones at that. To the extent that Durkheimian civic morale was also something of an 'ideology,' they shared the common motive of seeking a common spiritual basis for the nation. The Durkheimians just had more difficulty admitting this. They hid their ideological ambitions under the laboratory coats of science. In doing so, the Durkheimians had to draw a hard line between what they did with religion and the virtually identical work done by neo-Jews like Reinach.

In the end, then, the Durkheimians preferred most often to obscure their affinities with the religious modernists.[134] Referring dismissively to one of Loisy's confederates, the philosopher Edouard Le Roy, Durkheim dryly observed that as a religious "modernist" he was part of a "neoreligious movement."[135] In part, this preserved their stance of scientific neutrality within French academic and national politics. The Durkheimians, for instance, went to great lengths to conceal their anti-clericalism. Thus, in public debates during the modernist crisis, they scrupulously declined to take a stance on the merits of Loisy's case.[136] Loisy himself, in his memoirs, voiced suspicions that the Durkheimians sought to thwart his ambitions for academic advancement.[137] More to the point, however, the Durkheimians were jealous of sharing the stage of social or religious reform with plausible competitors, such as the religious modernists. The Durkheimians manifestly relished polemics with their religious brethren. In a letter of 1898, Hubert revealed how he relished the disruption that his and Mauss's work on sacrifice would cause among the religious powers of the day. Writing to Mauss, Hubert said: "We are condemned, my dear fellow, to make religious polemics. We shouldn't miss a chance to make trouble for these good, but badly informed, souls. Let's stress the direction of our work, let's attend to our conclusions—so that they be pointed, sharp like a razor, and so that they be treacherous. Let's go! I do love a battle! That's what excites us!"[138] With attitudes like these, plus their own ambivalence, as 'scientists,' about being ideologues for a new morale, it is small wonder the Durkheimians tried to keep religious modernists at arm's length.

Jewish conservatives, on the other hand, still operated as if the exigencies of life in the modern world made no difference to the nature of Jewish religious life and practice. For the Durkheimians, traditional Judaism was still a 'religion' and therefore something of an evolutionary survival. It did not pretend, like liberal Judaism, that it might successfully adapt to the modern world and challenge other modern ideologies to treat the spiritual needs of the day. Unlike the traditional religious visions of conservative Jews, the liberal view could not so easily be dismissed as 'backward.' It was, after all, 'modern' in the sense of being open to science and democratic values. In taking this stance to the modern world, neo-Judaism thus threatened to 'play in the same league' with Durkheimian liberalism, to compete with Durkheimian ambitions to establish a secular ideology for the Third Republic.

Ironically, because the Durkheimians were more traditionally 'religious' and made no pretense as to their modernity, they did not regard theologically conservative figures, such as Israël Lévi or Sylvain Lévi, as potential competitors. They split their intellectual and spiritual worlds. The conservative Jews remained encased within a world of more or less positivist philological and historical scholarship, on the one hand, and a purely traditional religious world, on the other. Neither Israël Lévi nor Sylvain Lévi entered the modernist competition to provide an answer to the 'problem of religion' question. They both knew that for them and their community, traditional Judaism answered that question—much as traditional Catholicism answered this for its conservative adherents. Thus, what also bound Durkheimians to their conservative Jewish intellectual contemporaries was the ideal of *scientific* inquiry into the nature of religion. Even though in a way more 'religious' than their liberal coreligionists, the moderate Jewish conservatives whom the Durkheimians followed were generally more chaste regarding the scientific purity of their scholarly work in religion than were the liberals. This may partly result from the fact that in feeling that neo-Judaism was in accord with science, they confused religion (or ideology) and science. They were on the whole closer to more conservative Jewish scholars, such as the great Talmudic scholar Israël Lévi or that master of ritual studies in his day Sylvain Lévi, because in their scholarship these Jewish conservatives were doing more science than were neo-Jewish propagandists such as Reinach.

Let me now lay out the historical background of that world of scholarly study of religion, a world in which Jewish contemporaries of the Durkheimians thrived in Paris and of which the Durkheimians themselves formed a small part.

4

HOW DURKHEIM READ THE TALMUD

Another sign of Durkheim's essential Jew-
ishness might be an undying nostalgia for a Jewish golden age
or 'mythical' Jewishness. Did Durkheim wax nostalgic for the
glories of ancient Israel, for the supposed pristine simplicity of
classic Hebrew culture and religion? Once more, Edward Tiryakian provides a stimulating point of departure for such inquiries. He urges us to look at Durkheim's sociological interests in
'the primitive' as inspired by a nostalgia for the primitive community of an idealized ancient Israel. In particular, Durkheim
was stirred by William Robertson Smith's image of the coherent
organic religious life and the social stability of the 'primitive'
Hebrews as depicted in Robertson Smith's *Lectures on the Religion
of the Semites*. Tiryakian believes that as a result, Durkheim began
to "rediscover his own roots in orthodox Judaism with its rich
symbolism and rituals,"[1] ultimately then using this Jewish image
to inform his equally idealized representation of Australian abo-
rigines in *The Elementary Forms of the Religious Life*.[2] For Durkheim,
this journey into the realms of primitive religion thus was in
reality a "recherche de la société perdue"—a pursuit of the Judaism he had discarded in his ambitious chase after an academic
career in the secular Third Republic.[3]

Despite Tiryakian's show of lively historical imagination, he
displays a commonplace indifference to the nature of Judaism

Émile Durkheim with
Marie Halphen and the
infant Claude Halphen,
October 1914. Photo
courtesy of Étienne
Halphen.

in Durkheim's own time and to Durkheim's relation to this Judaism. Such an approach once again plays down the role of affinities in the makeup of Durkheimian thought and ignores the
kind of "argumentative context" to which the Durkheimians
addressed themselves; this approach favors what amounts to a
nostalgia for an imagined past.[4] Once more we see how scholars
like Tiryakian seem to prefer constructing an imagined relation
to a mythic past to Durkheim's lived experience of affinities with
the Jewish contemporaries making up his academic social world.
I do not think Tiryakian's position can meet the test of initial
plausibility, even if there may be merit in the related view that
the Alsatian (and thus more conservatively reared) Durkheim
cherished the Jewish nostalgias of his childhood. Such nostalgias
would have been for a close provincial family life with its domestic rituals and strong internal bonds, not for a 'past' funded by

the lost world of a primitive Hebrew religion. Although some biblical scholars and religious modernists of Durkheim's day—both Gentile and Jewish—romanticized the primitive Hebrews and prophets, their reasons for doing so put them far from the kind of person Durkheim was. Instead, we find Durkheim praising the very Judaism anathema to these biblical scholars and theological modernists, whom we met in the previous chapter. We find Durkheim meditating on the wisdom of Talmudic Judaism.

The implications of this stance are intriguing for revealing a 'Jewish' Durkheim. Here, we see Durkheim acting against a subtle, and sometimes unintended, form of scholarly anti-Semitism in biblical scholarship, much as Durkheim acted against the anti-Semitic work of the 'anthroposociologist' Henri Muffang by expelling him from the *équipe*.[5] In defending the integrity and religious vitality of Talmudic Judaism, Durkheim actually supported the religious integrity of the only Judaism there was in his time—the real and concrete Judaism of his own day, however sociologically and religiously varied along regional lines. Paradoxically, Durkheim does so against those who are Jews themselves (modernist neo-Jews such as Salomon Reinach) or who are great scholars of Jewish religion (German biblical scholars such as Paul de Lagarde and Julius Wellhausen); nevertheless, Durkheim does not defend an abstract or essential Judaism or Jewishness. For although the likes of the Reinachs and Wellhausens were steeped in Jewish lore and learning, they were, for different reasons, equally well set against the prevailing real or concrete Judaisms of their own day. Their love of the prophets and of primitive Hebrew religion was always coupled with an equal and opposing contempt for the rabbinic and Talmudic Judaism of their own time—the Judaism of the Jews all round them. In this sense, they may be said to have been anti-Semitic—as indeed they have so been charged by their various critics.[6] Whatever his personal feelings about being Jewish himself, Durkheim in effect argued that concrete Judaism should be judged fairly and should not be caricatured for the sake of either a neo-Jewish or crypto-Christian theological agenda. This stance, however, was not 'natural' to the intellectual and social class that Durkheim occupied. As I will show, it marked Durkheim and his attitudes toward Judaism as notable for being especially sensitive to the real Jews and Judaism of his day. Thus, I find a telling characterization of Durkheim's relation to things Jewish, however unanticipated, ironic, and unresolved it may be, a characterization far more revealing than anything uncovered in the pursuit of the essential or hidden Durkheimian Jewishness that I have been criticizing.

Durkheim and the Durkheimians, as we will see, not only did not share this fashionable contempt for Talmudic Judaism, but they energetically and inventively defended it against scholarly anti-Semitism. Thus, rather than imagining that Durkheim's reading of Robertson Smith's account of the religion of the primitive Hebrews may have stirred up a nostalgia for a mythical idealized past, we should direct our attention to what Durkheim shared with the prominent Jewish champions of Talmudic Judaism of his time. In approaching Durkheim's Jewishness by way of Talmudic Judaism, I am not breaking totally new ground. Alexandre Derczansky, Jean-Claude Filloux, Louis M. Greenberg, Eugen Schoenfeld, and Stjepan Meštrović have all attempted to comprehend Durkheim's Jewishness in terms of Talmudic Judaism, with varying degrees of success.[7]

Recently, for instance, Schoenfeld and Meštrović have argued that Durkheim's moralism and his interest in a science of morals reflect Talmudic notions of justice.[8] Derczansky has urged us to see Durkheim's moral rigorism, puritanism, and resistance to social revolution as indicators of Durkheim's formation in the antimystical, antimessianic spirit of the Talmudic Judaism of the Troyes Talmudic school, in which Durkheim's father was educated.[9] Finally, Filloux has argued along different lines that Durkheim's conception of society, especially as expounded in the lyrical passages that Filloux appropriately calls "the hymn to society," matches precisely the Talmudic conception of God.[10] Each of these efforts falls short in key respects, but mostly because none of them engage Durkheim and the historical meaning of the Talmud for him and for the Jewish community of his time.

Let us consider Filloux first. Filloux argued that just as the Talmud's God is transcendent and immanent at one time, so too Durkheim's 'society' stands against its members, all the while exerting its strength from deep within our consciences. Just as the Talmud teaches the utter dependence of humanity on God, so also does Durkheim teach us of our dependence on society for all those things making us human—language, universal notions, moral norms, and so on. Finally, the relation of God to humanity in the Talmud is modeled on the love of a father for his children, thus making adherence to divine law a pleasurable matter. Accordingly, Filloux is not surprised to find Durkheim referring to the norms of society as ideals, sources of inspiration and goodness.

To anyone with the slightest acquaintance with nineteenth-century European (Protestant, as it happens) theology, Filloux's argument seems hardly worth taking seriously. These supposedly 'Talmudic' ideas of divinity are generic to several denominations of theism, particularly to the liberal theological milieu with which, as I have shown, the Durkheimians were conversant. Most, if not all, of these features of Durkheim's notion of society are equally represented in each of the theistic traditions found in the West. For example, Friedrich Schleiermacher, that powerful shaper of nineteenth-century Protestant theology, also spoke about the feeling of utter dependence of humanity on divinity.

Next is Schoenfeld and Meštrović's claim that Durkheim's supposed preference for 'justice' over 'charity' signaled his adherence to a 'Talmudic' or 'ideal construct' Jewish order of ethical priorities. This claim is odd not because the Talmud does not assert such a preference but because even if it did, and even if Durkheim agreed, for Durkheim to do so would hardly be distinctive. Contrary to what Schoenfeld and Meštrović imply, nothing is remarkable about Durkheim's affirming the importance of justice in a day when philosophical idealism made ethics a leading concern. Why, then, are we compelled to attribute this to the lasting impact of the Talmud? The ideal of justice was ready and available to thinkers of Durkheim's liberal persuasion, that is, to those who believed in the rule of law—especially at a time when both anarchist agitation and 'men on horseback' threatened the Third Republic. Were the semiofficial philosophers of the Third Republic, Charles Renouvier and Octave Hamelin, 'secret' Jews because they devoted major portions of their output to ethics?

More notable yet is the fact that contrary to what Schoenfeld and Meštrović say, Durkheim refused to dichotomize justice and charity, self-interest and altruism, and can therefore not be said to have preferred one over the other in the unqualified way stated by Schoenfeld and Meštrović. Altruism and egoism, according to Durkheim, are "two concurrent and intimately intertwining aspects of all conscious life."[11] The origins of Durkheim's position regarding the balance between duty or justice and charity or altruism can, moreover, be quite economically explained as virtually replicating the bourgeois moral positions of his philosophical mentor Renouvier, and his Bordeaux colleague, Hamelin. Significantly, neither Renouvier nor Hamelin appears in what must now be declared as Schoenfeld and Meštrović's profoundly unhistorical approach to Durkheim's Jewishness.[12] For example, Renouvier's metaphysics reconciled the individual with society by resisting tendencies to dichotomize the two. Our duty to others is our first duty to ourselves, according to Renouvier.[13] In like manner Hamelin disapproved of personal recklessness and absolute altruism.[14] "Duty toward oneself," argued Hamelin, is always subject to an appeal by a "better informed conscience"—namely one's own.[15] Hamelin accordingly noted with approval Renouvier's individualist view that the obligation to altruism is incumbent only on the saint. Ordinary people are expected to adhere only to their obligations.[16] Put in more abstract terms, Durkheim accepted that in practical terms, altruism or perfect civic self-sacrifice is an 'ideal' and thus something "that we may approach indefinitely without ever realizing" it.[17] When we try to live it in reality, Durkheim noted, self-sacrificing altruism throws up an "antinomy" between the "joy" of release from egoism and the "pain" of the real loss of pleasure—an "antinomy . . . so deep and so radical that it can never e completely resolved."[18] Durkheim never quite surrenders love and altruism from moral calculations even if he does force the *ideal* of charity and altruism to cohabit with the practical reality and desirability of concrete individuality and duty. Thus, as a moral philosopher, Durkheim identified himself with Renouvier and Hamelin, his neo-Idealist philosopher mentors and friends, rather than with some latter-day *porte-parole* for Talmudic morality or an 'ideally constructed' Judaism.[19]

By far the most useful discussion of Durkheim and Talmudic Judaism comes from Derczansky. He at least considers a particular historical context in which Talmudic Judaism might have grown into something having an impact on the young Durkheim and thus on the thought of the adult Durkheim. Derczansky's characterizations of the Judaism conveyed to the rabbinic students in Troyes, students like Durkheim's own father, suggest a distinctive social formation far from the essentialist abstractions offered by Filloux, Schoenfeld, and Meštrović. Here we can get our hands on one of the concrete Judaisms that very well may have been a factor in Durkheim's socialization. This is a Judaism of puritan, ascetic, antimessianic, antimystical religious practicality encouraged by the training at the rabbinic school of Troyes.[20] Durkheim's character certainly exhibits these traits, and thus his personality may well have been shaped by the kind of Judaism that influenced his father. It is worth noting that these features of Judaism are of course not 'essential' ones but are those formed in a certain context—just the kind of historically specific 'Jewishness' for which we have been looking.

If we then take Talmudic Judaism as forming a good portion of the probable context of Durkheim's Judaic past, we need to turn to the work of Greenberg. He, like some of the other participants in this inquiry, focused on the fact that Durkheim's father, Moïse, was a distinguished rabbi descended from a long line of men learned in the Talmud. Greenberg tells us that Moïse Durkheim was close to a distinguished Talmudic school (Troyes) that was known for having followed Rashi's principles of Talmudic interpretation. We also discover that Moïse Durkheim was probably a man of thwarted ambitions, a man unsuccessfully seeking to become a bigger part of the modern world of French nationalist Jewry. A photograph of the chief rabbi of the Vosges and Haute Marne shows Moïse Durkheim uncharacteristically beardless and in modern dress. This stimulates Greenberg to ask questions, which he is unable, however, fully to answer. How is it that the reputedly orthodox Moïse Durkheim consented to be photographed in the first place? Even though the Wissenschaft des Judentums had led directly to the birth of the reform movement in Germany, in contrast with France, the photograph of the beardless Moïse Durkheim fitted out in secular attire suggests that he may have been among the first to be tempted to follow the German example. Why is he not arrayed in traditional orthodox religious vestments? Although the French rabbinate was rather conservative when compared with the German rabbinate, Greenberg argues that Durkheim's father may have been an exception.

But Greenberg is unable to elaborate on the meaning behind Moïse Durkheim's talents and interests both in the "sciences and in philosophy"—ambitions never realized because of financial strictures laid upon the entire family.[21] Although the

French laity did not expect their rabbis to be men of broad learning and general culture, Moïse Durkheim was—and further wanted to be—just such a man. Although the French rabbis were not even expected to keep current with the latest developments in Jewish religious thought and scholarship, such as the liberalizing movements of the critical study of Judaism like the Wissenschaft des Judentums, we can well imagine that the inquisitive and adventurous Moïse Durkheim, who wanted to move to Paris to study science and philosophy, might have done so. Although the French rabbinate continued to avoid any contact with these new trends of the scientific study of Judaism well into the late nineteenth century and thus resisted the reforming potential of biblical criticism and other historical disciplines on the institutional religious life, Moïse Durkheim seemed at least headed in this direction. We lose track of Moïse Durkheim's development after his move to Épinal in the 1830s, but we do know that for most French Jews, liberalization came gradually from the mid-1850s.

In this chapter, I believe that I can move toward more certain answers for these questions by delving into the thought-world that such a 'modernizing' Jew as Moïse Durkheim might well have inhabited. This thought-world was dominated by that great cultural movement of Jewish intellectuals and scholars begun in Germany and carried over into France—the Wissenschaft des Judentums—or in its French incarnation, the Science du Judaïsme. I will not, however, be merely satisfied to speculate that Durkheim's father *might* have been influenced by the Wissenschaft des Judentums. We know for sure that at least Henri Hubert and Marcel Mauss enjoyed very close intellectual and personal relationships and affinities with Jews dedicated to the Wissenschaft des Judentums and that these relationships were fundamental to their intellectual formation. As for the Talmud, we will also see that those representatives of the Science du Judaïsme who were closest to Hubert and Mauss also had distinguished themselves in the intellectual world of their day as defenders of the reputation of the rabbis and Talmud. Remarkably, given their lack of Jewish piety and observance, the Durkheimians lined up alongside these representatives of the Science du Judaïsme to defend the honor of the rabbis and the Talmud. Thus, I suggest that rather than nurturing a childhood reverence for the 'real' Judaism of his youth—Talmudic Judaism—Durkheim 'read the Talmud' (that is, scholarship bearing on the Talmud) so favorably because he was thoroughly informed by the cutting-edge scholarship of the latter-day representatives of the Science du Judaïsme, who in turn did so much to educate the central members of the Durkheimian *équipe*, Hubert and Mauss, and thus eventually Durkheim himself.

Who were these Jewish contemporaries of the Durkheimians in the French version of the Wissenschaft des Judentums? And how did they come to occupy their positions in the French academic world? To begin with names, we should mention scholars such as the Islamicist Hartwig Derenbourg, the professor of Talmudic studies Israël Lévi, the Indologist Sylvain Lévi, and to a lesser extent, the philosopher Louis-Germain Lévy and the archaeologist, art historian, and all-round savant Salomon Reinach. All were active members of the Société des Études Juives and were supporters of the work of the learned journal the *Revue des études juives.* All, on the whole, held to a moderate form of Jewish observance. Although none of these men were Durkheimians themselves, they enjoyed fraternal, intellectual, and collegial relations with the Durkheimians, primarily in their capacity (with the exception of Lévy and Reinach) as mentors to Hubert and Mauss in the Fifth Section, the "religious sciences" section, of the École Pratique des Hautes Études. I believe that these relations reflect something about the reasons why Durkheimians wrote about otherwise déclassé Talmudic Judaism as they did. In short, I suggest that we can most plausibly account for the Durkheimians' nuanced and informed views on Jewish issues by reference to the chief defenders of Talmudic Judaism in the scholarly world of their day—to representatives of the progressive, scientific, Jewish learning of their milieu.[22]

Consequently in this chapter, we need to determine the nature of the historical and ideological bonds linking Durkheimian scholarship and the approach to Judaism practiced by the French heirs to the Wissenschaft des Judentums. Thus, I will sketch out the program and origins of this French version of the Wissenschaft des Judentums, naturally enough called the Science du Judaïsme. Then I will see how the Durkheimians approached Judaism in general and how these French Jewish scholars of Judaism themselves did. Since this comparison concerns attitudes to religion itself, we will be able to compare simultaneously both the 'styles' of historical inquiry and the 'contents.' What we find here is a remarkable community of interest between the French representatives of the Science du Judaïsme and the Durkheimians.

Let me begin by taking up the chase and following the trail from the German Jewish beginnings of the Wissenschaft des Judentums to the Science du Judaïsme and the major Jewish figures of our current discussion. As we will see, it was the French wing of this movement for the Jewish scientific study of Judaism that entered into an intimate relationship with the Durkheimians and their study of religion.[23] The nominally Catholic Hubert began his studies of the world religions with the Middle East. Hubert and Mauss apparently met as students of Hebrew in the late 1890s at the École Pratique des Hautes Études. In the same year, Hubert and Mauss begin their studies in the Fifth Section, studying under Israël Lévi and eventually Hartwig Derenbourg, among others. As the name implies, the Wissenschaft des Judentums was a phenomenon of the German-speaking world, promoting a critical, historically scientific study of Judaism. As articulated by the German Jewish scholar Immanuel Wolf in 1822, the commission of the Wissenschaft des Judentums was clearly scientific:

> [The] science of Judaism . . . treats the object of its study in and for itself, for its own sake, and not for any special purpose or definite intention. It begins without any preconceived opinion and is not concerned with the final result. Its aim is neither to put its object in a favorable, nor in an unfavorable light, in relation to prevailing views, but to show it as it is. Science is self-sufficient and is in itself an essential need of the human spirit.[24]

From the Jewish viewpoint, the situation in Germany was, on the whole, bad for the critical study of Judaism. Where Judaism was studied, Gentiles dominated the field. More typically, in the late eighteenth and early nineteenth centuries, when scientifically minded Jews wanted to follow the lead of the new critical studies of the Jewish and Christian Bibles, they were rebuffed by state institutions. When Abraham Geiger had proposed to establish Jewish studies in German universities, he was denied the opportunity.[25] Likewise, when Geiger sought to establish a Jewish faculty of theology at one of the universities, alongside Catholics and Protestants, he was similarly denied government approval.[26] Thus, in 1819, Leopold Zunz founded an independent and private organization for the scientific study of Judaism, the Verein für Cultur und Wissenschaft der Juden.[27] Geiger and Zunz launched the official organ of the movement, the *Monatschrift für Geschichte und Wissenschaft des Judentums;* it expressly aimed to publish original work on all aspects of the history of Jewish life around the world. Under the leadership of Geiger and Zunz in the first third of the nineteenth century, the Wissenschaft des Judentums movement took form.[28]

In the 1830s, the French became interested in developments within the German university system and sought actively to lure German scholars to France. Among those attracted by emigration to France were a number of German Jewish scholars connected to the group that Geiger and Zunz had assembled in 1819. Having refused to convert to Christianity in pursuit of higher careers in the German professional world, they had thus effectively stymied their careers. Hoping for the benefits of emancipation, some emigrated to France. Thus, within a short time of the establishment of the Wissenschaft des Judentums itself, the originally German movement was carried to France, subsequently to be transformed there.

Prominent among the new arrivals were two younger members of the *Monatschrift*'s original circle, Joseph Derenbourg and Salomon Munk. A younger member of the first generation of promoters of the Wissenschaft des Judentums, Munk (1803–67) arrived in Paris in the 1840s to assume a research post in Hebrew manuscripts as curator of Oriental manuscripts at the Bibliothèque Nationale and as professor of Hebrew, Chaldaic, and Syriac at the Collège de France.[29] At about the same time, the French-born but German resident Derenbourg (1811–95) joined Munk from Germany. In 1877, he became professor of Hebrew languages in the Fourth Section (philology) of the École Pratique des Hautes Études. One of the teachers of Hubert and Mauss, Derenbourg's son Hartwig, followed his father's lead and became professor of Arabic and Islam at the École Pratique des Hautes Études, Fifth Section.[30] It was there, as well as in Paris, that Israël Lévi (1856–1939), another scholar familiar to the Durkheimians, came under the influence of these first émigré members of the Wissenschaft des Judentums movement. Although the conservative French rabbinate kept these scholars somewhat at arm's length, they, like other Jewish scholars, found their intellectual homes in the great secular institutions of the French state such as the École Pratique des Hautes Études— where the Durkheimians too would seek to establish themselves.

The École Pratique des Hautes Études, Fifth Section, was unlike other institutions devoted to the study of religion. It was not aligned with any religious denomination. In conception, it emphasized historical and philological erudition at the expense of theological or philosophical polemics or speculation. It did so in part for nationalist reasons—namely to match the critical scholarly achievements of the German biblical historians. Indeed, since it was founded in connection with the disestablishment of the Roman Catholic school of theology at the Sorbonne, the Fifth Section even carried a certain anticlerical reputation. Although Alfred Loisy was no longer a priest at the time of his appointment at the École Pratique des Hautes Études, Fifth Section, public opposition to the appointment was made on the grounds that the history of religions was best taught by someone who had been a faithful, lifelong atheist. Devoted to "la science religieuse," the Fifth Section was a perfect match for the culture of scholarship already firmly established for some decades by the Jewish scholars at the Science du Judaïsme.

The world of parochial Jewish learning was different. Still determined to resist the new history and philology, French Jewry continued to develop its own institutions of higher learning. The scientific study of Judaism in France remained confined to the university, however. Thus, in 1856, the slightly more worldly Séminaire Israëlite was established in Paris, primarily organized to train young men for the rabbinate.[31] At best, the seminarians were permitted leave from their schools for a scant two hours a week and then only to visit Hartwig Derenbourg's class in Hebrew at the École Pratique des Hautes Études.[32] Thus, when Munk and Derenbourg arrived in France, French Jewish learning meant Talmudic training of a provincial and conservative sort—a fact, incidentally, that makes Moïse Durkheim's cosmopolitanism of the early 1830s all the more remarkable.[33]

It was not until Durkheim's generation at the end of the nineteenth century that the Science du Judaïsme had any impact at all on the seminary education of the traditionally conservative French Jewish community[34] and then only because of the initiative of Jewish scholars at the university.[35] Courses in Jewish and French history and literature were added to the curriculum that had prevailed at the earlier seminary in Metz.[36] Modern intellectuals like Paul Janet also lectured at the *séminaire*. But despite these efforts to modernize education there, the prevailing unscholarly and conservative 're-orthodoxing' trends of French Judaism at the end of the century prevented the student rabbis at the Séminaire Israëlite from becoming unduly influenced by the new secular scholarship championed by the Wissenschaft des Judentums.[37]

The conservatives, however, gradually saw a way to exploit the historical positivism of the Wissenschaft des Judentums for their own purposes. Some of the Jewish scholars whom the Durkheimians knew and revered date from this generation of learned Jewish students of Jewish life and thought. The new scholarship offered both liberals and conservatives a set of ground rules for debate about religious change, by providing a repertoire of precedents for ruling on current Jewish practice. All "legitimate reforms must be rooted in a respect for history."[38] Phyllis Cohen Albert has reported that Chief Rabbi Isidor, exemplifying this dominant mood of progressive "conservative innovation, based on historical awareness," wrote in 1885 that he had been "trying to imitate the Adam of the midrashic legend, who had two faces, one turned toward the past, and the other turned toward the future."[39] Thus, in an odd way, the Science du Judaïsme allowed both wings of French Jewry some measure of mutual accommodation.

Typical of this ability to reconcile piety with scholarship were the mentors of Hubert and Mauss, Rabbi Israël Lévi and Sylvain Lévi.[40] Both Israël and Sylvain, though critical scholars of the first order, tended to be more conservative about religious belief and practice than the extreme liberal partisans of neo-Judaisms, men such as James Darmesteter, Louis-Germain Lévy, or Salomon Reinach. This lingering conservatism of the Jewish scholars who most directly influenced Hubert and Mauss left indelible marks on them and on Durkheimian scholarship, as we will see. Thus, it was these advanced Jewish students of Judaism who read and argued about Durkheim, Loisy, Robertson Smith, Sir James Frazer, and Georges Sorel and about their theories on the nature of religion, whether Jewish or not. So when we think about the network of Jewish learning in Durkheim's day, we need to think in part about the tradition of scientific study of Judaism brought from Germany and about the members of the Jewish scholarly avant-garde who were its greatest practitioners. It was their 'reading' and practice of Judaism that the Durkheimians took as authoritative.

Perhaps the man who did the most to set the pace for these avant-garde French Jewish scholars was Salomon Munk. He directly influenced the approaches to Judaism and to religion in general taken by intimates and contemporaries of the Durkheimians like Israël Lévi and Sylvain Lévi. In doing so, Munk may very well have indirectly shaped the Durkheimian approach to the study of religion. For Munk, Judaism stood alongside other religious traditions such as Islam and Christianity as an equal—and equally powerful—object of scientific study, not as a separate autonomous entity. Were Munk alive today, he would place the study of Judaism within the comparative study of societies, religious studies, history of philosophy, or comparative cultural history and not within some supposedly autonomous discipline such as Jewish studies. To borrow a phrase from Jacob Neusner, Munk would "take Judaism for example."[41] Unlike his German Jewish mentors, but like the Durkheimians, Munk was a comparativist and an original proponent of interdisciplinary work. He sought to orient the study of Judaism toward the disciplines of archaeology, history of antiquity, and philology.[42] Munk showed, for example, how Jewish thinkers played important parts in making up the intellectual world of supposedly 'Christian' medieval philosophy. Likewise, the same desire to show how Judaism and Christianity nurtured each other may well have been one precedent guiding some of Israël Lévi's work, which we will see shortly. Lévi argued, for instance, that the sacrifice of Isaac was the model for Paul's sacrificial reading of the death of Jesus.

Much of Munk's spirit informed the institution that finally came to represent the ideals of the scientific study of Judaism in France, the Société des Études Juives. All major Jewish figures of this study—Israël Lévi, Salomon Reinach, the Derenbourgs, James Darmesteter, Isidore Lévy, and Sylvain Lévi—were members, as was the Gentile Ernest Renan. In 1879, Zadok Kahn had founded the Société des Études Juives as the French parallel to the original Verein für Cultur und Wissenschaft der Juden. From this base in the *société,* in the same year, Zadok Kahn launched the *Revue des études juives,* a perfect mirror of its German Jewish model, the *Monatschrift für Geschichte und Wissenschaft des Judentums,* recognized as such by the Germans.[43] In the inaugural number, the editors affirmed their "preoccupation with scientific truth"[44]—even if this risked inducing a certain "aridity" into the pages of the *Revue.*[45] Sounding even more like the Durkheimians, the editors declared that science was the "only thing" guiding them in the publication. Underlining their differences from the orthodox, they stated, "We are not in the business of making religious propaganda, nor are we even aiming at edification."[46] Founder Zadok Kahn declared that from its beginnings, the Société des Études Juives took charge of "all aspects of the Jewish past excluding dogmatic or purely denominational matters."[47]

But for Zadok Kahn, dedication to the ideals of a scientific study of Judaism did not entail indifference to specifically French Jewish values. First and foremost Zadok Kahn wanted to aid in building up the integrity of the Jewish community. He and others felt that both the Société and the *Revue* should and could spur the future evolution of Judaism—but should do so positively and "scientifically." Further, from the beginning, the editors clearly stated that they had certain "patriotic" interests as well. The editors said they wanted to create a "*French* library of Jewish science and literature." They wanted to "relieve France of its inferior position" in the study of the Jewish past.[48]

The *Revue* thus put into practice those values that Munk's scholarship asserted. Supporting Munk's opposition to Jewish studies as an autonomous endeavor, the editors of the *Revue des études juives* extended their appeal for the study of the Jewish past of France not only to Jews but also to "the public in general." They added, "We neither ask those who write for the *Revue* who they are, nor where they come from—only that they be serious and sincere."[49] Recalling as well Munk's Jewish universalism and his interests in seeing how Judaism played a role in the formation of modern European civilization, the *Revue* set out on the same path. The inaugural editorial of the *Revue* wanted, for example, to illuminate the nature of the French Judaism of the Middle Ages because, said the editors, this Judaism showed a native "Jewish universalism" and thus bore the "imprint of the French spirit."[50]

The *Revue* also seems to bear witness to Munk's belief in the importance of comparative studies, in an openness to the new disciplines of folklore and ethnography, and in the general tendency to emphasize the location of Judaism within the larger world of religious history—all trends evident in the contemporary efforts of the Durkheimian *L'Année sociologique*. Louis-Germain Lévy, for example, authored an early piece on totemism.[51] Reinach wrote articles on the accusations of Jewish ritual murder, the Inquisition and the Jews, the origin of prayers for the dead, and racism.[52] Under the leadership of Israël Lévi, the *Revue des études juives* published short notices and reviews of some Durkheimian publications—especially those written by members of the Durkheimian *équipe* who were also members of the Société des Études Juives, for example, Isidore Lévy. Israël Lévi himself published a comparative study of the sacrifice of Isaac and the death of Jesus.[53] In 1913, we will see how Israël Lévi took Sir James Frazer's *Golden Bough* to task for its insinuations about Jewish blood libel.

The desire for religious reform against the conservative forces of orthodoxy was not the only motivation behind the new critical history. Increasingly in the nineteenth century, positivist history helped Jews defend their traditions against what I will call scholarly anti-Semitism. French Jewish efforts to master the historical sciences anticipated and also reacted to the growing anti-Semitism of the late 1800s. It is here, in this context of anti-anti-Semitic history typical of members of the Société des Études Juives, that I believe we can locate the Durkheimians. Interestingly enough, the Durkheimians took positions identical to those proposed by the Science du Judaïsme. They were especially vocal against anti-Semitic attacks on the Talmud. One cannot help wondering what Moïse Durkheim would have thought, knowing that his son and colleagues kept current, as we will see, with the most advanced trends of Jewish 'scientific' rehabilitation of the reputation of his beloved Talmud and, in the process, relieved Talmudic Judaism of the common slanders laid on it by its detractors.

The strategy of these 'scholarly anti-Semites' cast Jews born in France as indifferent to their own traditions. These Jews could not be bothered to write their own history. As Romain Rolland said flatly, "The past does not exist for the Jews."[54] Sylvain Lévi, then president of the Société des Études Juives, well understood that such libels presented a "most pressing problem" to the well-being of the Jewish community. In 1904, he addressed the general assembly of the Société des Études Juives and argued that Jews should take their place in the world but without "re-nouncing their past or traditions." Giving eloquent voice to this ambition to write Jewish history—but within the context of hu-man history—Lévi added:

> When we rummage through libraries, decipher obscure scrib-bling, wrest bits of manuscript or fragments of inscriptions from the bowels of the earth, we mean to do work that is both fulfilling and positive, and to draw from these dead documents the secrets of our life. . . . Noble families of old kept in their archives the remembrances of the great deeds which had made them famous. And in so doing, they justified their social rank and fortune. To-day, the whole of humanity wants to ennoble itself. Humanity wants its own archives. And it is from the historians that it expects them—[and expects them to be] faithful and sincere. In solidar-ity with the whole world, can we—without misuse or nar-rowness—reclaim the Jewish past?[55]

Lévi answered Rolland's charges clearly and positively in the style made possible by the Société des Études Juives. Yes, Jews—especially those like himself—could write such a history of them-selves, because the "Jew is an historical being."[56] For Sylvain Lévi and others, this meant conducting the scientific history of religions stemming from the Wissenschaft des Judentums.[57] It meant, as we will see, treating the history of Jews and Judaism as a history of concrete social realities, located in specific times and places, bounded and constituted by particular institutions, rituals, and practices that in turn 'made' the Judaisms that there were and would be.

Thus, French Jews had to face more than the skepticism that they were both capable and interested in writing their own histories. They had to confront the fact that in France before the rise of the Science du Judaïsme, the study of the history and prehistory of Judaism was almost exclusively a Gentile operation and was often profoundly anti-Semitic. The efforts of Munk on the whole played in the shadows while the careers of Gentile Semiticists sparkled in full view of the literate public. We have only to recall the celebrated career of Ernest Renan. Before Darmesteter's 'Jewish' publications of a generation later, Renan was the leading spokesman for Jewish religion and the Hebrew Bible in France. Thus, when we speak of Jewish learning in France we should distinguish among scholarship done about Judaism by Jews, scholarship done about Judaism by Gentiles, and scholarship done about non-Jewish subjects by Jews. By "Jewish learning," I mean those Jews who studied religions, whether Jewish or non-Jewish. These distinctions generate three possible categories of scholars usefully distinguished in Durkheim's day.

1. Jews Who Studied Judaism

Specialists: Salomon Munk, Joseph Derenbourg, Isidore Lévy, Israël Lévi, Salomon Reinach, Theodore Reinach

Secondary figures: Sylvain Lévi, Marcel Mauss, Joseph Reinach

Learned Journal: *Revue des études juives*

Learned Society: Société des Études Juives

2. Jews Who Studied Non-Jewish Religions

Specialists: James Darmesteter, Hartwig Derenbourg, Emile Durkheim, Robert Hertz, Sylvain Lévi, Louis-Germain Lévy, Lucien Lévy-Bruhl, Marcel Mauss, Salomon Reinach

Learned Journals: *L'Année sociologique, Revue d'histoire des religions, L'Anthropologie*

Learned Society: Société Francaise de Philosophie

3. Gentiles Who Studied Judaism

Specialists (Roman Catholics): Alfred Loisy, Ernest Renan

In this way, Gentile command over Jewish scripture amounted to Gentile power to determine what was important and worth studying in the heritage of Jewish people. In 1892, this point was made by no less a figure of Jewish learning than James Darmesteter. Remarking that in France the Bible was "more celebrated than known," he noted that German "Protestant theologians" had led the way in these studies and had done so "exclusively."[58] This German Protestant dominance of biblical studies had resulted in religiously partisan scholarship, in studies that were in "the thraldom of theological and scholastic hierology."[59] Darmesteter here echoed the views of one of the founders of the Wissenschaft des Judentums, Edouard Gans, and thus recapitulated for French Jews the very reasons the Wissenschaft des Judentums had been founded in the first place. In 1822, Gans believed that Jews should be scandalized both by the dominance of Christian scholars over Jewish studies and by the partisan Christian uses to which the studies were put: "Any credible results [in the field of Jewish scholarship] are mainly due to the efforts of Christian scholars. But while the rabbis lacked the necessary freedom in their studies, the Christian approach to Judaism lacked independence: much too often it was turned into a discipline secondary, and merely ancillary, to Christian theology."[60] Gans did not mention the particular Christian scholars he had in mind. But Darmesteter would surely have had the major biblical scholars of his day in mind: Paul de Lagarde and Julius Wellhausen.

Beyond feeling somewhat overshadowed by these well-ensconced Christian students of the Jewish Bible, many Jews were sensitive to the anti-Semitic character of some Christian work—a conviction that goes back at least to 1818 with Leopold Zunz. This father of modern Jewish studies was quite clear about his feelings toward the treatment of the religion of Israel at the hands of some Christian theologians: "Nothing more distorted, more damaging, more dishonest has ever anywhere been written than that which has been written on the religion of Israel. The art of inciting malice has here reached its pinnacle."[61]

Such anti-Semitic scholarship was perhaps best exemplified by Paul de Lagarde (1827–91), a German Orientalist and, in his later years, 'theologian' of a neopagan Germanic religion.[62] Lagarde merged his own theological biases against Catholics and Jews with the German romantic primitivism of the *volkish* movement of which he was so important a part. For him, primordial religion was the best religion, since it originated in the simplicity and innocence of the beginnings, long before the decadent sophistication of civilization.[63] Pure religion exalts the joyous celebration of life, which Lagarde believed had characterized primitive Christianity before its 'pharisaic' corruption by Saul of Tarsus.[64]

A key Protestant biblical theologian figuring in these academic anti-Semitic trends of thought was Lagarde's student Julius Wellhausen (1844–1918), the founder of the higher criticism of the Bible and the mentor of Robertson Smith. Although undeniably renowned for his scholarly achievement, Wellhausen nonetheless furthered an anti-Semitic interpretation of Jewish history by attempting to weaken the work of Abraham Geiger and the Wissenschaft des Judentums movement. According to the *Jewish Encyclopedia,* his work was marred by "an unmistakable anti-Jewish bias." This refers to Wellhausen's lack of sympathy for Judaism outside the prophetic period. He believed that one could neatly divide Jewish history into "lofty" periods such as the prophetic age, which he (unlike Darmesteter)[65] took to be virtually independent from priestly influence.[66] Even though he tended to idolize the religion of the ancient Hebrews for its primitive vigor, Wellhausen offended Jewish sensibilities by pressing the view that the cult of the ancient Hebrews, however vital, was a crude nature religion with few redeeming virtues.[67] Following the lead of Wellhausen, even Ernest Renan, a member in good standing of the Société des Études Juives but also greatly in the debt of German Protestant biblical scholarship, refused to give the religion of Israel, much less Judaism, a worth in its own right. The religion of Israel had value only in terms of its being a preparation for the Christian gospel or universal humanism.[68] In Renan's view, the spiritual "vocation" of Israel had been, from the beginning, to establish the basis for the religion of humanity and then to disappear. "Has Israel fulfilled its vocation? Has it protected in the grand conflict of the nations, the position which was primarily confided to it? Yes, we reply without hesitation. Israel has been the trunk upon which the faith of the human race has been engrafted."[69] Thus, Jewish scholars had to face an accumlated mass of anti-Semitic opinion emanating from sources fundamentally hostile to real Judaism.

Going one step further beyond comparative history proper, adherents to the Science du Judaïsme extended their efforts in the direction of writing Jewish *pre*history. Thus, like the Durkheimians, they enthusiastically responded to the new ethnographic data that flooded into Europe during the late nineteenth and early twentieth centuries. A decade or so before the publication of *The Elementary Forms of the Religious Life,* Salomon Reinach reported, "One of the most significant and most curious phenomena of contemporary science is that anthropology, ethnology and sociology are on their way to transforming traditional philology."[70] Reinach had in mind the comparative anthropological methods first employed in obscurity by the German scholar Wilhelm Mannhardt (1831–80) and later taken over and popularized by Frazer and, less so, by Robertson Smith.[71]

In the hands of Jewish reformers like Reinach, the new ethnography was used to encourage Judaism to reform itself in the same way as we have seen ordinary history used by such figures as Zadok Kahn. Reinach felt that the new methodologies provided him a powerful means of exposing the nature of a religious tradition that he felt badly needed reform. He, like Frazer, tried to undermine the legitimacy of certain modern religious beliefs and practices by claiming that they were survivals of certain unsavory prehistoric practices. Thus, even earlier than the Durkheimians, but often for such different purposes, the Jewish scholars began incorporating the new cross-cultural ethnographic writing into Jewish historical work. What was to become a trademark of Durkheimian work seems, then, already to have been put to use by proponents of the Science du Judaïsme.

Partly driving this engagement with prehistoric religious materials was the desire of Jewish scholars to counter anti-Semitic scholarship. Typical of those who made such an anti-Semitic politics of prehistory were, of course, the Aryanists, chief among them Paul de Lagarde.[72] On the face of it, Lagarde wanted to discover *the* ancient German religion;[73] his deeper intention was to define it in dialectical opposition to Jewish religion. To be an Aryan was by definition not to be a Jew.[74] Indeed Lagarde hoped that by establishing this 'pure' Aryan identity, he would eliminate any claims of Jewish contribution to the foundations of Western civilization. Accordingly, Aryanists like Lagarde emphasized the value of the peasant culture of Europe in the formation of the European mind. The peasants represented 'survivals' of a pre-Christian 'old' Europe, uncontaminated by Jewish elements.[75] On the other hand, the contributions that Jews made to the formation of Europe could be minimized or passed over as 'superficial' and foreign. Europe's real lore was thus folklore, the Eddas or the old Norse myths, not the traditions of Jewish and Christian Europe; the real 'bibles' were not the Jewish and Christian scriptures but some sort of Aryan bible, identified eventually as the Vedas.[76] The threat that such views represented to French Jews and their ideology of French nationality was obvious. Since the Jews did not stem from the peasant stock of 'old Europe,' they had therefore never really belonged to Europe.

In response to the Aryanists, Jews sought to take charge of their own prehistory by participating in its writing. Significant for us was the fact that in France, the first to engage and appropriate the work of Robertson Smith and Frazer were not the Durkheimians but the Jewish scholars, whether modernists or not, such as Salomon Reinach, Louis-Germain Lévy,[77] Isidore Lévy, and Israël Lévi. Here were men, in the tradition of the Science du Judaïsme, who wanted Jews to command the writing of their own prehistory. Indeed the new Jewish excursions into prehistory appeared in the same venue as routine studies of Jewish history—the *Revue des études juives*. Thus, when the new folkloric and ethnographic work hit Europe in the middle of the nineteenth century, certain Jewish scholars were ready to explore it and publish its implications for the Jewish tradition.

Typical of this kind of defense of Judaism was Israël Lévi's vigorous attack on the French edition (1918) of Frazer's *Golden Bough*.[78] Frazer had written that ancient Hebrew human sacrifice and the death of Jesus were part of a 'surviving' Jewish culture trait of bloody sacrificial victimization. Such primitive practices survived and were even reinforced, wrote Frazer, in the Purim symbolic hanging of Haman. Frazer added that human sacrifice was a continuing part of Jewish tradition. Making the bad situation of accusing Jews of bloodlust and ritual murder even worse, Frazer in effect claimed that the institution of Jewish ritual murder further survived in the death of Jesus. Although Frazer disavowed any anti-Semitic implications in his work in a letter to *The Times* (11 November 1913), the matter greatly dismayed Jewish scholars, not only because the great Frazer had lent his reputation to vulgar scholarship but also, and most of all, because anti-Semitic scholarship seemed to have produced real-world effects. Frazer's discussion occurred, for instance, around the time of the prosecution in Russia of a blood libel charge against Mendel Beilis.[79]

This intrusion of popular anti-Semitism into the aristocratic world of scholarship sent shockwaves through the French Jewish scholarly community in Durkheim's day. Chief among those moved to respond to this phenomenon was no less a figure than Israël Lévi.[80] In his review in the *Revue des études juives*, Lévi made it clear how stunned he was by Frazer's dalliance in the vulgar discourse of Jewish blood libel. To Lévi, Frazer's complicity marked him as an intellectual inferior: it demonstrated the "poverty of the mind of the accusers."[81] And at least from this point on, many Jewish scholars increased their alertness to anti-

Semitism in otherwise 'high' scholarship. A contemporary, the Romanian-born Jewish folklorist Moses Gaster (1856–1934), for example, kept a sharp eye out for the same anti-Semitic tendencies in ethnographic literature.[82] I believe we should include the Durkheimians in this number. Although Hubert and Mauss, for example, often operated from different first principles than Israël Lévi, their work on Jewish prehistory and folklore recalls the spirit of Israël Lévi's reaction to scholarly anti-Semitism. Mauss's 1926 contribution, "Critique interne de la 'légende d'Abraham,' " to Israël Lévi's.[83]

The Durkheimians and the liberal Jewish heirs of the traditions of Munk and the Science du Judaïsme can, therefore, be brought into an even closer relationship to each other by considering their community of shared interests in combating the scholarly anti-Semitism of such figures as Lagarde and Wellhausen. In general, the Jewish members of the Durkheimian *équipe* had little or no active interest in the reform of Judaism by way of critical history or the new ethnography. They did, however, care a great deal about scientific history and social justice. They thus opposed anti-Semitism whether in politics or in the 'politics' of scholarship.[84] The evidence indicates that at least two key Durkheimians, Hubert and Mauss, were substantially informed by this critical and historicist Jewish history of religions. Both Hubert and Mauss, for example, studied under Jewish mentors at the École Pratique des Hautes Études, Fifth Section. I believe a remarkable community of interest is here to be found between the French representatives of the Science du Judaïsme and the Durkheimians. To wit, although we know something about Durkheim's views of anti-Semitism,[85] we know almost nothing about how his thought and the opinions of members of his *équipe*, like Hubert and Mauss, were situated within the thought-world of the advanced Jewish scholarship at the Fifth Section. In this connection, I claim, first, that the issue of anti-Semitism became for our Jewish scholars of religion a factor in how and why they wrote about Judaism and, second, that the Durkheimians occupied the same positions on these issues themselves. I will consider two such areas of anti-Semitic focus: Talmudic Judaism and the so-called blood libel. I want to consider both Jewish and Durkheimian reactions to these two foci of anti-Semitic scholarship and compare them with each other.

In the end, critiques of Talmudic Judaism amount to critiques of religion as ritual and, indeed, of all 'embodied' or collective forms of Jewish religious life. This is why both the attacks on ritual in Talmudic Judaism coincided with equally vehement attacks on the synagogue. This is also why the critics of Talmudic Judaism—critics such as Wellhausen and, following him, Robertson Smith—interpreted ritual sacrifice among the ancient Hebrews as a 'disembodied' spiritualized act of communion between humanity and deity. Ritual was for them a groping attempt to approximate an ideal that would be realized only explicitly as humanity progressed up the evolutionary ladder. And so these critics had basically driven a wedge between the pure 'spiritualized' rituals and the degenerate 'materialist' rituals of Talmudic Judaism. For them, ancient Hebrew sacrifice was not really a ritual like the rituals of Talmudic Judaism; it was a profoundly spiritual act of communication. Returning to a leitmotiv of my earlier discussion of the historical situation of Judaism in late-nineteenth- and early-twentieth-century France, we see that critics of Talmudic Judaism were essentially attacking real Judaism—Judaism as an *embodied* reality.

Despite its distance from the ritualistic religion of the priestly traditions of ancient Israel, Talmudic Judaism was made to bear most of the burdens that, without German romantic primitivism's love of the primordial, would have been laid on ritual religion itself. Talmudic Judaism was the Judaism disliked by both prominent Christian and prominent Jewish biblical scholars for its so-called desiccation of primitive Hebrew religion. Such views were even propagated by 'enlightened' Gentile students of Judaism such as Ernest Renan—himself a member of the Société des Études Juives. Propagating Wellhausen's view of the gradual loss of the Jewish religious spirit in Talmudic Judaism, Renan said: "Judaism goes forth, contracting itself and fortifying itself more and more. The liberty, the simplicity, of the ancient Hebrew genius, so foreign to every scruple and casuistry, give place to the littleness of Rabbinism. The scribe succeeds the prophet. A strongly organized priesthood stifles all profane life."[86]

Further typical of Wellhausen, Renan saw, in the development of Judaism out of the religion of ancient Israel, a steady departure from ancient values. A prominent symptom of decline here was the Jewish ritual life evident for him in Talmudic Judaism. "The practice of particular devotion," said Renan, "had for the ancient Hebrews little attraction." And in the process of developing new ritual forms, Judaism "obliterated the ancient foundation." Likewise, the synagogue had little value because it is an institution of Judaism, not ancient Israel. Renan noted, "We find no trace [of it] before the captivity, and . . . the institution is only to a small extent in harmony with the Mosaic spirit."[87] Speaking from his own pious, anticlerical, free thinker's heart, Renan warned, "The *synagogue* becomes what in later ages is to be the *church;* a sort of constituted authority against which all independent thought hurls itself."[88]

Talmudic Judaism was, of course, the target of choice for the virulent anti-Semitism of late-nineteenth-century France, as can be observed in the writings of Edouard Drumont. It not only taught Jews to hate non-Jews, Drumont claimed, but also enjoined Jews to kill Gentiles and to seize their wealth.[89] It was also criticized by Jewish anti-Semites, like Bernard Lazare, who during his anti-Semitic phase attacked the Talmud for its supposedly desiccated nature. Interestingly enough, the attacks of Drumont's *La France juive* (1886) and Lazare's *L'Anti-Semitisme* (1894) had much in common. Jewish modernist reformers, such as Darmesteter and Reinach, also took aim on the Judaism of the rabbis.

These attacks came in many forms, but typically in debates about (against) what became known in the Jewish community as "ritualism"—the dietary interdictions, the Sabbath observance, and the synagogue.[90] At the height of his anti-Semitic phase, Lazare laid out an ideal-type scenario opposing the "Mosaic Israëlites" to the "Talmudic Jews."[91] It was these Talmudic *Juifs,* Lazare argued, who provoked anti-Semitism. By their arrogant insistence on being themselves determined by their laws, they brought Gentile hatred down on themselves and all Jews.[92] Similarly Salomon Reinach carried out a protracted public campaign within the Jewish community against adherence to dietary proscriptions, ritual obligations, and the Sabbath rest. To the liberal Reinach, all these "ritualistic" trappings of Talmudic Judaism kept French Jews from their "internal emancipation." Ritualism kept Jews tightly bound within the spiritual ambit of a primitive religion of "scruples"—taboos or interdictions. Instead, reflecting the antisocial sentiments of many liberal Jews, Reinach thought that "true religion is a matter of feeling, not practices."[93]

Given that this critique of Talmudic Judaism was fashionable in the liberal and enlightened scholarly circles in which the Durkheimians moved, it is striking that the Durkheimians totally rejected the liberal position. They not only resisted the criticism of Talmudic Judaism but even made a virtue of the so-called ritualism. In this, as we will now see, the Durkheimians surprisingly mirrored the scholarship of a major conservative representative of the Science du Judaïsme, the editor-in-chief of the *Revue des études juives* and president of the Société des Études Juives, a future grand rabbi of the Central Consistory and chief historian of Talmudic Judaism, a mentor of both Hubert and Mauss: Israël Lévi.

Ironically enough, just at the time that Talmudic Judaism was most out of fashion, it was recognized as an area deserving special study in the French academic world. This doubtless reflected the growing strength of the more conservative forces in the Jewish and Gentile academic communities, since the creation of all such posts was politically sensitive in France.[94] In 1896, the first chair in "Judaïsme talmudique et rabbinique" at the École Pratique des Hautes Études, Fifth Section, was established, with Israël Lévi as its first incumbent. Lévi was for many reasons an excellent choice for the chair, not the least because he tended to avoid the extreme liberalism of the neo-Jews, who dominated the secular Jewish intellectual scene in Paris. As we will see, he disagreed with the extreme liberalism of the founders of the Wissenschaft des Judentums, such as Wilhelm Geiger, on important theological points.[95] Thus, as a rabbi himself, learned in the techniques of the new critical scholarship of the Science du Judaïsme, he was a natural defender of Talmudic Judaism.[96]

Lévi defended Talmudic Judaism by advancing four theses. These in turn were incorporated into the self-understanding of modern French Jews and thus were commonly rehearsed in scholarly comparisons of Judaism and Christianity.[97] As we will soon discover, Lévi's theses correspond exactly to Durkheimian views about the status of Talmudic Judaism. First, Talmudic Judaism, thus contemporary Judaism, was the equal of Christianity. It had developed out of the ancient Hebrew religion parallel, chronologically and theologically, to Christianity. Talmudic Judaism was not Christianity's precursor but, rather, a viable historical alternative to it.[98] Second, Talmudic Judaism was thus at least as religiously vital and theologically sophisticated as Christianity. Talmudic Judaism did not represent the 'old' testament but, rather, a tradition of teaching that was continuously renewed and embellished by the rabbis. Thus, Talmudic Judaism represented maturity, growth, and development, not decay.[99] Third, even though Talmudic Judaism was not Christianity's precursor, the success of Christianity depended in large part on the institutions and social networks produced in the Gentile world by diasporate Jewish communities.[100] Fourth, Talmudic Judaism was more wholesome and rounded than Christianity because it gave a prominent place to a wider range of religious life than did Christianity. Since Talmudic Judaism valued ritual, morals, and culture—in short, the practical and 'embodied' dimensions of religion—it was in fact less prone to the scholastic desiccation that perennially seemed to afflict Christianity.[101] Thus, rather than a mark of its weakness, the ritual, collective, and thus 'embodied' nature of Talmudic Judaism represented its strengths. As we will now see, the work of the Durkheimians on Judaism presupposed this sympathetic framework of interpretation of Talmudic Judaism worked out by Israël Lévi.

To appreciate how informed the Durkheimians were by Israël Lévi's defense of Talmudic Judaism, consider what the Durkheimians wrote about the subject, remembering all the while how even observant avant-garde Jews found it hard to consider Talmudic Judaism sympathetically in Durkheim's day. Against the fashionable liberal currents, the Durkheimians shared Lévi's view that Talmudic Judaism was a vigorous and vital form of Jewish religion and, against opinions such as Renan's, that its social embodiment in the synagogue only affirmed its vitality and stature.

Although the Durkheimians did, for the most part, share the spirit of Robertson Smith's view (via Wellhausen) that ancient Hebrew religion consisted primarily in a joyful, totemic, communion sacrifice, they did not deny the same vitality to Talmudic Judaism, nor did they interpret the ancient Hebrews as 'primitives.' In this vein, Mauss produced an interesting contribution to Israël Lévi's Festschrift; writing in the *Revue des études juives* on the legend of Abraham, Mauss argued that just because Jewish culture had at times a pastoral and migratory structure, this in no way meant that its cultural creations were inferior to those of more settled folk.[102] Mauss tellingly added, "*We* are far from the savages depicted by MacLennan or the rustics Renan understood us to be."[103] In light of the close association of Mac-Lennan and Robertson Smith, Mauss may very well have been directing yet another of his several reproaches at the great Protestant biblical scholar to whom the Durkheimians otherwise owed so much. The Durkheimians thus did not follow the lead of the German Protestant biblical scholars, such as Lagarde, who felt that the ancient Hebrew religion was 'primitive' and that it was the only Jewish religion of value.

Further, they did not accept the corollary that postprophetic Judaism consisted more or less of a gradual desiccation of a primitive religious spirit. When the Durkheimians considered Talmudic Judaism in their reviews and articles, they dwelled on *its* dynamogenic features—the same vitality that Robertson Smith, Lagarde, and Wellhausen saw restricted to the ancient Hebrews. Mauss argued that magic was one sure sign of the vitality of a religion. But if so, and since it survived into Talmudic Judaism at the highest levels in the magical use of the tetragrammaton, Talmudic Judaism too must embody the dynamogenic qualities usually attributed only to 'primitive' religions. Talmudic magic was employed, for example, as a countermagic and thus as an integral part of the struggles of Talmudic Judaism against opposing forms of religious magic.[104] Therefore, along with the use of phylacteries, prayers, and conjury, Talmudic Judaism presented a religion alive in a battle among forces in the spiritual world. Moreover, even though the Talmudic Jewish magic of Jerusalem represented borrowings from Babylon, it drew equally from indigenous Jewish magical traditions. Later Judaism, no less than the 'primitive' Hebrew religion beloved of the Protestant detractors of Talmudic Judaism, was thus radiant with religious vitality.

As we have seen, the synagogue represented everything that critics of Talmudic Judaism found undesirable. Many modernist Jews too, like Lazare, saw the synagogue as the spiritual center of a Judaism hated for its supposed lack of vitality, mysticism, and prophetic energy—in short a Judaism lacking all those dynamogenic qualities the Durkheimians would be eager to see there. But the Durkheimians found the synagogue, as the social body of Talmudic Judaism, to be a source of sociological inspiration. Mauss, for example, criticized a study of Jewish religious movements of Jesus' time for stressing the importance of relatively trivial social realities, such as the Jewish sects, and for failing to bring out the decisive fact of the formation of the synagogue.[105] For Mauss, the synagogue was "the mother of Judaism—neither a sort of vague Judaism, nor a religion of the priestly code or that of the gods and the wise."[106] For Isidore Lévy, the Jewish Durkheimian contributor both to *L'Année sociologique* and to the *Revue des études juives,* the synagogue was nothing short of "a Church capable of surviving the destruction of the nation and temple—in which the destiny of the religion had always seemed to be bound up."[107]

For the Durkheimians, the synagogue, in addition to its service to the survival of Judaism, was essential to the genesis of Christianity. The synagogue's ancient forms of worship, for example, passed directly to Christianity.[108] In particular, Mauss felt that Christianity's exploitation of the religious value of prayer owed much to the spiritual trends already set in motion by the Judaism of the synagogue. He noted

> the fact that Jesus's prayer and that of the Galilean community did not differ from the Jewish prayer of the same epoch. This is to be sure most important. Their terminology is the same; their material and form are identical; only the spirit seems to have changed. This could explain many things: it may throw light on the origin of Christianity, on the one hand, while also shedding light on the quite extraordinary birth in Judea of free, individual prayer, on the other. . . . The role of Christ was precisely to have distilled from [the prayer life of the synagogue] . . . a sort of condensed scheme of prayer, serving individual piety in place of the more reserved spirituality of prayer in the synagogue.[109]

Mauss also developed a rather sophisticated line toward the synagogue in his study of prayer. He rated the religious life of the synagogue at least higher than the priestly Judaism of the temple, if not higher than that of the ancient Hebrews. Mauss noted, for example, that it was not until the synagogue that prayer really entered the mainstream of Jewish religious practice. As far as the religious life of the temple was concerned, "prayer itself was foreign to the ritual of the temple, to the Levitic ritual. Non-verbal rituals seemed to have absorbed all the efforts of the people. Prayer was . . . only present in places which were not truly holy. Until the destruction of the temple, for example, prayers were only said far from the sanctuary." But the synagogue was different. "The synagogue, on the contrary, seems to have been above all a congregation of the people joined together for prayer. . . . From this perspective and before anything else, the synagogue is a praying society."[110]

Thus, the synagogue, far from being a desiccated institution, was the very source of the religious vitality of the West, encompassing both what we now call Judaism and, in some real sense, Christianity as well. What struck Mauss as he looked at the synagogue through his Durkheimian eyeglasses was how, because of its prayerful religious practice, the religious life of the synagogue showed all the creative 'effervescent' power typical of the kinds of societies the Durkheimians loved. The synagogue created the Judaism that followed—including as well the peculiar deviant Judaism that we now call Christianity. Mauss continued: "This movement toward supplication animates the synagogue and [animates] as well the intense movement of the sects. . . . [It] animates messianic preaching—both John the Baptist's and Jesus's. Inside the praying community, other communities develop—Ebionites, Essenes, Christians."[111]

In considering Durkheim's Jewishness in this chapter, I have tried to show how the Durkheimians, in their treatment of Judaism, and especially Talmudic Judaism, replicated much of the substance and style of the French heirs of the Wissenschaft des Judentums, even though it would have been more 'natural' for the Durkheimians not so to do. Salomon Munk's refusal to isolate Judaism and Jews from the great ebb and flow of the world's cultures, his embrace of comparison as an essential tool in understanding the religion and history of the Jews, set standards that Israël Lévi, Hartwig Derenbourg, and Sylvain Lévi would all follow. As we have noted, these standards can be seen most clearly in Durkheimian views of the vitality and historical status of Judaism in relation to Christianity and in Durkheimian acuity about the nature and value of the synagogue and ritual practice.

But beyond seeming to emulate the style and substance of the Science du Judaïsme, Durkheim and Mauss, at least, came to act and look increasingly more Jewish by consistently arguing against anti-Semitic positions in their scholarship. One should note, for instance, that in his scholarship, Durkheim never joined the ranks of the vocal critics of the actual Judaism of his time or even of Talmudic Judaism, its proscriptions and practices, no matter how unobservant the Jewish Durkheimians were of them then. I have also argued that Durkheim and some of his Jewish confederates, such as Mauss, seemed to move in the direction of identifying themselves as Jewish—however partially and tentatively this movement had progressed by the time of Durkheim's death. We should recall that they might well have followed other courses. With the rise of anti-Semitism in France from the 1870s, a kind of modernist anti-Talmudic zeal would have fit the profile of the Durkheimians as easily as it fit the likes of Salomon Reinach or Bernard Lazare. Or, as men of the Left, even after the Dreyfus Affair, the Durkheimians might easily have followed the well-worn anticapitalist and anti-Semitic track trod by Jean Jaurès, the great socialist leader and intimate of Durkheim's. After all, even though Durkheim was a Dreyfusard, he was so on humanist grounds and certainly distanced himself from many of its more exuberant manifestations—even to the point of telling his students not to join the great public demonstrations that marked the cause.[112] Alternately, the Durkheimians might have embraced the Enlightenment cosmopolitanism of Salomon Reinach, who saw no good in the particulars of 'primitive' elements of the Jewish tradition—especially its Talmudic 'ritualism.'

Yet contrary to expectations, the doctrine and methods of the rather more conservative and observant scholars like Israël Lévi turned out to be most congenial to the Durkheimian way of studying Judaism.[113] The Durkheimians defended the embodied social nature of religion, using, for example, the synagogue as a prime example of an institution of religion as it should be. Likewise, they granted a permanent, if qualified, place to ritual in religion and in Talmudic Judaism in particular. Whether his affinities for the Jewish conservatism of the time expresses Durkheim's nurture at the hands of his rabbi father, his affiliation with the French champions of the scientific study of Judaism in his circle of acquaintances, or his sense of his own Jewish identity emerging as a reaction to the growing anti-Semitism of the day, we will probably never know. But whatever the source, these views show us a Durkheim who was informed by the avantgarde of Jewish scholarship, a Durkheim who manifested 'Jewishness' not because some eternal 'Jewish' trait surfaced in the midst of his thought, and certainly not because his thought was in some way *determined* by his 'Jewishness,' but because he identified, intellectually and morally, with a particular segment of

French Jewish opinion. Even though Durkheim's professional scientific loyalties would undoubtedly have induced him to adopt the positions of the anti-anti-Semitic scholars associated with the Science du Judaïsme, there may have been more to his identification with them than pure science. Scholars like Israël Lévi were at the top of their class, but so also were the anti-Semites, even someone who might in part be labeled this way, such as Ernest Renan. Durkheim would have had very good scientific, ethical reasons for supporting them—their Jewishness notwithstanding. Perhaps, then, this respect for the scholarly integrity of real (observant and somewhat conservative) Jews helped Durkheim in turn regard Talmudic Judaism—the real French Judaism of his day—with the same respect. That this required Durkheim to 'read the Talmud' against the spirit of an age that scoffed at it was a price that Durkheim, as a scientist of religion, apparently paid without any trace of regret. If we then want to ask why apostates like Durkheim and Mauss cheerfully defended real Jews and the stuff of real Judaism against anti-Semitic slanders, we need, I believe, to go beyond professional ethics and the personal respect they bore for real Jews such as Israël Lévi or Sylvain Lévi. We need to consider the ways that anti-Semitism reinforced or even created a sense of Jewish identity that was, up to that point, weak or moribund.

We know, for example, that during his youth in eastern France, Durkheim observed firsthand the reality of anti-Semitism.[114] I would here suggest that he and his *équipe* may have arrived at a point where even their resistance to Jewish identification reached a limit. This would especially be so given the scholarly nature of the anti-Semitism to which Israël Lévi and the Durkheimians reacted. Consider this suggestion in light of Durkheim's discussion of anti-Semitism with Henri Dagan in 1899, in which Durkheim theorized on the differences between French and German or Russian anti-Semitisms. French anti-Semitism was occasional and superficial, primarily an emotional mob response to national economic or political crises. By contrast, German and Russian anti-Semitism was deliberate, chronic, and, tellingly, "aristocratic."[115] The appearance of a well-thought-out, scholarly, and thus aristocratic anti-Semitism doubtless shook the Durkheimians, much as Frazer's dalliance with the blood libel had shocked Israël Lévi. The appearance in France of such scholarly anti-Semitism might have begun

Durkheim's development of a Jewish identification not present up to that point.[116] Why should Durkheim (and Mauss as well) have been immune from such notoriously potent sources of identification as anti-Semitism? Anti-Semitism may have worked on the Durkheimians as it did on many others before and since, creating a sense of transnational Jewish identification that was virtually lacking in them up to that time. This would explain the puzzles of Durkheim's dismissal of Muffang for his Aryanist writings in 1900, or Mauss's defense of Jewish civilization in 1926, or Durkheim's membership on the board of directors of the Society for the Aid of Jewish Victims of the War in Russia.[117]

Here we may be able to mark the beginnings of a new French Jewish identity distinct from the neo-Jewish and regional ones rejected by Durkheim and Mauss up to that point. In this connection, we would do well to link this movement toward a Jewish identity with the stirring words of a younger-generation Jewish Durkheimian, Robert Hertz, as he went off to war. Anti-Semites charged that Jews, such consummate bourgeois individualists, were all too willing to sacrifice *others* and to save themselves from the dangers of death in battle. Stung by this charge, Hertz declared himself willing to die on behalf of France in order to prove the devotion of French Jewry. Hertz "had the presentiment," a contemporary report said, "that he would not return. But this presentiment changed into a determination to become a sacrifice. Jewish by origin and French by all the thoughts of his mind and strivings of his moral being, he reckoned that the blood of the men of his race and of his own conscience would be usefully shed to liberate their children from all reproaches of egoism, particularist interest and indifference in the eyes of a suspicious France."[118]

If younger-generation Jewish Durkheimians could speak and act so to claim a Jewish identity, could the older generation, headed by Durkheim, formed though he was in the high season of passionate devotion to French nationality, have been far behind? This may be why in 1916, against charges that the Russian Jewish refugees had been disloyal to France, Durkheim proudly reported to the minister of the interior:

> As soon as hostilities took a threatening turn, the societies of Jewish émigrés launched an enthusiastic appeal to fellow Jews, pointing out all that Judaism owed to France. "If we are not yet

French by law," it was stated, "we are so in heart and soul and our most sacred duty is to place ourselves forthwith at the disposal of this great and noble nation in order to play a part in its defence. Brothers, it is time to pay our debt of gratitude to the country in which we have found moral emancipation and material well-being. Jewish immigrants, do your duty. Long live France!"[119]

Was Durkheim here also speaking for himself—for his Jewish self—as had Hertz? The tantalizing nature of this question is equaled only by our inability to answer it conclusively.

5

SYLVAIN LÉVI:

MAUSS'S "SECOND UNCLE"

Paradoxical though it may seem, there is no better way to conclude this study of Durkheim and the Jews of France than to dwell on the relations between Marcel Mauss and Sylvain Lévi. Mauss was, as I have noted earlier, in many ways Durkheim's alter ego. Aside possibly from Henri Hubert, no one was closer to Durkheim than Mauss. Both Durkheim's nephew and coreligionist, Mauss hailed from the same eastern regions of France as Durkheim and collaborated on many projects with his uncle in Bordeaux while pursuing his first degree in philosophy there with Octave Hamelin. When Mauss moved to Paris and the École Pratique des Hautes Études, Fifth Section, he (along with Hubert) became the organizer for Durkheim's great journal *L'Année sociologique* and the director (along with Hubert, again) of its sections devoted to religion. Some historians of Durkheim's 'team' justifiably claim that the collaboration extended far beyond officially coauthored works to such works as Durkheim's *Suicide* and his magnum opus, *The Elementary Forms of the Religious Life*. In the latter, Durkheim repeated Mauss's positions first articulated in his inaugural lecture of 1901.[1] So in considering Mauss's relation to things Jewish, we can assume that we are not far from Durkheim's relation to things Jewish as well.

Now what of Sylvain Lévi? Of all the great intellectuals con-

Marcel Mauss, 1918.
Photo courtesy of
Étienne Halphen.

sequential for Durkheim and his team, Lévi was doubtless both the most observant and the most self-consciously Jewish. Who else could possibly compete for such honors? James Darmesteter, Israël Lévi, and Salomon Reinach can hardly be said to compare in influence to Gentile thinkers like Immanuel Kant, Charles Renouvier, Sir James Frazer, Herbert Spencer, and so on. Unlike the apostate Durkheim and most of the (at least nominally) 'Jewish' Durkheimians, Lévi was an active, observant, and enthusiastic Jew. At different times, he served as president of the anti-Zionist Alliance Israëlite Universelle and the Société des Études Juives; he wrote occasionally on Jewish subjects for the *Revue des études juives;* and he was a critical figure in trying to conceptualize the relation of French Jews to a future Zionist state.

Furthermore, Mauss considered Sylvain Lévi, after Durkheim, to be the most important intellectual influence of his life. Contemporary observers of the Durkheimians similarly tell us that Lévi's seminal *La Doctrine du sacrifice dans les brâhmanas* (1898) exerted a "great influence on the sociology of religion."[2] In a sweeping discussion of the nature of the study of religions, Lévi said: "The history of the church is therefore the *necessary* introduction to the study of religion; it is the center around which gravitates or radiates the active imagination of the faithful."[3] Echoing this judgment, Mauss said of Lévi's masterpiece of Oriental erudition: "We have greatly drawn upon it."[4] The example of Sylvain Lévi shows, once more, how much more fruitful it is to concentrate on the network of real relations among the Durkheimians and Jewish thinkers than to focus on speculations about an 'essential' Jewishness. If the claim of Lévi's importance is believed, his influence would amount to the best-attested case of a Jewish scholar shaping Durkheimian thought in ways that can meaningfully be called 'Jewish.'

One might immediately object to my use of Lévi as an exemplary 'Jewish' thinker, since Lévi was so thoroughly a professional Indologist—indeed, by any standard, one of the most distinguished Indologists of his time.[5] Like many others of his day, Lévi seemed to have compartmentalized his life into professional academic and private religious domains, ruling the lecture hall with his Indological expertise while keeping his Judaism to himself. His books deal only with South Asian matters; none of them treat a Jewish subject. Under Sylvain Lévi, Hubert and Mauss studied classic Indology—not Judaica. How, then, can we call Lévi a 'Jewish' thinker regarding the intellectual influence he may have had? How, then, can we say that some sort of 'Jewish' content passed on to Mauss and the other Durkheimians through Indology? How, then, can an appeal to Lévi further our present inquiry into the *Jewishness* of Durkheimian thought?

And even if I could make the case that Lévi as Indologist was in some meaningful sense a 'Jewish thinker,' how could I call him and his thought 'Jewish'—without myself falling back into talk of a secret Jewishness or some sort of essentialism, which I have attacked? In this case, I would be assuming that Jewish authors necessarily produce 'Jewish' books, regardless of the explicit subject. Or I would be arguing that a kind of subtle Jewishness passed automatically to the Durkheimians from the person of Sylvain Lévi. These assumptions would play too neatly into the hands of modern racist-biological anti-Semitism. After such an auspicious beginning, we seem to have more questions about the Jewishness of Lévi's thought and the Jewish influence exerted on the Durkheimians than encouraging answers.

I believe we can make headway in understanding and assessing Lévi's Jewishness and its relation to Durkheimian thought by promoting two main theses. First, Lévi neither desired nor in fact achieved segregation of his Jewish identity from much of his career as an Indologist. Instead, Lévi spoke in a kind of symbolic code: he talked *about* the religion and life of the Jews by talking *with* the religions of India. Second, I want to show how the relationship between Lévi and the Durkheimians was in part informed by Lévi's Jewish agenda of interests peculiar to his own historical time and place. In this way, I think that Lévi's Jewish Indological agenda facilitated the concern of the Durkheimians with ritual and with the late Durkheimian conception of a positive and material sacred. In light of these discussions, I therefore think we can inform the idea of the Jewishness of Durkheimian thought in a way that has a historical basis. But who exactly was Sylvain Lévi, and how was he connected with the Durkheimians?

As noted previously, Mauss considered Lévi, after Durkheim, to be the most important intellectual influence of his life.[6] Nothing better describes the deep personal and professional relationship between the great Indologist and Durkheim's nephew than the words of Mauss himself. He noted that Lévi was his "second uncle."[7] Lévi "did more for us and all of you who have followed us [than one might imagine]." Sylvain Lévi was a patron of the entire *équipe*, especially in the all-important École Pratique des Hautes Études, Fifth Section. For instance, Mauss recounted how Lévi oversaw the careers of each of his students.

> He never separated a concern for our careers from the administration of our progress, work and our science. One of his great "merits" was that he thought about each one of us in material, fatherly, and fraternal ways. . . . In a letter which he had written [recommending Mauss for a position in the Fifth Section] he wrote: "I am happy to be able to introduce Marcel into the regular cadre, into a position for which he was made." Then he added: "I should say however that although I do not doubt his

genius, he can be erratic!'' This last comment was to prove prophetic. It showed how well he gauged each one of us and thus
placed us in our careers exactly as was appropriate to each one
of us—not just as this concerned our studies, teaching career
and science itself, but most of all for our own sakes and for his
as well.[8]

Beyond being responsible for Mauss's election to the Fifth Section, Lévi also ensured that Henri Hubert would win a post there
as well.[9]

Born in Paris of Alsatian parents, Lévi was educated in the
traditional, rather conservative Jewish learning of the time. So
adept was the youth at these early studies that leading scholars
of the day saw in Sylvain Lévi France's first great Jewish Semit-
icist; Grand Rabbi Zadok Kahn even wanted to employ Lévi to
tutor his own children in Judaica.[10] But however great Lévi's talents for Jewish studies, he instead chose Indology. Deciding on
an area specialty proved to be more difficult. Lévi sought the
advice of Ernest Renan, himself a former *élève* of the Indologist
Eugene Burnouf. Renan had a special affinity for Indian studies,
in no small part because he tended to follow German fashions
of thought, one of which, as we will see later, was the so-called
Aryanist movement.[11] The Aryanists were not only great promoters of the glories of Indian civilization but also scholarly anti-
Semites, as was the young Renan in his own way.[12] Renan confided to Lévi that the resident Sanskritist, Abel Bergaigne,
needed students at the time and that he would therefore eagerly
welcome an opportunity to take Lévi as his *élève*. Thus, by way
of a series of accidents, Lévi began, at age nineteen, what would
prove to be an illustrious scholarly career.[13]

After finishing with Bergaigne, Lévi was unable to find a
suitable academic post in his field. But the leadership of the
same rather conservative rabbinic school in Paris where he had
done his own seminary training was eager to have Lévi on its
faculty. So when the school offered Lévi a position teaching traditional seminary subjects, he accepted, partly out of a sense of
obligation to his Jewish faith.[14] After several years of teaching
seminary students, Lévi eventually succeeded Bergaigne in the
chair of Sanskrit at the École Pratique des Hautes Études, Fifth
Section. By 1894, he was elevated to the Collège de France in

Sanskrit Language and Literature, where he remained until 1935.

Sylvain Lévi's scholarly interests were broad. He wrote books on the history of Nepal, the first systematic study of classic Indian theater, studies of classic Buddhist idealist philosophy, and among other things, his masterpiece, *La Doctrine du sacrifice*. Lévi also traced cultural influences across Asia and between Asia and the West even into modern times. Later in his life, he acted on these scholarly interests by taking a leading practical role in establishing cultural ties between France and Asian nations such as India, Japan, Nepal, and Vietnam.

Sylvain Lévi was also a great patron of Jewish learning and close friend of Israël Lévi. In addition to his leading scholarship in Talmudic studies and his leadership role in the Société des Études Juives, Israël Lévi would become the grand rabbi of France. In Jewish matters, Sylvain Lévi was an active leader in the Paris Jewish community, for many years serving as president of the Société des Études Juives. Given both the dense documentary style of his scholarly writing and his close affiliation with the leadership of the Science du Judaïsme, Sylvain Lévi fits naturally within the movement of critical historical scholarship of Jewish learning derived from the Wissenschaft des Judentums.[15] As for his approach to the study of religion, Sylvain Lévi seemed indelibly marked by the example of that seminal figure of the French branch of the movement, Salomon Munk. By contrast with his mentors in the Wissenschaft des Judentums, Munk was from the beginning a comparativist; likewise, Sylvain Lévi led the way in the comparative study of Indian and Jewish religions.

This dedication to studying all the religions (including Judaism) in the context of the other religions led Lévi to reject an exclusive concentration in Judaica. Both Munk and Lévi stood Judaism up alongside the great 'world' religious traditions like Islam and Christianity as equal in cosmopolitan history and thus as an object worthy of scientific study. From this location of Judaism among the religions of the world, Lévi seemed further to echo what Munk had argued years before—namely that Jewish studies belonged to the established disciplines of archaeology, history of antiquity, philology, and the science of religion rather than in a special autonomous venue.[16] The Durkheimians seem to have shared this perspective of Judaism as one of the great world religions, neither reserved for special treatment nor dismissed as unimportant. One way Lévi appeared to take this lesson to heart was by studying Judaism from the scholarly base of Indology, not in spite of it. Lévi wrote, for instance, on the global spread of Jewish communities as far afield as India.[17] He reclaimed a place for Jewish life in the making of world history by arguing, for instance, that the biblical Ophir lay at the mouth of the Indus. By arguing in this vein, Lévi showed how German Aryanist Indologists' attempts to pit 'Aryans' against 'Semites' used a dichotomy that failed to meet historical tests. In this way, Lévi and Munk seemed joined in the common project of showing how Jewish thought contributed to other civilizations.

On top of his universalist scholarship, Lévi demonstrated how perfectly at home he was mediating the world of the university with his personal world of Jewish piety, community affiliation, and scholarship. Sylvain Lévi's active life of Jewish philanthropy and religious practice is little known. Because of his Parisian birth and cosmopolitan beliefs, one might assume that Lévi was more the (French-born) *Isräelite* than the (separatist) *Juif*. Lévi thus reflected Munk's devotion to the values of 1789 — humanism and enlightenment married to a strong French nationalism.[18] Furthermore, like Darmesteter, he interpreted Judaism 'prophetically'—as exemplifying those very same universalist reforming values represented by the Revolution. Even much of Lévi's Jewish philanthropic activity seemed motivated by the universal humanist spirit of French Jewish associations such as the Alliance Israëlite Universelle and later the Comité des Étudiants Étrangers.[19] Deeply "shaken" by the Dreyfus Affair, Lévi was an early defender of the Jewish Captain Alfred Dreyfus.[20] Publicly, he, like Durkheim, joined the defense as a universalist humanist, typical of members of the Ligue des Droits de l'Homme.[21] Further, as a member of the Central Committee of the fervently anti-Zionist Alliance Israëlite Universelle, Lévi resisted political (as opposed to cultural or social) conceptions of Palestine as the Jewish national homeland.

Like many sincere French Jews of his generation, Lévi was genuinely divided about his Jewish religious identity. Though associated with the modernist Judaism of Darmesteter, he was considerably more observant and particularist than neo-Jews like Louis-Germain Lévy or Salomon Reinach.[22] Sylvain Lévi was also deeply disturbed by the anti-Semitism of the last decades of the

nineteenth century.[23] This began for him a period of active political life in behalf of causes near and dear to the Jewish community. In addition to his concern for the welfare of French Jews,
he directed even greater efforts toward aiding foreign Jews, especially those fleeing the Russian persecutions toward the end
of the nineteenth century. After the pogrom of Kichineff in
1905, for example, many young Russian Jewish scholars fled to
France. Legend has it that Lévi solicited funds door to door for
the relief of these young refugees, even though he met with
personal rebuffs and indignities along the way.[24] Linked perhaps
with a renewed sense of Jewish particularism, Lévi was also devoted to certain specifically Jewish religious causes. Here one
may number his many articles advocating the renewal of ritual
life among the French Jewish community. In 1900, in *Archives
israélites,* Lévi wrote both "Rituel du Judaisme" and "La Régéneration Religieuse,"[25] practical guides to religious practice, under the regular rubric "Études de culte."

Despite his devout nature, Sylvain Lévi should not be confused with the 're-orthodoxed' Jewish traditionalists, who had
grown in strength in the last quarter of the nineteenth century.
Instead, he tried to blend reformist and conservative elements
into his Jewish life. Perhaps best called a 'progressive,' Lévi saw
Judaism as alive and continually developing. It carried the baggage of its past, but it also 'repacked' this baggage and sometimes jettisoned what was no longer needed. As the Durkheimians revealed in their defense of both synagogue and Talmudic
Judaism,[26] he accepted a changing Judaism but without feeling
contempt for the past. For Lévi, the 'glass' of Judaism was 'half
full.' Exemplifying this mood of progressive innovation, Phyllis
Cohen Albert reports, Chief Rabbi Isidor "had been trying to
imitate the Adam of the midrashic legend, who had two faces,
one turned toward the past, and the other turned toward the
future."[27]

Thus, unlike Reinach, Lévi did not fear or dislike the new
Jews from eastern Europe or their ritualist religion. Indeed as
the son of religiously conservative and economically modest Jews
(his father was a haberdasher from Alsace), Sylvain Lévi was,
after a fashion, more like these 'new' Jews than most of the
French-born gentrified Parisian Jews of his acquaintance in academe. In a biographical sketch of Lévi, Mauss further tells us
that despite universalist beliefs, Sylvain Lévi was far more tradi-

tional than many of the other French-born Jews of his peer group and generation. As Mauss put it, Sylvain Lévi was

> a patriot, *un Français, un petit Parisien du Marais,* a descendant of Alsatian Jews—who showed in practice how much he felt himself to be a man both of his milieu and his work. He never wanted to break with his race, with his traditional milieu, from which he never wanted to be completely emancipated. And indeed during these times of trouble, he wanted to surpass the limits of duty. But he was also a citizen of the world, someone chosen by the universal spirit. . . . His will for peace, his intimate knowledge of people, the power of his thought, shaped all his activities. Alongside the life of a *savant,* friend, husband and father, Sylvain Lévi had another life as well.[28]

Therefore, unlike the nonobservant Durkheim, Lévi died a "saint" and "witness to his faith."[29]

The religious example of the personal life of Sylvain Lévi seems to have affected Mauss, although exactly how much is hard to determine.[30] Mauss tells us that because of Lévi's ill health in his last years, Mauss accompanied him to meetings of the Alliance Israëlite Universelle. So strong was Lévi's influence on Mauss that the young atheist also tells us of an apparent change in his own attitude to Judaism. At Lévi's personal request, Mauss too joined the Central Committee of the Alliance in 1931, although up to that point, Mauss tells us, he never would have done so because of his previous "prejudices."[31]

Here we should pause to open a parenthesis and note that by the 1930s, we may assume that at least one of the Durkheimians—Marcel Mauss—began to identify as Jewish. How early this identification started is hard to determine, although Mauss's contribution to the Festschrift for Israël Lévi pushes this date back into the mid-1920s. There, in considering the ancient Hebrews, Mauss explicitly registered his identity as Jewish when he indignantly noted, "*We* are far from the savages depicted by MacLennan or the rustics Renan understood *us* to be."[32] How much Durkheim shared this sense of identification is impossible to tell, since he had at that point been dead for nearly a decade. But we would do well to recall our discussion, in the previous chapter, of how Durkheim's own sense of Jewish identity seemed to have been excited by the scholarly anti-Semitism of the late nineteenth and early twentieth centuries. Anti-Semitism or something similar was clearly making the Durkheimians reconsider, indeed perhaps create, their Jewish identities. Whether this emerging sense of Jewish identity shows up in their work—and if so, when—are parts of the puzzle I have tried to solve in this book.

How did Sylvain Lévi's Jewish piety and interests fit with his Indological career? Lévi's mind was profoundly, if subtlety, polemical—and especially so when it came to the defense of the integrity of Judaism. Interestingly, he defended Judaism by trading on a certain symbolic equivalence made between Israel and India. For him and others of his scholarly generation, the history of the religions of India constituted a parallel universe of symbolic discourse for speaking about the history of Israel and Judaism. Establishing this symbolic equivalence allowed Lévi to speak (implicitly) about one of these religious worlds while seeming to speak (explicitly) about the other. For us, this symbolic way of talking meant that what in Lévi often seems to be discourse referring explicitly and exclusively to India alone really, for him, resonated with what he wanted to say about the Jews. Thus, in teaching about the religions of India, Lévi passed on to the Durkheimians certain lessons about the nature of Judaism.

It was natural for Sylvain Lévi to associate Israel and India because a previous generation of scholars had already done so by opposing the two countries—to the consequent detriment of Israel. Such opposition was primarily the work of the German Aryanists, whom Lévi probably first encountered in the work of the young Renan.[33] For Renan and his German teachers, 'Aryan' and 'Semitic' starkly opposed one another as civilizational ideal types, with the Semitic type representing most of what was negative about the present state of Western civilization. In his inaugural lecture at the Collège de France in 1862, Renan spoke of the "fearful shallowness of the Semitic spirit narrowing the human mind and closing it to all subtle ideas."[34] Thus, India was no pure and autonomous domain of disinterested intellectual inquiry. The Aryanists had already, since the mid–nineteenth century, made India a vast realm of symbols, rife with ideological significance, for their campaign against the Jewish presence in Europe. With India, they in effect staked out another "argumentative context" alongside their efforts in biblical studies, both of which contexts were designed to cut Judaism and the Jews out from the heart of European civilization, as the pioneers of the Wissenschaft des Judentums had always feared.

The Aryan/Semitic opposition recalls the anti-Semitic ideology of biblical scholarship promoted by Paul de Lagarde and Julius Wellhausen. Here, instead of attacking the Talmudic basis of contemporary Judaism by deflecting it off the glories of ancient Hebrew religion, these writers cast Judaism into the shadows by comparing it with the supposed brilliance of ancient Indian religion, such as the Vedas.[35] India was believed to be the homeland of the Aryans. Since European languages in large part derived from a linguistic 'Aryan' root—what we today call Indo-European—the Aryanists declared India the homeland of European, and thus German, culture. Indian religious traditions were thought as well to be the most ancient of any in history and thus, for some, the embodiment of religious traditions even more venerable than those of Israel.[36] The Aryanist thinkers felt that India represented a complete alternative to and superior mirror image of the Jewish traditions of the West. Thus, in speaking about the religions of India, the Aryanists did so with the opposite ideal type of Judaism in mind.

Given the sensitivity of the leadership of the Science du Judaïsme to anti-Semitic scholarship, and given what we already know of Lévi's devotion to the cause of Jewish history writing, we might well imagine that Lévi undertook Indological studies fully aware of the anti-Semitic nature of these symbolic relationships. Many of his minor writings clearly show that Sylvain Lévi actively competed in the arena of nationalist and racial polemics put into play by Indological scholarship.[37] He did so using at least two rhetorical strategies: he either turned anti-Semitic discourse on its head or he undercut it.[38] Thus, just like the Aryanists, Lévi could advantageously dichotomize Aryan and Jews by speaking *of* one thing (the Jews) while speaking *with* another (India). Here, as we will see, what Lévi *said* worked to defend Judaism from Aryanist anti-Semitism.[39]

Typical of Sylvain Lévi were his efforts to undercut Aryanist ideology by undermining the divisions upon which it was based and which the anti-Semites used to demonize the Jews in Europe.[40] "We have," he tells us, "thought too exclusively of India from the Indo-Aryan viewpoint. It is fitting that we remember that India is a great maritime country, open to an immense *bassin* which is as well its Mediterranean—certainly a Mediterranean in proportion to its dimensions—but that we have for a long time believed was closed off at the south."[41] Using Buddhism here as a metalanguage to undermine cultural polarization, Lévi worked to deny the anti-Semitic Aryanists the advantage they wanted.[42] Lévi did this cleverly. First, even while affirming the Indian identity of Buddhism, he undercut claims as to its 'pure' Aryan roots. How could Buddhism be thought to be Aryan when, Lévi argued, it reflected a religious character quite unlike that of the Vedas?[43] Where in the Vedas do we find the world renunciation, inwardness, and concern for psychological problems typical of the Buddhists? The 'conventional wisdom' of scholars of the time, who automatically assumed that everything Indian was Aryan, revealed a prejudice symptomatic of the dominance of the Aryanist view of India. For Judaism, the subtext of such arguments was not far below the surface: if the civilization of 'Aryan' India was now no longer so purely Aryan, perhaps the so-called Aryan roots of European civilization were likewise intertwined inextricably with others. Thus, if the isolation of India could be broken, the isolation of the Jews would be broken as well.[44]

In line with Munk's comparativism for the Science du Judaïsme, Lévi showed that neither ancient Indian nor ancient Jewish civilizations mutually excluded one another, as the Aryanists had wanted to establish. On the contrary, they *shared* many of the same cultural features—especially those prized Western activities such as philosophical thinking. Lévi even tried to chart historical connections between the schools of Greek philosophical speculation in Jewish Alexandria and those of classical India. Perhaps with the polemics against Talmudic Judaism in mind, Lévi insisted on likening medieval Talmudic schemes of thought with the complex systematic philosophy of the Indian Middle Ages.

The Durkheimians were well attuned to this sort of cryptic polemic discourse, as they showed in their handling of German scholarship on the Talmud and in their own engagement in the Aryanist controversy, culminating in the dismissal of Henri Muffang from *L'Année sociologique*.[45] Thus, as I have argued in the previous chapter, Durkheim joined a particular Jewish agenda of interests in contesting scholarly anti-Semitism aimed at undermining the status of Jews in Europe. As they did in these early defenses of Judaism, the Durkheimians stood alongside Lévi in his resistance to Aryanism. In this spirit, Hubert and Mauss too placed India and Israel alongside one another as comparable cases by devoting equal portions of their treatment of sacrifice to Indian and Jewish examples. Not surprisingly, they cited Lévi's influential work on sacrifice, *La Doctrine du sacrifice*, throughout their work. It is within this context of symbolic relations defining scholarly discourse about ancient India and Judaism that I believe we should locate Lévi's *La Doctrine du sacrifice* and thus begin to shed some light on the Durkheimian ideas of religion, ritual, and the like. This part of our story concerns Lévi's approach to the oldest scriptures of Indian civilization, the Vedas, and the Aryanist controversy itself.

The Aryanists saw the Vedas as embodying the wisdom of an Aryan golden age. The Vedas formed their 'bible' and thus were to displace the Jewish Bible from its place of honor in Western civilization.[46] Two corollaries flowed from this perspective: first, by contrast, all the rest of India's religious tradition (the Upanishads excepted) was judged 'degenerate'; second, this 'degenerate' Hinduism was symbolically identified with Talmudic Judaism. Talmudic Judaism was like Hinduism in 'decline' after the glory of the Vedic period but before the philosophical renaissance of the Upanishadic 'reform.' On another plane, the Aryanists perpetuated the anti-Semitic rhetoric of German biblical scholars like Lagarde and Wellhausen, who had paired their admiration for a long-gone ancient Israel with an equal distaste for Judaism proper—Talmudic Judaism.[47] Taken together, these strategies sought to offer an alternative (Aryan) foundation for the religious traditions of the West and at the same time vilify standard contemporary Judaism. Thus, whatever Sylvain Lévi or any other scholars might say about the Brahmins and medieval Hinduism would bristle with symbolic significance for the real Judaism of the day.

Picking up these symbolic implications against Talmudic Judaism, Lévi reacted by challenging Aryanist doctrine regarding the sacrosanct status of Vedic religion. The language of the Rig Veda was, by Indological standards, notoriously 'barbaric'; the very existence of something called a 'Vedic society' remained unproven; claims about its archaic character had been refuted by the discovery of the pre-Aryan Indus Valley civilization of Mohenjo-Daro.[48] In sum, the Vedas were far from anything

marking a golden age of religion in India. From this it also followed that, for Lévi, the religion of such later texts as the *Brâhmanas*, treated in his *La Doctrine du sacrifice*, was not necessarily
a degenerate form of religion. In tandem with this defense of
the integrity of post-Vedic Indian religion, and despite his 'natural' tendencies to religious liberalism, Lévi became a staunch
defender of the religious value of Talmudic Judaism. Given this
parallel with Durkheim's defense of Talmudic Judaism, it is
tempting to think about Lévi as Durkheim's model of resistance
to scholarly anti-Semitism.

What is particularly interesting was how the rather liberal
Sylvain Lévi managed to rub against the grain of his universalist
orientations to justify the integrity of a more conservative Judaism.[49] Although Lévi endorsed Darmesteter's notion of 'prophetic' Judaism, he also had many fine words for the more 'conservative' sorts of Jewish religion. Lévi managed to defend the
integrity of both poles of these religious traditions by first refusing to accept that their differences were, in effect, essential or
permanent. Predictably, Lévi celebrated 'prophetic' Judaism for
its originality and enlightened universalist virtues, much as he
rallied to the liberal, neo-Jewish piety of his own milieu.[50] In
a 1918 address before the Ligue des Amis du Sionisme, "Une
Renaissance juive en Judée," Lévi said that this prophetic, universal Judaism held out "a fraternal hand to humanity to march
in concert, anticipating the triumph of justice." Sealing a pact
with the Enlightenment, Lévi immediately added: "French genius with its passion for universal humanity which expresses itself in its classics as well as in the Revolution is the closest relative
of this messianic spirit. It is its natural safeguard against sectarians who have never renounced its suppression."[51]

In this very same address, however, we need to note that
Lévi praised the particularist 'Mosaist' aspect of Jewish life and
history with equal force, linking it with the lessons that Theodor
Herzl drew from the anti-Semitic fury of the Dreyfus Affair
in 'enlightened' France.[52] Without rejecting prophetic ideals,
Lévi unapologetically spoke in behalf of that Judaism of religious particularity, that 'Mosaist' aspect of Judaism that drew
inward for its own protection, and resisted the universal Judaism
of the liberals and prophets. Mosaism was that 'aspect' of the
fluctuating movement of the perennial rhythms of Judaism in
which Judaism "tends to regroup the chosen people into its eth-

nic isolation, to multiply the barriers which separate it from the nation."[53] Although it was everything that 'prophetic' Judaism was not, Mosaism flourished in its own time and place and was not to be gainsaid. Liberal or prophetic Judaism and the more conservative Talmudic Judaism did indeed oppose one another, but only as 'aspects' of a perennial ebb and flow in a long religious history. At any given time, one or another aspect of a religion would come to the fore as needed.[54] Instead of the then fashionable evolutionist talk of irreversible historical 'stages,' Sylvain Lévi spoke only of aspects in the fluctuating life of a religion. The courses of Hindu and Jewish religious histories, for instance, moved to different, equally harmonious, rhythms.

If we return to the question of the sense in which one might call Sylvain Lévi, *as Indologist,* a 'Jewish' thinker pursuing a 'Jewish' agenda of scholarly and other interests, we can now see how Lévi shows himself to be a Jewish thinker, engaged in a particularly timely Jewish agenda of issues. Insofar as Lévi pursued an Indological agenda of scholarship, and insofar as this scholarship was embedded in a cultural polemic initiated by the Aryanists, Lévi's work on India functioned indirectly to defend the interests and integrity of Judaism in Europe. Lévi's Indological writings were motivated and informed to counter the anti-Semitism found in that specialized field of study—much as we saw, in the previous chapter, Durkheim's support of the integrity of Talmudic Judaism as a response to anti-Semitism. As a pious, practicing, and alert Jew, Lévi well knew of the cryptic anti-Semitism encoded in much of the Indological literature of his milieu. To read him and some of his Indological work as a 'Jewish' reply to Aryanism is no more far-fetched than to read Aryanist Indology, folklore, and the rest as anti-Semitic. Lévi wrote as he did against Aryanism as a way of asserting the dignity of his own Jewish community. He conducted Indology scholarship from a perspective informed by affiliation with the Jewish community.

In this merging of intellectual and worldly projects, Sylvain Lévi and Mauss (and Durkheim and Hubert as well)[55] seemed to be of a common mind. A student of Mauss's, the great French anthropologist Louis Dumont, has spoken from his own experience of the often concealed political nature of overtly nonpolitical Durkheimian work:

Mauss was a fascinating personality. It is impossible to speak of the scholar without recalling the person. Probably the secret of his popularity among us was precisely that for him, unlike so many academics, knowledge was not a separate branch of activity. His life had become knowledge and his knowledge life; that is why he could exert, on some individuals, at least, as great an influence as a religious teacher or a philosopher.[56]

Thus, both Lévi and the Durkheimians engaged an entire series of cultural issues through the symbolic medium of academic writings. When we think about the 'Jewishness' of Durkheimian thought, I believe we should focus on the specific Jewish agenda of scholarly and public interests of the time, which despite formal religious differences, men like the conspicuously Jewish Lévi advanced and which the apostate Durkheimians shared.

How did all this make a difference to what the Durkheimians wrote? How did Sylvain Lévi's 'Jewish' Indology make a difference to Durkheimian thinking—about religion in particular? I will argue that the Durkheimians' societist conception of religion, their view of religion as a concrete 'thing,' their ritualism, and their positive and palpable idea of the sacred all point to origins in Lévi's Indology and thus in his specific concerns about the integrity of Judaism.

To some, this will hardly be a remarkable claim. Indeed, it would seem to reinforce the essentialist view by saying how *essentially* Jewish concerns for ritual, society, and a living, tangible sacred percolate through all the vicissitudes of historical change endured by Judaism. But as we know from the Jewish liberal/orthodox debates, the larger Jewish community was in turmoil itself as to whether or not these positions were quintessentially Jewish. After all, many Jews of Durkheim's day, such as those imbued with the spirit of Judaism as a 'prophetic' faith, rejected the entire agenda of Lévi and the Durkheimians. Thus, we will return to the paradox of the Durkheimians' rejection of the antiritualist, individualist, and abstract modernist theological proposals of the Jewish liberals and their adoption of theological proposals of a far more conservative sort embraced by Sylvain Lévi.

Let us first consider the Durkheimian idea that religion is a concrete, socially embodied reality rather than a spiritual thing, idea, or abstraction. Such a 'spiritualized' notion of religion was generally the norm among the neo-Jews of Durkheim's day, as well as among the leading students of religion (chiefly liberal Protestants) of the École Pratique des Hautes Études, Fifth Section. Typical of the aversion to the concreteness of religion was the University of Leiden liberal Protestant Cornelis P. Tiele, one of the most influential figures for members of the Fifth Section, where Sylvain Lévi made his academic base. Tiele felt that the superiority of the spiritual to the bodily was manifest because it rested on what was, for him, the indubitable experience of a spiritualized personal identity: "While I hold that the content of doctrine and the forms of worship are by no means matters of indifference in religion, I can no more admit that they pertain to the essence of religion than I can regard my body as pertaining to the essence of my human nature, or suppose the loss of one of my limbs or organs would really impair my personality or true humanity." A truly religious person will inform their sensibility with a religious "spiritualism," which results from a "more elevated moral and religious sense."[57] Lévi, in his Jewish-Indological meditations on religion, intentionally mounted an argument against this prevailing spiritualist conception of the nature of religion. In this way, he at least reinforced the Durkheimian tendency to do the same.

For the Durkheimians, the sacred was instead something one might even call palpable, material, and bodily. Citing Lévi with approval, Mauss agreed that sacrifice and the forces it liberated were socially embodied. Sacrifice thus " 'was a mechanical action, which acts by means of its own deep-seated energy.' It has its abode in the act, and finishes with the act."[58] Indeed, if we take Hubert and Mauss at their word, Lévi directly influenced them to think about religion as something socially embodied. For them, the sacred was, in the words of François Isambert, "a 'milieu' one enters and leaves."[59] Such a spatio-temporal sacred is precisely how Durkheim finally conceived of it—something concrete rather than spiritual, as the mainstream of the study of religion in France saw it. Durkheim's sacred as an *idée force* and system of forces basically conveyed the notion of the sacred urged by Lévi in his Indological work.[60] Here as well, Lévi took his place among other forward-looking Jewish thinkers of the Parisian intellectual milieu, men such as Maurice Liber and Hyppolite Prague, who were advancing similar conceptions of the nature of Judaism in what seems an altogether distinctly Jewish effort of the epoch.[61] Liber's view that Judaism was much more than "great ideas" but was as well a social and ritual entity—"culture . . . work . . . art"—was shared by other leaders of the Paris Jewish community.[62] In 1900, *Archives israélites* editor Hyppolite Prague asserted the right of French Jews to concrete group identity. Judaism was their "laws and practices," he asserted,[63] not something 'hyperspiritual' like Christianity.

As he did in defending Judaism against Aryanist anti-Semitism, Sylvain Lévi used the language of Aryanism to explore larger problems. He believed, for example, that India was the source of a rich humanism, an alternative to our somewhat abstract universalist and disembodied humanism. We try, Lévi said, to "do away with local and national creeds," in reality only another expression of "Roman power."[64] Indian humanism, by contrast, is incarnated in actual social and cultural realities: it sanctifies the local and makes a human center of the "family house,"[65] understood as a nexus of "kinship" relations realized in the "joint family."[66] Rehearsing his proposals for a Jewish national homeland in the code provided by Indian civilization, Lévi pointed out how Hindus have celebrated a notion of humanity that stresses "the continuity of men submitted to laws established and enforced by themselves . . . on the same piece of ground where their forefathers were living who originated them."[67] Even the Buddhism that he dearly loved Lévi regarded as a "secondary episode" from the viewpoint of Indian civilization taken as a whole;[68] Buddhism too should be seen as having sprung from Brahminical interpretations of sacrifice.[69] Thus, in linking Lévi's belief in the superiority of religions embodied in society or culture, we pick up again the nationalist thread. Here Lévi's conviction that religions ought to be collectively and concretely embodied (if they want to survive) stemmed not from his French nationalism but from his emerging *Jewish* cultural nationalism, from the beginnings of his slow and cautious movement toward a cultural, rather than political, Zionism.

Although Lévi dearly esteemed the egalitarian ideals of the prophets, the French revolution, and Buddhism, he had to concede that Brahminical Hinduism—the Hinduism of caste inequality and brutal ritual sacrifice—had preserved Indian civilization by making itself increasingly concrete. It turned away from a conception of itself as an abstract system of ideas—like the 'neo-religions' of French religious modernists such as Louis-Germain Lévy, Salomon Reinach, and James Darmesteter. It was solidly embodied in the societal and cultural realities of the caste system and in sacrificial ritualism. Thus, however unlikable these realities might be to a religious liberal, they provided Hindus with the materials of cultural distinctiveness, a "means of defense against menacing absorption" by invading Muslim forces.[70] So though Lévi had reservations about Brahminical India, he found reasons to esteem it, at least in part because of its success at embodying itself societally.[71]

For Lévi, Buddhism was symbolically equivalent to the kind of Judaism represented by Darmesteter's 'prophetic' Judaism. Extending the comparison, Lévi saw Buddhism also as analogous to classic Greek civilization. Just as Western renaissance humanism resulted from the influx of Greek scholars into the Roman world, so also India, through Buddhism, had exported its culture throughout the Asian world.[72] For Lévi, Buddhism was worldly and cosmopolitan, rich in the same mystical and philosophical wisdom, lofty and compassionate morality, that he cherished in Darmesteter's prophetic Judaism. Thus, just as Darmesteter conceived of a universal and humanist Judaism, Lévi noted that "although brahminism represent[ed] the national genius of Indian civilization," Buddhism expressed "what was universal in it."[73]

Significantly, Lévi stopped short of unambiguously extolling these universalist qualities in Buddhism. In the case of Buddhism, Lévi in effect tested his earlier conclusions rendered in connection with Brahminical Hinduism: that collective embodiment and particularity are necessary for the viability of a religion. A religion that had lost touch with its native 'soil'—such as the Buddhism of India—would simply disappear—as indeed had the Buddhism of India.[74] For a while, even when Buddhism aspired to be universalist, it maintained its ties with the Indian subcontinent and Indian culture. At a certain point in its development, however, Buddhism severed its ties with Brahminical social structures and indeed with anything linking it to Indian cultural and societal particularity. Indian Buddhism then "more and more lost its national character . . . in order to take on a more and more human aspect."[75] In its Mahayana developments, for example, Buddhism even cheerfully dissolved its ties with India as a historical and geographic entity. The "new Buddhas" were in effect socially disembodied, according to Lévi; they inhered in nothing, since they "had no sacred geography."[76]

Although jettisoning the 'dead weight' of fixed geography and sociocultural particularity might seem liberating (as apparently it was to early Christianity), Lévi felt that it spelled disaster for Indian Buddhism. Buddhism flourished in India only when it was embodied, such as when it brokered Indian society and culture with the larger, outside world.[77] Without ties to India, Buddhism could no longer do this and thus ceased to enjoy the side benefits of dealing in cultural 'trade.' One thinks of similar benefits accruing to Christianity, for example in some missionary situations, where its prestige was enhanced as a broker of Western society with its medicine and education. Furthermore, in universalizing, Buddhism lost much more than mere cultural identification; it "lost the inspiration which had animated it from its beginnings: it ceased being a church and became a school . . . a philosophical school."[78]

Buddhism, in effect, became a 'religion' in the sense that our neo-Jewish modernists imagined *the* religion to be—a universal and 'spiritual' thing without the cultural, social, and material forms or 'particularities' that came with having a legal code, ritual life, or national character. This was modernist universal religion, devoid of "any concern with social formation."[79] In Lévi's eyes, this socially disembodied 'religion' was a poor thing indeed and was doomed to certain extinction. Even a Judaism embodied in forms that affronted certain values (like caste Hinduism) was better than one that was reduced to a philosophy, to something like an abstract, universalized 'neo-Judaism.' At least socially embodied religions survive. Disembodied Judaism, like Indian Buddhism, would only weaken and then gradually disappear from Europe. Finally disembodied, purely 'spiritual' conceptions of religion could not therefore be the bases of a theory of the nature of religion. These conceptions might characterize 'philosophy,' but they could not do justice to the nature of 'religion,' which, as we know, Durkheim in the end argued was society with its 'system of forces' lodged in time and space.

In seeing both Buddhism and religion as embodied realities, Sylvain Lévi was thinking along the same lines as those that informed his thinking about the nature and extent of Jewish nationalism.[80] During the years just before and after the First

World War, Lévi was the "official spokesman on the Zionist question to French Judaism."[81] Michel Abitbol reports that Lévi, consistent with the high-minded idealist philosophical culture of his milieu and his adherence to the Franco-centric ideals of the Alliance Israëlite Universelle, approached Zionism with "great discretion."[82] Since Lévi also found day-to-day politics distasteful, he saw the fate of the world's Jews by and large as a problem of the "moral sphere."[83] Lévi's desire for a socially embodied Judaism in Palestine did not, therefore, constitute a break with his liberal universalist, idealist Judaism, since he never became a Zionist in the political sense.[84] Although he felt that Jews should be free to migrate to Palestine, to reconstruct Jewish life there, even to cultivate Jewish culture there as well, he thought that founding a separate Jewish state in order to further the renewal of Jewish life in Palestine was neither necessary nor desirable. To him, political Zionism was the "work of sectarians"; it would create intractable problems with Palestinian Arabs. Furthermore, it would encourage the immigration of Russian Jews and their tendencies toward radical revolutionary politics, and it would make Jews the world over suspects of divided national loyalties.[85] Political Zionism, furthermore, betrayed the universal and humanist ideals of the Alliance Israëlite Universelle and the kind of Judaism he embraced as a French-born Jew. Consonant with the vision of "Les Amis du Judaïsme," Lévi's vision of a Jewish *"foyer national"* in Palestine was to be a cultural, not political, entity. While embodied and particularist, Judaism was a cultural reality, a 'religion,' not a matter of satecraft, politics, or ethnicity. He thus distinguished the ideal of a Jewish *"foyer national"* from a Zionist state. Together with the leadership of the Alliance, he carried his fight against Zionism right to the highest councils of French and Jewish leadership, in the end only to be swept aside by the force of events.

By 1918, however, Lévi's views had changed. He now favored a Jewish national homeland in Palestine, although he still opposed a political 'state' of Israel. Like some other liberal Jews of his milieu, such as the 'palestinophile' Grand Rabbi Zadok Kahn,[86] Lévi had by this time begun to think that the idea of a Jewish homeland showed a certain wisdom.[87] If Jews happened onto bad times in liberal France, how much more did Jews have to fear in other nations? These views seem to have crystallized in Lévi's remarkable report about his trip to Palestine in 1917–

18. Full of admiration for what he had seen that Jews could do for themselves, Lévi applauded plans to settle Palestine with Jewish "colonies."[88] He thrilled at the renewal of Hebrew: "verbal effervescence responds to a boiling up of ideas and doctrines on their way to being realized."[89] He marveled at Jewish enterprise in all areas of commerce and agriculture and especially at how intellectuals worked the land as a way of recovering their Jewish identity.[90] The orthodox may have denounced, as "impious," the efforts of the liberal Alliance Israëlite Universelle to rescue Jews, but Lévi was all praise for the way Jewish endeavor had surpassed the Alliance in sheer "boldness."[91] France should support its Jews in Palestine in the same way it rushed to the aid of its Christians in Lebanon.[92] And he sought to do just that for the remainder of his life. Together with Chaim Weizmann, Sylvain Lévi took part in the ceremonial laying of the cornerstone of the Hebrew University of Jerusalem.[93]

Perhaps it was the Dreyfus Affair that startled Lévi, like other liberal Jews of his generation, into a new appreciation of the difficulties of Jewish collective identity—even if he did not go all the way to a political solution.[94] The ideal of a socially embodied religion, in touch with its own 'soil,' informed his scholarly judgment about the status of Buddhism set adrift from its home as much as it informed his attitude toward Judaism. Despite French national policies decreeing that Judaism was just a 'religion' alongside other 'religions,' historical events seemed to turn Lévi toward the view that this could not in practice ever be so. Although drawing well short of Zionism, Lévi took his place alongside the Jewish opinion-makers and asserted that Jews were a 'people' and should assert their collective identity. The 'law' of his thought was that as much as his universal aspirations favored Buddhism, the Enlightenment, and modernist, prophetic Judaism, the reality of a life of social embodiment put him closer to the side of particularity—traditional India and Judaism. In this way, Lévi's newfound enthusiasm for a particularist Judaism embodied in a Jewish homeland seems cut from the same cloth as his arguments for conceiving religion, in general, as socially embodied. Confirming this link from German Jewish sources, David N. Myers points out how Peretz Smolenskin, the Jewish intellectual and founder of the Zionist monthly (Vienna) *Ha-Shahar*, explicitly argued in the same way—namely that the concern for a socially embodied sense of Jewish religious identity could not be separated from Zionist intellectual trends. Myers notes:

> Much of Smolenskin's importance . . . derives from his emphasis on the social existence of the Jewish people. Jewish scholars in the nineteenth century increasingly portrayed their fellow Jews as members of religions or spiritual community. Smolenskin perceived that such terms would not qualify the Jews as a nation, at least not by the standards of the day. His words in the opening volume of *Ha-Shahar* challenged Jewish scholars not only to assert their right to self-representation, but to change the organizing principle of their study of the Jewish past. It was not the spiritual but the material foundation of the Jews that should stand at the center.[95]

Aside from reflecting Sylvain Lévi's conviction that the key to the survival of a religion is its ability to be a socially embodied 'thing,' the Durkheimians agreed with Lévi in saying that religion ought to be studied as a 'thing' as well. Indeed Marcel Mauss, at any rate, was convinced of this by Lévi, even if Durkheim had in all likelihood already tried to impress this view on him. This, then, would be the second great debt the Durkheimians owed to Sylvain Lévi and is another place where we can see his involvement in a Jewish agenda of scholarship.

To approach religions as 'embodied,' concrete realities was already typical of—although not necessarily unique to—the Science du Judaïsme.[96] This is not to deny that Mauss, like some of the other thinkers of his day, was not also moved toward this collectivism and concreteness by other figures and forces at the same time; I am merely saying that it seems that Sylvain Lévi was the one who provided a timely and historically attested intellectual rationale for what Mauss would do with religion. By what devious routes did such influence pass?

Students of the Durkheimians often see the work of Hubert and Mauss as defying the prevailing positivism of the day. Indeed, their contemporary critics saw them as rank ideologues and thus anything but out-and-out exponents of a kind of *"histoire historisant"* that we might connect with Lévi and the Wissenschaft des Judentums.[97] But students of the Durkheimians know as well that works like Hubert and Mauss's *Sacrifice* also provide models of the Durkheimian methodological conviction for getting in touch with 'things.' Thus, although Hubert and Mauss presumed that theory preceded data, they also believed that controversies about the nature of the concept of sacrifice should be submitted to a neutral court of appeals—should be restricted to the 'facts.'[98] They were thus as much in the camp of the positivist love of things and facts as they were still in the Cartesian camp of ideas. I am arguing, then, that this positivist 'half' of Mauss's epistemological 'heart' seems to come directly from Sylvain Lévi and thus from the Jewish *"historiens historisants"* of the Science du Judaïsme who trained Lévi. It would become for Mauss as much a lasting feature of his intellectual character as his theoretical and philosophical side.[99] This also confirms Robert Alun Jones's claims as to the *ultimate* importance of German thought in the Durkheimian circle.[100] The history practiced by the Jewish historians of the Science du Judaïsme was a deliberate Jewish adaptation of the text-critical historical methods of early-nineteenth-century German history, essentially the same (and ultimately German) as the historiography learned by Hubert from his Catholic modernist historian mentor, the great Catholic church historian Monseigneur Louis Duchesne.[101] Duchesne in turn had learned his craft from Renan, who had mediated the same German traditions of historical criticism of the Bible to Catholic scholars in France. The story of how Maus became a historian in the spirit of the Science du Judaïsme is a real conversion story and is worth telling for insight into the significance of his move from Cartesian idealism to a historicist concern with 'things.'

The setting is Paris 1896 at the École Pratique des Hautes Études, Fifth Section. After working with Durkheim in Bordeaux, Mauss moved to Paris to do his doctorate with Sylvain Lévi. His account of Lévi as "guru" paints an admirable and intriguing picture of the great Indologist, telling us what Lévi meant to Mauss as a scholar.[102] The experience gave a completely "new direction" to his career, Mauss said.[103] But originally Mauss did not take to this "new direction" easily. In addition, Mauss did not explicitly name this "new direction." But from what we know of the Science du Judaïsme and of Lévi's affiliation with it, Mauss, in submitting to an education at the hands of Lévi, was submitting to the 'discipline' of 'scientific' history writing. "As we conceive it the science of religion is not a branch of philosophical studies," said Hartwig Derenbourg, Lévi's colleague, coreligionist, and second-generation descendant of the French founders of the Science du Judaïsme.[104]

The main obstacle barring Mauss's reeducation was his youthful 'Cartesian' philosophical formation. Unlike Hubert, who was already *agrégée* in history when he and Mauss met at the Fifth Section,[105] Mauss did not at all take naturally to history. He required conversion from philosophy. He needed to acquire a taste for details and particulars, a taste that would in time be characteristic of his own work and that, as we have seen, was characteristic of the Science du Judaïsme.[106]

Thus, Mauss came to Sylvain Lévi puffed up with the pretensions of the cosmopolitan idealist philosophy he had imbibed from his *maître* at Bordeaux, Octave Hamelin.[107] Mauss tells us that the time he planned to commit to plugging away at Indian culture with Lévi would be short and uncomplicated. He thought he would exploit Lévi for a few 'typical' facts and force them onto the Procrustean bed of theory that he had brought with him from Bordeaux. In that order, he would write his doctoral thesis on prayer "past and present all over the world"[108] and move on to the real business of producing the grand theoretical synthesis.

Mauss's plans were, however, rudely upset. Early in his career as a student of Lévi's, Mauss presented the idea he and Hubert had conceived for *Sacrifice*. Lévi's immediate reaction was to reproach his inconstant pupil for having produced a mere piece of abstraction. Even though Hubert had given the prototype his firm historical touch, much remained to be done for it to meet the standards of the kind of history Lévi practiced.[109] Thus, far from indulging his rationalist philosophizing tendencies, Lévi made Mauss "plunge into a sea of facts." And after two years of submission to Lévi's historical method, no end was in sight. Mauss confessed in exasperation, "I kept on collecting and sifting facts."[110]

If Mauss's words can be trusted, the abstract universalizing tendencies of his philosophical inclinations gradually gave way to a historical and cultural particularism—what Jones seems to have in mind when he refers to the Durkheimian devotion to 'things.' The galloping speculation of philosophy was harnessed to a respect for particulars, a respect characteristic of the historical positivism of the Science du Judaïsme. By this route, Lévi's more conservative Judaism, partly as mediated through his historiographical practice and learned at the feet of the masters of the Science du Judaïsme, seems to have formed Mauss's devotion to the collective, concrete, and embodied approach to religion typical of the Durkheimians.

Sylvain Lévi's emphasis on the collective and concrete had two further consequences for the Durkheimian agenda for the study of religion, consequences that in turn owe debts to the Jewish intellectual world constructed by and around Lévi. These two are the Durkheimians' ritualism and their new idea of the sacred.

When Mauss arrived to study in the Fifth Section in 1896, Durkheim's *équipe* was a year or so from being formed, and plans for *L'Année sociologique* were just being made from Durkheim's provincial post in Bordeaux. In 1896 as well, Sylvain Lévi was doubtless in the midst of researching and perhaps writing his classic work *La Doctrine du sacrifice,* published in 1898.[111] Mauss would not meet Hubert until about a year later, in 1897. Their great collaboration on ritual sacrifice, *Sacrifice: Its Nature and Functions,* was two years from publication in 1898 as "Essai sur la nature et la fonction du sacrifice," one of two "Mémoires originaux" at the head of the second volume of *L'Année sociologique.* It was a seminal time indeed. From what we can tell, Lévi started Mauss straight off learning the lessons of historicist scholarship on religion with the subject of ritual sacrifice. Partly for the sake of chronological order and partly to keep the logic of the development of Mauss's thought clear, we need to separate two steps in Lévi's thinking about religion. First, Lévi was committed to the view that rituals were fundamental in understanding religion—at least Vedic religion. His *La Doctrine du sacrifice* further argued for the supreme importance of sacrifice in religion. He believed that of all rituals, sacrifice was marked with special importance for the nature of religion. Second, these commitments contributed in no small degree to the articulation of the notion of the positive force known as 'sacred' as the essence of religion. Both themes will be recognized as central to Durkheimian studies in religion. For our purposes, we will see that they shed light on the question of the Jewishness of the thought of the Durkheimians and, of course, of Lévi. First we turn to Sylvain Lévi's ritualism.

Lévi taught his *élèves* that Hindu texts should be read as indicators of rituals rather than as philosophical arguments.[112] In this way, Lévi seems to have introduced Mauss (and perhaps the Durkheimians at large) to 'methodological ritualism.' Lévi in effect argued that the right way to study religion was to study its rituals. Lévi thus directed Mauss from the study of philosophy to a study of 'concrete,' socially embodied religion—in this case ritual sacrifice.[113]

Given the conclusions reached about the particular importance of ritual for Durkheimian thought, essentialists will be tempted to say that Durkheimian methodological ritualism proves how essentially Jewish the thought of both Lévi and the Durkheimians was. In essence, Jewish religious *practice* is deeply ritualist; therefore we might expect the approach used by Jews in studying religion to be likewise ritualist. This is not necessarily so, however, and history again holds the key. After all, until the arrival of the Russian Jews in the last decades of the nineteenth century, French Jews did not stand out as particularly ritualistic. Catholics of the same period were as equally ritualistic in their religious practice as most (old and new) French Jews.[114] And from what little we can gather about Durkheim's own religious nurture, his father seems to have shown signs of liberal—and thus antiritualist—tendencies.

What is interesting, as we come to know the historical context of Durkheim's day, is that being Jewish at the time and place in question did seem to count in favor of methodological ritualism—in ways that are totally unexpected to the essentialists. The real background of this methodological move toward ritual is to be found in that symbol-laden domain of Orientalist thinking that was so much a part, as we have seen, of French Indology and in the agendas of scholarly anti-Semitism that perennially came into play there. The tendency by some French Jewish scholars to adopt methodological ritualism may just as easily have derived from the commitment to the ideal of religions as socially embodied, a commitment made by certain key representatives of the Science du Judaïsme since at least the time of Darmesteter. Let me elaborate.

Methodological ritualism seems to have taken its lead from Sylvain Lévi's own teacher, the Vedicist and Indologist Abel Bergaigne. Bergaigne's methodological ritualism in turn seemed to have been occasioned by his stiff opposition to Max Müller's Aryanist mythological reading of the ancient Indian texts.[115] According to Bergaigne, the hymns of the Vedas should be read against the backdrop of the performative context of their settings; Müller, on the other hand, felt that the Vedic hymns had only "incidental dramatic value."[116]

Paul Mus notes that Bergaigne started a "heresy in traditional Indianism" by "showing that one ought above all to interpret the Vedas as explaining a ritual."[117] Salomon Reinach reported that in France, this trend represented the same victory of anthropological study over philology as had occurred in England. For example Andrew Lang, a principal critic of Müller, argued that myth should be seen within its native setting of folk culture and lore.[118] The French movement included partisans of the Science du Judaïsme such as Darmesteter, who as early as 1886 went to India to study Oriental languages in their concrete contexts.[119] Subsequently, the reputation for methodological ritualism would pass to William Robertson Smith. The French critics of Müllerism also took exception to the standard opinion of "brahminical Hinduism" that stated the Vedas were "a profound philosophy."[120] In a testimony of intellectual conversion remarkable in the history of science, Bergaigne tells us of being "suddenly stopped on the road leading to Damascus" shortly after his article on Vedic mythology, written in the solarist style of Müller, went to press. "What was it," Bergaigne asks, "if not the evidence of the texts, or in any case, something which appeared to me to be such, that could have been the reason for the change?"[121] Bergaigne no longer believed: "I ultimately came to recognize that exclusively solar interpretations, just like exclusively meteorological interpretations . . . when they applied to the analysis of the Rigvedic myths, almost always leave behind a liturgical residue, and that this residue . . . is exactly the most important portion from the point of view of the exegesis of the hymns."[122]

Mauss first realized these lessons very early in his career as a student of Sylvain Lévi. To gauge his intellectual judgment, Lévi assigned Mauss to assess Bergaigne's *Religion védique*—a text totally unknown to Mauss at the time. After three days of intense reading, Mauss reported a favorable reaction, although he did so with some trepidation. Mauss concluded that if Bergaigne was correct, all other Vedicists were wrong. Lévi was duly pleased, and Mauss gained the confidence of his teacher.[123] Thus, through the classics of the Indological scholarship of Bergaigne, mediated by Lévi, the Durkheimians began taking ritual seriously as a key to the study of religion.

This deepens the historical support for Isambert's view that the principal carriers of the new ritualist view of the sacred passed down the line from Bergaigne to Sylvain Lévi to Hubert and Mauss. One does not need to deny Robertson Smith's possible impact on Durkheim (and thus on the Durkheimians), who from 1895 always credited Robertson Smith with certain principal theoretical insights of *The Elementary Forms of the Religious Life*.[124] But the lines are nowhere as clear as have been made out. This is especially true in light of the fact that Bergaigne's example was faithfully followed by his student Sylvain Lévi, who introduced Mauss to Bergaigne's ritualist study of the Vedas.

After this conversion to a kind of methodological ritualism, the next and decisive step toward the formation of key aspects of the Durkheimian approach to religion came in 1898 with Hubert and Mauss's *Sacrifice*. As director of Mauss's studies, Lévi selected the topic of ritual, especially ritual sacrifice, for special study by Mauss. In doing this, he also directed the course that Hubert and Mauss would take in their study of sacrifice later to appear in *L'Année sociologique*. Mauss tells us explicitly of Lévi's care and influence in this matter: "His course on the *Brâhmanas* was personally destined for me. His *Idea of Sacrifice in the Brâhmanas*—his chief work—had been made for me. From its first words, it delighted me with a decisive discovery: 'the entry into the world of the gods'; there, right under our noses, was the starting point of the labors which Hubert and I realized in *Sacrifice*. We were only bearing witness.''[125] Thus, to the nucleus of the Durkheimian *équipe*—Hubert and Mauss—Sylvain Lévi was a positive source of influence urging them on to serious study of ritual. This influence bore fruit in the first extensive study of a religious 'institution' undertaken by the Durkheimians, Hubert and Mauss's *Sacrifice: Its Nature and Functions*. Sylvain Lévi's impact on Hubert and Mauss's *Sacrifice* is recorded, in effect, in the teachings of his theoretical *La Doctrine du sacrifice*.

But Lévi's influence did not stop there. Beyond seeing ritual as a methodological key for understanding religion, Lévi also regarded it as a key to understanding the very causal processes of religion. First, ritual did so by explaining how the gods came to be. Although the Durkheimians seem to have been more confused than Lévi about the priority of ritual to myth and word,[126]

Lévi certainly taught the Durkheimians that ritual, not the idea of gods, was the key to the origins of religion.[127] Sylvain Lévi says that the *nature* of the religion revealed in the Brahmins is constituted by sacrificial ritual. Thus, sacrifice "is God and God *par excellence.*" Further, sacrifice "is the master, the indeterminate god, the infinite, the spirit from which everything comes, dying and being born without cease."[128] So potent is the sacrifice that even if gods are relevant, those very gods are "born" from sacrifice, are "products" of it.[129] Behind the figure of Prajapati, a major Hindu creation deity, is the sacrifice: "Prajapati, the sacrifice is the father of the gods . . . and its son."[130] Lévi in effect argued what Renou calls the "omnipotence" of ritual,[131] what can be termed 'causal ritualism.' This differs from the methodological point made by Robertson Smith that to understand primitive religion, we should begin by trying to understand ritual life. Here the issue is the nature and origins of religion itself, not how to go about studying it. What ultimately matters, of course, is that Marcel Mauss at least recognized this point—something he duly records in his review of *La Doctrine du sacrifice.* There Mauss recited the lessons of Sylvain Lévi's view of the causal power of rituals, including the power to create the gods themselves.[132] Although it is also true, at least in part, that Hubert and Mauss were methodological ritualists, the methodological point is secondary to the causal one.

Second, because the gods themselves were the causal consequences of sacrificial ritual, the *definition* of religion could be separated from a belief in the existence or even the idea of God. Instead of the idea that the gods defined religion, the notion of a sacred power, behind the gods and empowering them, took over. Little imagination is required to see here the Durkheimians' *sacré*, which for Mauss was "fundamental."[133] For Sylvain Lévi, this power—the *brahman* of Indian thought—was a property of sacrificial ritual itself, an "impalpable and irresistible power which is released . . . like electricity."[134] Lévi reported that like Hubert and Mauss's new dangerous sacred, the "force of sacrifice, once released, acts blindly; he who does not know how to tame it is broken by it."[135] Critical for us is the fact that in 1906, Hubert and Mauss concluded their reflections on the meaning of their earlier work on sacrifice by saying, "The ultimate aim of our researches [was] the sacred." In the same breath they added that the sacred was also the "highest reward of our work on sacrifice."[136] Thus, the conclusions Hubert and Mauss reached about sacrifice were, for them, internally related to those reached about the new positive sacred that characterized Durkheimian thought after 1895 or so. They were part of this same theoretical breakthrough. Thus, if we can understand the origins of one, we might very well be in a position to understand the origins of the other.

Sylvain Lévi did not address the problem of the definition of religion as directly as did the neo-Jews and other religious modernists. Yet in effect, he provided the Durkheimians with the materials for what would become the Durkheimian solution of the "problem of religion" debate in terms of the idea of the sacred. Significantly, when Durkheim made the point, in *The Elementary Forms of the Religious Life,* that religion must be defined in terms of the sacred and therefore cannot be defined by reference to God, he virtually cited Sylvain Lévi by citing the great man's teacher Abel Bergaigne.[137] Further, he employed Lévi's domain of expertise, Buddhism, to demonstrate his claim that a science of religion must therefore be methodologically atheistic.[138]

Third (and in strongest contrast with Robertson Smith, for example), Sylvain Lévi believed that ritual was not simply a necessary feature of primitive religion but was something that could be seen as *perennially* characteristic of religion—even religion with philosophical aspects. Lévi took special delight in demonstrating the ritualism of the Vedas against "the defenders of Aryan bible."[139] Moreover, at the same moment that this ritualism reached its peak among an elite class of Brahmins, so also did philosophical speculation. The ritual sacrifice of the Brahmins could not thus be seen as symptomatic of a "long and profound degeneration of religious feeling."[140] Rather, despite the brutality of Brahminical sacrifice, the ritual contained a theological system and speculation that gave immediate rise to the lofty philosophical speculations of the Upanishads.[141] Sylvain Lévi thus struck at the heart of the theory of religious evolution typical of Robertson Smith, who took it over from Wellhausen and the *volkish* Lagarde.[142] It seems, therefore, that Sylvain Lévi is the one who should be named the father of modern perennial ritualism.

In sum, the position on the sacred originated by Hubert and Mauss and put into play by Durkheim himself is quite distant from the views of the typically antiritualist, 'iconoclast' Jewish modernists exemplified by Salomon Reinach. Against the antiritualist position of such Jewish (and other) religious liberals, Hubert and Mauss adopted a *causal* ritualism: religion *is* its rituals, not just its beliefs or even morality. Ritual is the locus of the positive power of the sacred that injects effervescence, energy, and power into people and that causes people to be religious at all. Thus, sacrifice is for them what makes (things) sacred, as the root meaning of *sacri-ficium* testifies. Sacrifice even creates the gods. Sacrifice performs a positive function of creating the religious life of people. Ritual is, then, religion in social form and thus "religion made visible and tangible."[143] Considering Lévi's teachings about the priority of ritual to theism, the idea of religion as a source of energy, and the perennial power of ritual action, we can see that Sylvain Lévi was one of the key figures influencing the development of Durkheimian thought about religion and thus about ritual, especially ritual sacrifice. As mentor, patron, and personal friend to both Hubert and Mauss at the École Pratique des Hautes Études, Fifth Section, Sylvain Lévi was perfectly positioned to understand what the Durkheimians wanted to do.[144] The great Indologist was thus well placed to influence the course of the Durkheimian revolution in our thinking about religion in ways that, for example, Robertson Smith never could.

Although we have seen how Mauss adopted a religious study style typical of the Science du Judaïsme by way of Lévi, how does all of this address the notion of the possible Jewishness of Durkheimian thinking? Just because Lévi was a pious Jew who learned his history by writing within the Jewish context of the Science du Judaïsme and just because his student Mauss was Jewish by nurture does not mean that the way Mauss then studied religion can itself be said to be a 'Jewish' way of doing so. Or does it? First, whatever else may be true, I do not think we can say that Mauss's way of studying religion was *essentially* or originally Jewish, any more than was Sylvain Lévi's. The historicism that informed Lévi's approach to religious data, that is, the historicism of the Science du Judaïsme, was derived from a kind of history pioneered by German Gentiles and—as we have seen—in many cases by anti-Semitic German Gentiles as well. But by dismissing theses of essential and eternal Jewishness in the study of religion, we have been freed to concentrate on the more fruitful lines of inquiry into 'real Judaism and real Jews,' which I have emphasized from the beginning of this book. Simply because Mauss's newly learned way of studying religion was not essentially Jewish does not mean it is irrelevant to the real history of the Jews of France. Indeed, the opposite is true. There were, for example, very good *Jewish* reasons why the founders of the Wissenschaft des Judentums adopted techniques developed by German critical historians. In the minds of the reformers, critical history would help Judaism become stronger. Likewise, in Sylvain Lévi's engagement with the issues of a Jewish homeland or in his polemics against the scholarly anti-Semites, there were also very fine *Jewish* reasons why he found the critical, socially and materially sensitive historiography of the Science du Judaïsme useful. It permitted him to come to terms with the peculiar power of concrete religiousness, of social embodimen—a power that in the case of India he exploited in thinking about the issue of Zionism and the nature of Judaism as a religion. We really cannot say how much these Jewish reasons mattered to Mauss, a latecomer to Jewish identity. But this does not diminish the character of the particular French Jewish context in which his move to the socially concrete, to ritualism, and to a new definition of the sacred came into being.

6

WHERE DO WE STAND?

In the course of this book I hope we have come to see much less of an essentially Jewish Durkheim and more of a Durkheim poised variously in relation to a community of French Jewish scholars and their concerns in his time. Sometimes he surprises us by assuming positions indistinguishable from those championed by the very Jewish contemporaries with whom he should have had the least in common. Here I refer to his learned defense of Talmudic Judaism, a defense that ran against the grain of the expectations one might rightly have for a liberal of Durkheim's ilk. At other times, he drew a sharp line between what he stood for and what prominent liberal Jewish contemporaries, such as Louis-Germain Lévy, Salomon Reinach, and Henri Bergson, represented. Then sometimes the Durkheimians moved close to their Jewish academic contemporaries, such as Israël Lévi and Sylvain Lévi. Some Jews, like Sylvain Lévi, left such indelible intellectual marks on the Durkheimian project of moral and social inquiry, arguably attributable to their own Jewish consciences and social agendas, that one is tempted to think that some deeper religious or ethnic link might account for their kinship and mutual regard. But at other times the Durkheimians showed no inclination to follow the leads of conspicuously Jewish scholars, such as Salomon Reinach and his liberal Jewish colleagues.

In this sense, Durkheim played the same ambivalent role in
the midst of his natural religious and ethnic kin as he played
in other domains where he had been expected to show more
partisanship. He was never socialist enough for the socialists and
certainly was not Marxist enough for the Marxists of his day. He
was too philosophical and theoretical for the historians of his
time, although he saw sociology as the natural successor of the
standard historicist history. He was too wedded to the power of
the concrete and social to please the philosophical rationalists
of his generation, although he rose from their ranks and felt
that his sociology represented the best scenario for the future of
that philosophy itself. In speaking to the free-thinker humanists
close in sympathy to his own humanism, he championed the
rights and integrity of traditional religion; in turning to the free
believers, he reminded them of the requisites of science as the
dominant culture of the time. As a fervent French patriot who
reviled German ideologues for their chauvinism, Durkheim nevertheless always greatly admired German sociability and scientific scholarship. Thus, in his systematic ambiguity to kin and
kindred, Durkheim's equally ambiguous place with respect to
Judaism and Jewishness falls right into place. Durkheim refused
to be neatly pigeonholed on an entire range of issues, Jewishness
among them.

We would be mistaken, then, to see Durkheim as a systematic or consistent Jewish thinker. Some of what he thought may
remind us of positions taken up by explicitly Jewish thinkers
working out what they, at least, considered to be expressly Jewish
intellectual agendas. But such impressionistic judgments have
no historic value. They have nothing to say about Durkheim or
his thought processes, whether conscious or unconscious. They
are no more than claims about what something suggests to us.
Durkheim was no secret Jew. His thinking was not a secularized and perhaps cryptic form of Jewish thought. I hope this
book at least lays to rest this method of analyzing Durkheim
and Durkheimian thought. But more than that, I hope it also
serves as a model of how to regard other attempts to classify
thinkers and their thoughts in terms of their particular racial,
ethnic, or religious origins. It takes more than the accident of
birth to form thought processes with the same character—if
such character even exists. To prove this, simply offer a 'blind

test' challenge to anyone claiming to be able to read people's
'roots' from their academic writings.

Instead of meditating on Durkheim's so-called Jewish soul
or the supposed Jewish character of his thought, I have tried to
introduce readers to a lost generation of Jewish thinkers with
whom Durkheim was in some relation. In doing so, I have
scratched only the surface of all there is to know about the vital
French Jewish intellectual community of the fin de siècle. Other,
little-known thinkers are waiting to be more thoroughly treated
by those interested in the study of religion and culture. They
merit our attention because they lived as Jews in more 'normal'
times than we can easily imagine since the Holocaust. It is my
hope that Jews of the future may find that living in more 'normal' times will be their lots too. Although one must keep in the
foreground of memory the genocidal catastrophe of this century, and especially how carefully targeted for extermination
were our Jewish brothers and sisters, leading Jewish thinkers of
our own time have already begun to move in new directions. In
a recent interview in the *Los Angeles Times,* rising Israeli Labour
Party leader Avraham Burg expressed such a new direction:

> I don't want the relationship between myself and my brothers
> to be based on traumas. Look, I'm married to my wife. I love her.
> She says she loves me. I don't know why, but she says she loves
> me. We have our moments—it happens with every *normal* couple.
> We have our moments of love and anxiety and happiness. Every
> now and then she turns to me and says, "Avraham, will you take
> out the garbage?" It's a *normal* life. There is no anxiety about it,
> no hysteria.
>
> But, we've developed in the Jewish people a kind of relation-
> ship that we express ourselves only when we have a problem. Give
> me a good crisis. . . . They express love only when there are prob-
> lems. Our real test is *normal life.* The "take out the garbage" life.[1]

Collective memory can be built up of many different kinds of
contents. When the hoped-for "normal" times come, perhaps
the situation will ripen so that the voices I have let speak will
gain the audiences they deserve. And perhaps new entries into
the collective memory of the Jewish communities of the future
will be discovered. When that time comes, I imagine that we will

need to know even more about the figures I have brought to life again in this book.

Still, readers less concerned with the Jews of France and more interested in the Durkheimian aspect of this book may ask how these revelations help us read Durkheim anew. First of all, and in general, I hope my book makes readers come more directly to terms with the thought of Durkheim as it really was—not as we might wish it to have been. I hope that I have undercut attempts to read Durkheimian thought as a specific product of *any* ethnic sort of thinking—Jewish or otherwise. This means that friendly and unfriendly critics alike must play by new rules: Durkheimian thought can neither be written off nor applauded for its being 'Jewish,' 'French,' or whatever. That Durkheim was 'Jewish' (whatever that may mean) is neither a good reason to damn what he says nor a good reason to celebrate it. Durkheim's thought is neither necessarily limited by a supposed 'Jewishness' nor especially praiseworthy for it. Durkheimian ideas need to be evaluated in terms of their own merits or liabilities in explaining social life. Appeals to 'Jewishness' simply derail our taking seriously the proposals Durkheim himself wanted to make. My book thus seeks to turn us back to a serious confrontation with Durkheim's proposals about the nature of social life.

As a consequence of refusing to pigeonhole and thus render irrelevant the theoretical proposals made by Durkheim, I believe I have contributed to a new reading of Durkheim in a number of particular areas. One is the location of Durkheim among the theological liberals or religious modernists of his day in my discussion of Durkheimian symbolist discourse. Reading Durkheim's language of symbolism as a 'dialect' of the language of religious modernism suggests that we read much of what Durkheim wrote differently than do those who would read Durkheim either in strictly secular terms or as a kind of radical religious primitivist *avant le lettre*. Durkheim shows himself as a liberal in religion, much as we have come to appreciate his liberalism in economics and politics. Just as we now no longer strain to show what a socialist Durkheim was, so my work entails that we put aside attempts to show what a radical primitivist he was in the domain of religion. To Durkheim and his confederates, *sociologie religieuse* offered a worldview similar in most respects to the so-called liberal-modernist religious worldviews of their Protestant, Catholic, and Jewish contemporaries.

Durkheimian symbolic hermeneutics thus represents a variant on the religious reformist trends of the time—not, as Edward Tiryakian argued, a species of avant-garde thinking, mirrored in the radical artistic and literary movements such as the symbolist movement. There is no mysticism or irrationalism in Durkheimian symbolism. Durkheimian symbolist thought is not an anticipation of the religio-social radicalism of self-appointed successors of Durkheim such as the Collège de Sociologie. We thus should not let Durkheimian talk of 'symbols' distract us from reading Durkheim as a cultural liberal, whose writing steered clear of direct revolutionary applications. I also believe that such location changes our appreciation of what Durkheim wrote—from a view in which Durkheimian liberalism stood only for a political position in the world of the Third Republic to one in which we see Durkheimian thought participating with equal interest in the religious controversies of the day, usually seen only as internal matters of the business of particular religious traditions. Among other things, this location should give pause to those who would see the Durkheimians as the kind of social and religious radicals their successors constituting the Collège de Sociologie were to become. The Durkheimians were reformers, both political and religious, not revolutionaries. Thus, attempts to read Durkheimian interests in primitive religion as indicators of revolutionary cultural tendencies are mistaken. What mattered to Durkheim in considering the primitive was contemporary society. Despite an admiration of the ritual life of the French Revolution, the Durkheimians would never have imagined joining with George Bataille in his plans for promoting human sacrifice in the Place de la Concorde. For the Durkheimians, ritual sacrifice was worth understanding and studying because it was organically continuous with our own practice of civic sacrifice. It is no coincidence that what was to be Durkheim's great culminating work was not *The Elementry Forms of the Religious Life* but the never-completed *La Morale.*

In reading *The Elementary Forms of the Religious Life*, we should shift from a nearsighted 'primitivist' ethnographic focus on totemism and recapture more of Durkheim's own farsighted modernist sociological priorities in his writing about totemism at all. Durkheim told us as much on the very first page of *The Elementary Forms of the Religious Life*. In registering interest in totemism, Durkheim made it clear that his concerns were only strategic to his contemporary sociological goals. "The man of to-day. . . . There is nothing which we are more interested in knowing," Durkheim declared.[2] Then, trying to allay fears that he had wandered off among the glades of primitivist exotica in discussions of Intichiumas, Corroborris, Witchety Grub clans, and such, Durkheim added: "We are not going to study a very archaic religion simply for the pleasure of telling its peculiarities and its singularities." Durkheim aimed, rather, to keep faith with his earlier interests in the big sociological issues of modern society: "If we have taken it [totemism] as the subject of our research, it is because it has seemed to us better adapted than any other to lead to an understanding of the religious nature of man, that is to say, to show us an essential and permanent aspect of humanity."[3] What I have unearthed about Durkheim's relation to the clerical modernists of his day should push these priorities into the foreground of our reading of Durkheim.

Another way I believe my analyses affect the way we read Durkheim is in the extent to which French national issues and French nationalism shaped his intellectual agendas. In general, commentators on Durkheim's works have not much noticed the national or nationalist content in Durkheim's writings until his explicit wartime pamphlets and addresses.[4] Further, interpreters of Durkheim have been content to read only those pieces that are explicitly concerned with national issues, such as public education, or Durkheim's patriotic writings for such content. On the contrary, beyond Durkheim's involvement in the business of the Third Republic, the nationalist revival of the late nineteenth and early twentieth centuries also may have shaped Durkheim's interests in ways that are neither immediately evident nor immediately explicit. In arguing, for instance, that both Durkheimian and French Jewish societism ought to be read against the backdrop of the French nationalist revival of the late nineteenth and early twentieth centuries, I have argued that the nationalist nature of other Durkheimian work needs also to be read more widely in the Durkheimian corpus than heretofore has been done. Thus, sometimes when Durkheim says 'society,' we should read him to mean 'nation' as well or even above all else.

For example, we know that Durkheim's "Individuals and the Intellectuals" proposed a political ethic valuing the individual as a sacred being. Further, we know that Durkheim felt that the sacredness of the individual depended directly on eminently French *social* norms. On the face of it, the individualist ethic proposed by Durkheim actually should be read as a national ethic devised to serve Durkheim's own progressive proposal of what a French nationalism might be. I say this because, first, this ethic is explicitly justified in national terms. Durkheim associates the sacredness of the individual to norms that, he declares, define French national identity. And second, this ethic is implicitly nationalist. Durkheim and those like him believed that France could mount a successful war effort only if it could unify the nation around some common acceptable national value. Without mentioning preparations for war, Durkheim, paradoxically but brilliantly, argued that this *common, social,* 'national' value was (Durkheimian) individualism.

The same rhetorical strategy can be detected in how the Durkheimians nuanced their theory of sacrifice. Thus, what I have argued about the national and nationalist character of some of Durkheim's thought in trying to understand his societism can help us read his attitude toward sacrifice. As for the national pertinence of a theory of sacrifice such as that developed by Durkheim and significantly by his confederates Henri Hubert and Marcel Mauss, the case is quite straightforwardly a matter of national political rhetoric. Sacrifice becomes a critical rhetorical notion in the affairs of state because it is often the way that duty under extreme conditions, such as warfare, is justified. Thus, we can check my suggestion that Durkheim's theory of individualism has nationalist content by seeing if the same would be compatible for his theory of sacrifice. This means that the debate about the nature of sacrifice is the *same* as the debate about the nature of the individual. This further means that Durkheimian theories of sacrifice appearing in *The Elementary Forms of the Religious Life* or in Hubert and Mauss's *Sacrifice: Its Nature and Functions* can usefully be seen as conditioned by the same nationalist debates of the late 1800s as was "Individuals and the Intellectuals."

Let me elaborate. In periods of nationalist agitation, the question of how far an individual may be obligated to the nation inevitably arises. In the late 1800s, French intellectuals debated this duty of the individual to 'sacrifice' oneself. The extreme right wing of patriotic Catholics and free-thinker nationalists, in large part, were arrayed in favor a national ethic of annihilating self-sacrifice—an ethic that also surfaced among anti-Dreyfusards, who called for the 'sacrifice' of Dreyfus (even if innocent) for reasons of state. Ironically, for the extreme French nationalists, Durkheim's denunciation of the collectivism of the German Heinrich von Treitschke rehearsed the same logic as his critiques of Catholic integralism.[5] At the same time that he attacked these right-wing Catholics, Durkheim let loose a volley against Treitschke's statist annihilationism: "Individuals, Treitschke says besides, 'should sacrifice themselves to that collectivity upon which they depend. *The state is that which is the highest in the order of human collectivities . . . it is for that reason, that the Christian duty of self-sacrifice to the highest end does not really exist:* because in the whole course of universal human history one finds nothing higher than the State.' " On such statist fulminations, Durkheim tartly observed: "Indeed, concerning humanity and the duties of the state toward humanity [Treitschke] has nary a word. . . . And thus it is clear why Germans learn to repeat from their earliest infancy that famous formula, *Deutschland Über alles.*"[6] On the whole, Protestants and Jews resisted such extreme collectivism, although sometimes even their friendly critics saw this as lacking a proper feeling for the needs of the national society.[7] Thus, Durkheim fits well within the range of opinion of some Jews concerning the articulation of a nationalism that sought to be consistent with the sacredness of the individual.

This rhetorical strategy might also lead one to read Durkheimian attempts to propose a gift theory of sacrifice in *The Elementary Forms of the Religious Life* as shaped in part by the nationalist politics of Durkheim's day. In his theory of sacrifice, Durkheim attempted to avoid the political extremes both of annihilationism (equivalent to the negation of the self for the nation) and of egoism (equivalent to the refusal to die for the nation). Thus, Durkheim felt that individuals need prudently to give *of* themselves rather than absolutely to give *up* themselves. So, when Durkheim speaks of sacrifice sustaining the powers, gods, and such or when he reinstates oblation as a primitive element of sacrifice (displacing William Robertson Smith's alimentary communion),[8] Durkheim in effect slides over into the modified gift theory first explicated by Hubert and Mauss in their *Sacrifice*. As Durkheim himself concluded:

> If the Australian makes offerings to his sacred beings, there is no reason for supposing that the idea of oblation was foreign to the primitive organization of the sacrificial institution and later upset its natural arrangement. Of course, the sacrifice is partially a communion; but it is also, and no less essentially, a gift and an act of renouncement. . . . Perhaps the oblation is even more permanent than the communion.[9]

Durkheim felt that it made sense for him to resort to the modified gift theory of sacrifice, I believe, because of his profoundly liberal bourgeois worldview and social location. From that perspective, exchange or gift fits the individualist values that the Durkheimians themselves never surrendered despite the curiosity they may have had about the extreme politics and economics of their day. Thus, if the sacredness of individuals is placed at the center of social life, we may expect *exchange* to appear as the typical way in which relationships are articulated and even created among people. To the extent that individuals are sacred, they have ontological integrity and thus can be real actors. Exchange between and among such individuals is one of the actions they may perform. Likewise *sacrifice* is one of the actions individuals may perform. Much the same implication arises if one views the relation of individualism and exchange theory in reverse: to the extent that one thinks of human relations in terms of transactions such as exchange, one will think of the relations established or encouraged there as between and/or among individuals. This follows trivially from the fact that exchange requires an 'other' and assumes the reality of duality, the integrity of plural parties. This is precisely what we find in Hubert and Mauss's *Sacrifice* and later in Mauss's *The Gift*, in which the sacredness of the individual is coordinated with the logic of sacrifice and gift. The victim protects the "sacrifier" and the sacrificer from having to give up themselves; prudence in giving of oneself is encouraged, whereas the perfection of self-giving, for example, the sacrifice of the god, is viewed by Hubert and Mauss as an asymptotic ideal, never reached but held up as a model for all the compromised sacrifices we make in the real world. As if proposing a theory of sacrifice tailor-made for liberal bourgeoisie members, which they were, Hubert and Mauss noted:

> In any sacrifice there is an act of abnegation since the sacrifier deprives himself and gives. . . . But this abnegation and submission are not without their selfish aspect. The sacrifier gives up something of himself but does not give up himself. Prudently, he sets himself aside. This is because if he gives, it is partly to receive. Thus sacrifice shows itself in a dual light; it is a useful act and it is an obligation. Disinterestedness is mingled with self-interest.

Ironically, after all this is said and done, to the extent that the Jews of Durkheim's acquaintance in Paris were themselves exemplary bourgeois individualists, Durkheim's individualism—not his collectivism—would be the likelier mark of his 'Jewishness'!

A final area of Durkheim's writing that my work has illuminated is his view of the sacred. By locating the origins of Durkheim's idea of the sacred in the context of the multifaceted researches of Sylvain Lévi, I have urged that we need to speak about the Durkheimian sacred as an embodied reality. If I am correct in linking the notion of the embodied sacred through Mauss to Durkheim, though it was originally developed in Lévi's writings on Zionism, on the demise of Buddhism in India, or on sacrifice in his *La Doctrine du sacrifice dans les brâhmanas,* then we will have to take seriously the material, spatial, and temporal identity of the Durkheimians' notion of religion and its essence—the sacred. For them, to speak of the sacred as necessarily needing to be embodied was part of their elementary conception of religion. This is, then, to add my own confirmation to Robert Alun Jones's arguments about the centrality of Durkheim's concern with 'things.'[10] What we have not perhaps fully grasped is that Durkheim's passion for the concrete, for 'things,' extended to religion as well and thus to the sacred. In all things, Durkheim was far less often the airy idealist he is sometimes imagined to be and far more often a thinker constantly assessing social reality in terms of its being well grounded. We forget, or simply are unaware, that Durkheim rejected the utility of the (Comtean) ideal notion of the society in favor of the concrete 'societies' almost from the beginning of his career. Thus, Durkheim said in his inaugural lecture at Bordeaux in 1887: "We are told it [sociology] should study *Society;* but Society does not exist. There are just societies, classified into genus and species, just like vegetables and animals."[11] In this sense, beyond a shared concern with the social, it makes perfectly proper sense to see the material focus of the work of the *Annales* historians as a natural evolution of the Durkheimian impulse in religious scholarship. For the *Annales* and for the Durkheimians, the sacred was not just a quality radically opposed to the profane or simply a characteristic of our ideals or morals. It was essentially an embodied reality, part of the world of concrete things, places, and events. Thus, in his great study of religious healing, Marc Bloch explores the way the sacred was mediated through a "sacred touch."[12] And in his sweeping account of the feudal world, he is trying to show us not only a *mentalité* but also how the sacred world of the Middle Ages entailed divisions of time and space.[13]

Perhaps still suffering from the attempts of American sociologists of an earlier generation to discredit Durkheimian theory in the name of its assertion of a "misplaced concreteness," we have overlooked Durkheim's commitment to a fully concrete and embodied conception of religion.[14] Indeed, how can we see religion socially if we do not see it in terms of the life of actual social groupings—in terms of their rituals, divisions of the calendar, organization of living space, and so on? If my connection of the concreteness and embodied view of religion developed by Sylvain Lévi can help us see more of this aspect in Durkheim's writing, I believe that my location of Durkheim's views of religion against the background provided by the Jews of France will have served an informed reading of Émile Durkheim very well.

NOTES

ONE

1. See references to "[Jonah David] Goldhagen's essentialist view" of the Germans as a nation of necessarily eliminationist anti-Semites in Omer Bartov, "Ordinary Monsters," review of *Hitler's Willing Executioners: Ordinary Germans and the Holocaust,* by Daniel Jonah Goldhagen, *New Republic,* 29 April 1996, 35.

2. Deborah Dash Moore, "David Emile Durkheim and the Jewish Response to Modernity" *Modern Judaism* 6 (1980): 287–300, is by far the most sophisticated version of the latter. There she says, "Durkheim's blend of politics, morality and science intersected with a Jewish perspective on modernity" (289). For the best skeptical treatment of Durkheim's 'essential' Jewishness, see W. S. F. Pickering, "The Enigma of Durkheim's Jewishness," in W. S. F. Pickering and Herminio Martins, eds., *Debating Durkheim* (London: Routledge, 1994), 10–39.

3. Eugen Schoenfeld and Stjepan Meštrović, "Durkheim's Concept of Justice and Its Relationship to Social Solidarity," *Sociological Analysis* 50 (1989): 113, 117. On religious tolerance, see Moore, "David Emile Durkheim," 297.

4. Jean-Claude Filloux, "Il ne faut pas oublier que je suis fils de rabbin," *Revue française de sociologie* 17 (1976): 259–66. For references to "Talmudic" features, see pages 260ff. Schoenfeld and Meštrović, "Durkheim's Concept of Justice," 112, 125, as well as Greenberg and Derczansky, see less piety and more the thought structures of someone raised in the Talmudic culture of Durkheim's day. Louis M. Greenberg,

"Bergson and Durkheim as Sons and Assimilators: The Early Years," *French Historical Studies* 9 (1976): 626; Alexandre Derczansky, "Note sur la Judéité de Durkheim," *Archives des sciences sociales des religions* 35/ 69 (1990): 158.

5. Derczansky, "Note sur la Judéité de Durkheim," 158.

6. Moore, "David Emile Durkheim," 295.

7. Filloux, "Il ne faut pas oublier que je suis fils de rabbin," 259–66.

8. See in particular Moore, "David Emile Durkheim," 295. Jacob Jay Lindenthal, "Some Thoughts Regarding the Influence of Traditional Judaism on the Work of Emile Durkheim," *Tradition: A Journal of Orthodox Thought* 11 (1970): 41–50.

9. Compare, on the other hand, the list of essentially Jewish features produced in Werner Sombart's *The Jews and Modern Capitalism* (1917), trans. M. Epstein (Glencoe: Free Press, 1951), 255, 258, 264–68.

10. Émile Durkheim, *The Evolution of Educational Thought: Lectures on the Formation and Secondary Education in France,* 2d ed. (1938), trans. Peter Collins (London: Routledge and Kegan Paul, 1977), 289. This was called to my attention by Robert Alun Jones and Douglas A. Kibbee, "Durkheim, Language, and History: A Pragmatist Perspective," *Sociological Theory* 11 (1993): 164.

11. On the strange congruence of some anti-Semitic polemic to recent anti-anti-Semitic polemic, Omer Bartov observes: "And what are the implications of such a notion that there exists a nation of ingrained murderers? How useful is this assumption for explaining an historical phenomenon? To what extent is this a bizarre inversion of the Nazi view of Jews as an insidious, inherently evil nation?" (Bartov, "Ordinary Monsters," 37).

12. Robert C. Grogin, *The Bergsonian Controversy in France: 1900–1914* (Calgary: University of Calgary, 1988), 119, quoting Gilbert Maire, "Crise pédagogique et anarchisme universitaire," *Mercure de France* 100 (1912): 278.

13. Yosef Hayim Yerushalmi, *Zakhor: Jewish History and Jewish Memory* (Seattle: University of Washington Press, 1982), 92.

14. Ibid., 96.

15. Bartov, "Ordinary Monsters," 37. See also Lionel Kochan, *The Jewish Renaissance and Some of Its Discontents* (Manchester: Manchester University Press, 1992), 20, for a spirited attack on the essentialist characterization of Jews by social scientists like Thorstein Veblen.

16. For a balanced account of the difficulties of determining the role of Durkheim's personal Jewishness in his thought, see W. S. F. Pickering, *Durkheim's Sociology of Religion: Themes and Theories* (London: Routledge and Kegan Paul, 1984), 14–18.

17. Schoenfeld and Meštrović, "Durkheim's Concept of Justice," 120.

18. Ibid., 113, 117. On religious tolerance, see Moore, "David Emile Durkheim," 297.

19. John Dunn, "The Identity of the History of Ideas," *Philosophy* 43 (1968): 85.

20. See John Dunn's attack on such "reified abstractions" in ibid., 85.

21. Robert Alun Jones, "On Understanding a Sociological Classic," *American Journal of Sociology* 83 (1977): 291.

22. I thank Professor Richard Hecht, University of California, Santa Barbara, for advice on these 'essentials.' For a daunting list of other such 'essentials,' see as well Pickering, "The Enigma of Durkheim's Jewishness," 30–31.

23. On the difficulties of constructing an ideal type of Jewishness or a Jewish mentality, see Peter Gay, *Freud, Jews, and Other Germans* (New York: Oxford University Press, 1978), 178–79.

24. Pickering, "The Enigma of Durkheim's Jewishness," 16.

25. Émile Durkheim, *La Science sociale et l'action,* ed. Jean-Claude Filloux (Paris: Presses Universitaires de France, 1970), 301.

26. Robert Alun Jones and W. Paul Vogt, "Durkheim's Defense of *Les formes Élémentaires de la vie religieuse,*" in Henrika Kuklick and Elizabeth Long, eds., *Knowledge and Society: Studies in the Sociology of Culture, Past and Present,* vol. 5 (Greenwich, Conn.: JAI Press, 1984), 48, quoting Steven Lukes, *Emile Durkheim* (New York: Harper and Row, 1972), 44.

27. Durkheim's observation was made in the course of his examination of the doctoral thesis of Louis-Germain Lévy, cited in Lukes, *Emile Durkheim,* 627.

28. Pickering, "The Enigma of Durkheim's Jewishness," 16.

29. Stjepan Meštrović, *Emile Durkheim and the Reformation of Sociology* (Totowa, N.J.: Rowman and Littlefield, 1988), 6, and Pickering, "The Enigma of Durkheim's Jewishness," 16.

30. Marc Bloch, *Strange Defeat,* trans. Gerard Hopkins (New York: Norton, 1968), 177–78.

31. Greenberg, "Bergson and Durkheim," 626–28.

32. Gay, *Freud, Jews, and Other Germans,* 99.

33. Moore, "David Emile Durkheim," 289.

34. Durkheim to Octave Hamelin, as quoted in Lukes, *Emile Durkheim,* 366.

35. Lucy S. Dawidowicz, *The Jewish Presence: Essays on Identity and History* (New York: Holt, Rinehart and Winston, 1977), ch. 1.

36. I say this in light of the fact of the destruction of most of Durkheim's personal records and correspondence. New biographical evi-

dence will not likely come to light about Durkheim's youth and his Jewish home life or about his conception of what being Jewish meant to him then or later in his life. The data have simply not survived. So, we might as well start from where we are.

37. See, for instance, Durkheim's active concern in behalf of Russian Jews in the years around World War I. "Appendix: Durkheim and the Committee for Russian Refugees" and Durkheim's "Report on the Situation of Russians in France in 1916" (first published as "Rapport sur la situation des Russes en France" in "Émile Durkheim, défenseur des réfugiés russes en France," presented by N. Elkarati, *Genèses*, 2 December 1990, 168–77) in Pickering, "The Enigma of Durkheim's Jewishness," 10–39.

38. In the course of this book, I will refer extensively to the works of these writers.

39. Robert Alun Jones, "On Quentin Skinner," *American Journal of Sociology* 81 (1981): 458. On the proper use of context, see also Robert Alun Jones, "Durkheim in Context: A Reply to Perrin," *Sociological Quarterly* 15 (1975): 552.

40. Sylvain Lévi, *La Doctrine du sacrifice dans les Brâhmanas* (Paris: Leroux, 1898).

41. Robert Alun Jones, "Demythologizing Durkheim: A Reply to Gerstein," in Kuklick and Long, *Knowledge and Society*, 5:75.

42. Quentin Skinner, "Meaning and Understanding in the History of Ideas," *History and Theory* 8 (1969): 47.

43. Ibid., 49.

44. Dunn, "The Identity of the History of Ideas," 87.

45. Ibid., 88.

46. Ibid., 87.

47. Skinner, "Meaning and Understanding," 49.

48. Ibid.

49. Jones, "Durkheim in Context," 558.

50. Dunn, "The Identity of the History of Ideas," 93.

51. Different from both context and authorial intention is the matter of 'influence.' If one wants to credit someone as an 'influence,' we can do so only if there is an awareness of this supposed influence, as well as a real dependence on the thought of the influence. See Jones, "On Understanding a Sociological Classic," 293.

52. John G. A. Pocock, "Introduction: The State of the Art," *Virtue, Commerce, and History* (Cambridge: Cambridge University Press, 1985), 9.

53. Ibid.

54. Jones and Kibbee, "Durkheim, Language, and History," 152–70.

55. Pocock, "Introduction: The State of the Art," 10.

56. Jones and Kibbee, "Durkheim, Language, and History," 152–70.

57. I thank Jonathan Z. Smith for this point. An extreme example of the differences within so-called Judaism can be seen in the Reform rabbi Simeon Maslin's recent declaration that reform and orthodox Jewry "have ceased to be one." Maslin goes on to say: "We must recognize that fact and proceed. . . . The time has finally arrived to stop deferring to an Orthodoxy that insults us at every opportunity" ("Rabbi's Speech Focuses on Rift within Judaism," *Los Angeles Times*, 6 April 1996, B6).

58. Michel Abitbol, *Les Deux terres promises: Les Juifs de France et le sionisme* (Paris: Olivier Orban, 1989), 32.

59. George Condominas, "Marcel Mauss, père d'ethnographie française," *Critique* 297 (1970): 130f.

60. Ibid.

TWO

1. Here I borrow the term coined by W. Paul Vogt in "The Politics of Academic Sociological Theory in France, 1890–1914" (Ph.D. diss., University of Indiana, 1976), 23.

2. Ibid., 29–30, quoting Émile Durkheim, review of *Essais sur la conception matérialiste de l'histoire,* by A. Labriola, *Revue philosophique* 44 (1897): 645–51, reprinted in Émile Durkheim, *La Science sociale et l'action,* ed. Jean-Claude Filloux (Paris: Presses Universitaires de France, 1970), 245–60.

3. Robert C. Grogin, *The Bergsonian Controversy in France: 1900–1914* (Calgary: University of Calgary, 1988), 119, quoting Gilbert Maire, "Crise pédagogique et anarchisme universitaire," *Mercure de France* 100 (1912): 278

4. John M. Cuddihy, *The Ordeal of Civility: Freud, Marx, Lévi-Strauss and the Jewish Struggle with Modernity* (Boston: Beacon, 1974), 8.

5. Peter Gay records the willingness of German Jews to stereotype 'Jewish' characteristics in equal measure as German anti-Semites. See Gay, *Freud, Jews, and Other Germans* (New York: Oxford University Press, 1978), 99. 101.

6. Émile Durkheim, *The Evolution of Educational Thought: Lectures on the Formation and Secondary Education in France,* 2d ed. (1938), trans. Peter Collins (London: Routledge and Kegan Paul, 1977).

7. Émile Durkheim, *Suicide* (1897), trans. John A. Spaulding and George Simpson (New York: Free Press, 1951), 55f., 158, 167, 170.

8. Durkheim, *The Evolution of Educational Thought,* 289. This was called to my attention by Robert Alun Jones and Douglas A. Kibbee,

"Durkheim, Language, and History: A Pragmatist Perspective," *Sociological Theory* 11 (1993): 164.

9. See in particular Durkheim's denial of the racial status of Jewishness, cited by Henri Peyre, "Durkheim: The Man, His Time, and His Intellectual Background," in Kurt H. Wolff, ed., *Essays on Sociology and Philosophy by Emile Durkheim et al.* (New York: Harper, 1960), 27. What physiognomic likenesses there may be are the results of social causes (28).

10. Ibid. Peyre cites Renan's *Le Judaisme comme race et comme religion* (Paris: Calmann Lévy, 1883).

11. Hubert showed, for example, that education could be extraordinarily formative in shaping human behavior. See Henri Hubert, "Introduction à la traduction française," in D. Chantepie de la Saussaye, *Manuel d'histoire des religions,* trans. Henri Hubert and Isidore Lévy (Paris: Colin, 1904), xxvii, xxix. Further, Hubert concurred with scholarly consensus showing that socialization can produce what would seem to be biologically rooted racial characteristics. In Hubert's view, if Armenians, Basques, Huguenots, Jews, etc., display physiological regularities, it must be because of the '*habitus*' created by their social isolation, frequent intermarriage, and continual occupation of a certain place (Henri Hubert, *L'Année sociologique* 5 [1902]: 187). Under Hubert's direction, race passes from a zoological to a sociological designation, thus, in principle, even breaking the monopoly of this supposedly zoological term within its own domain. For a fuller discussion of Hubert and racial science, see Ivan Strenski, *Religion in Relation: Theory, Application, and Moral Location* (London: Macmillan, 1993), ch. 10.

12. Vicki Caron, *Between France and Germany: The Jews of Alsace-Lorraine, 1871–1918* (Stanford: Stanford University Press, 1988), 191.

13. For a highly nuanced and complete treatment of Alsatian Jewish identity, see ibid.

14. Lewis A. Coser, *Masters of Sociological Thought* (New York: Harcourt, Brace and Jovanovich, 1971), 161–63; Durkheim, *Suicide,* 159f.

15. Michel Abitbol, *Les Deux terres promises: Les Juifs de France et le sionisme* (Paris: Olivier Orban, 1989).

16. On the general theme of Judaism as an embodied religion, see Howard Eilberg-Schwartz, *The Savage in Judaism* (Bloomington: Indiana University Press, 1990).

17. On Jewishness and Jewish religion, see Jacob Neusner, "Back to the Fold, Not to the Faith," *Los Angeles Times,* and David Brion Davis, "The Other Zion," *New Republic,* 12 April 1993, 29–36.

18. Mordecai M. Kaplan, *Judaism as a Civilization* (1934; Philadelphia: Jewish Publication Society of America, 1981), 333.

19. Indeed, Irving Kristol has argued just the opposite. See Irving

Kristol, "The Spiritual Roots of Capitalism and Socialism" and "The Disaffection with Capitalism," in Michael Novak, ed., *Capitalism and Socialism* (Washington, D.C.: American Enterprise Institute, 1979), 1–33.

20. Here, I have in mind Durkheim's defense of individualism in his celebrated "Individualism and the Intellectuals" (1898). Furthermore, for a thoughtful treatment of the place of the bourgeois revolutions of the nineteenth century and the character of newly emancipated Jews, see Pierre Vidal-Naquet, *The Jews: History, Memory, and the Present* (New York: Columbia University Press, 1996), 68.

21. Vogt, "The Politics of Academic Sociological Theory"; Brian J. Turner, "The Social Origins of Academic Sociology: Durkheim" (Ph.D. diss., Columbia University, 1977).

22. Vogt, "The Politics of Academic Sociological Theory," 24.

23. Ibid.

24. Jones and Kibbee, "Durkheim, Language, and History," 152–70.

25. Vogt, "The Politics of Academic Sociological Theory," 29.

26. Ibid., 35ff.

27. Émile Durkheim, "Individualism and the Intellectuals" (1898), in W. S. F. Pickering, ed., *Durkheim on Religion* (London: Routledge and Kegan Paul, 1975), ch. 4.

28. Vogt, "The Politics of Academic Sociological Theory," 32.

29. Ibid., 33.

30. Émile Durkheim, *Socialism* (1928), trans. Charlotte Sattler (New York: Collier, 1962), 285.

31. Turner, "The Social Origins of Academic Sociology," 277, 282, 292.

32. Ibid., 292, 324ff.

33. Ibid., 282.

34. Ibid., 271–73.

35. Jones and Kibbee, "Durkheim, Language, and History," 163.

36. Ibid., 164.

37. Ibid.

38. Ibid. (my emphasis).

39. Émile Durkheim, "La Philosophie dans les universités allemandes," *Revue internationale de l'enseignement* 24 (1887): 333, quoted in ibid., 163.

40. Ivan Strenski, *Four Theories of Myth in Twentieth-Century History* (Macmillan: London, 1987), ch. 3 and pp. 46–48, 67.

41. Turner, "The Social Origins of Academic Sociology," 144.

42. Perhaps due to Hamelin's interest in the socialist Hegel, the philosopher surprisingly took much the same stance against Cartesian

abstractness and individualism as did Durkheim and his societist fellow travelers. See Ivan Strenski, "Durkheim, Hamelin, and the 'French Hegel,' " *Historical Reflections/Refléxions Historiques* 16 (1989): 135–70.

43. Dominique Parodi, *La Philosophie contemporaine en France* (Paris: Alcan, 1919), 449.

44. See Hamelin's papers in the Bibliothèque Victor Cousin. Discussions of moral philosophy include Armand de Quatrefages's "Universality of Moral and Religious Sentiments" (October 1888) (Côte 352 C9), the undated notes entitled "Études critiques sur la morale de Kant" (côte 352 C9), and thirteen lectures of his "Cours de Morale" (côte 352 E), which range from 1883–84 to 1888.

45. Octave Hamelin, *Le Système de Renouvier* (Paris: Alcan, 1927), ch. 18, especially 356–58.

46. Ibid., 358.

47. Octave Hamelin, *Essai sur les éléments principaux de la représentation* (1907) (2d ed., Paris: Alcan, 1925), 451.

48. Ibid., 452.

49. Hamelin holds instead a theory of obligation in which it is reason itself that presents itself as obligatory (ibid., 450).

50. Ibid., 454.

51. See the correspondence between Charles Andler, Herr, and Hamelin in the Bibliothèque Victor Cousin (Côte 356/2a).

52. Yet he rejected what he called "absolute socialism" for moral reasons. See "Études critiques sur la morale de Kant" (Côte 352 C9), leçon V, Bibliothèque Victor Cousin. Hamelin added: "Our conception of justice is eminently socialist. . . . Social things always encompass a relation with something other than oneself!" (ibid.). Also see parallel passages in Hamelin, *Essai,* 451.

53. Marcel Mauss, introduction to the first edition of Durkheim, *Socialism,* 32.

54. "The goal of education, as Durkheim defined it, was to fulfill society's needs" (Turner, "The Social Origins of Academic Sociology," 85).

55. Ibid., quoting Durkheim, "Education," in Ferdinand Buisson, ed., *Nouveau Dictionaire de pédagogie et d'instruction primaire* (Paris: Hachette, 1911), 536.

56. John Dunn, "The Identity of the History of Ideas," *Philosophy* 43 (1968): 87–88.

57. Émile Durkheim and Ernest Lavisse, *Lettres à tous les français* (1916), ed. Michel Maffesoli (Paris: Armand Colin, 1992); Émile Durkheim, *"L'Allemagne au-dessus de tous": La Mentalité allemand et la guerre* (1915; Paris: Armand Colin, 1991).

58. Caron, *Between France and Germany,* 186, 187.

59. Salomon Reinach, *Cultes, mythes, et religions,* 1st ed., vol. 5 (Paris: Ernest Leroux, 1923), 438.

60. Deborah Dash Moore, "David Emile Durkheim and the Jewish Response to Modernity," *Modern Judaism* 6 (1980): 287–300.

61. Michel Despland, "A Case of Christians Shifting Their Moral Allegiance: France, 1790–1914," *Journal of the American Academy of Religion* 52 (1984): 672–90.

62. Ivan Strenski, "L'apport des élèves de Durkheim," *La tradition française en sciences religieuses,* ed. Michel Despland (Québec: Université Laval, 1991), 109–27.

63. Theodore Zeldin, *France, 1848–1945: Intellect and Pride* (Oxford: Oxford University Press, 1980), 224.

64. Eugen Weber, *The Nationalist Revival in France, 1905–1914* (Berkeley: University of California Press, 1959).

65. Steven Lukes, *Individualism* (Oxford: Basil Blackwell, 1973), ch. 2.

66. Workers did not escape nationalist criticism either; their particular class problem was entropy. See Weber, *The Nationalist Revival in France,* 57. On the general sense of malaise in France at the turn of the century couched in terms of the illness of 'degeneration,' see ibid. and Daniel Pick, *Faces of Degeneration* (Princeton: Princeton University Press, 1988).

67. Weber, *The Nationalist Revival in France,* 58.

68. Ibid.

69. Strenski, "Durkheim, Hamelin, and the 'French Hegel,'" 154–56; Turner, "The Social Origins of Academic Sociology," 273, 326.

70. Durkheim, "Individualism and the Intellectuals," 59–73.

71. Zeldin, *France, 1848–1945,* 273.

72. Ibid., 272.

73. Michael R. Marrus, *The Politics of Assimilation: A Study of the French Jewish Community at the Time of the Dreyfus Affair* (Oxford: Oxford University Press, 1971), 141f.

74. Charles Péguy, *Notre Jeunesse* (Paris: Gallimard, 1933), 68.

75. Notice especially Caron's decisive critiques of Marrus's contention that French Jews were naively patriotic: see Caron, *Between France and Germany,* ch. 9, and Marrus, *The Politics of Assimilation.*

76. Yosef Hayim Yerushalmi, *Zakhor: Jewish History and Jewish Memory* (Seattle: University of Washington Press, 1982), 101.

77. Caron, *Between France and Germany,* 192f.

78. Ibid., 188, 190.

79. See the excellent work done by the following: Marrus, *The Politics of Assimilation;* Phyllis C. Albert, *The Modernization of French Jewry: Consistory and Community in the Nineteenth Century* (Hanover, N.H.: Brandeis

University Press, 1977); Frances Malino and Phyllis Cohen Albert, eds., *Essays in Modern Jewish History* (Rutherford, N.J.: Fairleigh Dickinson University Press, 1982); Paula Hyman, *From Dreyfus to Vichy* (New York: Columbia University Press, 1979), 23–28; Stephen Wilson, *Ideology and Experience: Antisemitism in France at the Time of the Dreyfus Affair* (Rutherford, N.J.: Fairleigh Dickinson University Press, 1982); Nelly Wilson, *Bernard-Lazare* (Cambridge: Cambridge University Press, 1978).

80. Arthur Herztberg, *The French Enlightenment and the Jews* (New York: Columbia University Press, 1968), 9.

81. Gay, *Freud, Jews, and Other Germans,* 95.

82. Paula Hyman, "French Jewish Historiography since 1870," in Frances Malino and Bernard Wasserstrom, eds., *The Jews in Modern France* (Hanover, N.H.: University Press of New England, 1985), 335.

83. The Parisian Sanhedrin, "Doctrinal Decisions," in Paul Mendes-Flohr and Jehuda Reiharz, eds., *The Jew in the Modern World* (Oxford: Oxford University Press, 1980), 123–24.

84. Hyman, *From Dreyfus to Vichy,* 5.

85. The Parisian Sanhedrin, "Doctrinal Decisions," 123–24.

86. James Darmesteter, "Essay on the History of Judaism" (1880), *Selected Essays of James Darmesteter,* trans. Helen B. Jastrow, ed. Morris Jastrow Jr. (Boston: Houghton and Mifflin, 1895), 270.

87. My use of the term "becoming a religion" conforms generally with the idea of "differentiation" employed by Cuddihy in *The Ordeal of Civility,* 10–14.

88. Louis Dumont, "Religion, Politics, and Society in the Individualistic Universe," *Proceedings of the Royal Anthropological Institute for 1970* (London: Royal Anthropological Institute, 1971), 31–41.

89. On the growing importance of beliefs, see The Parisian Sanhedrin, "Doctrinal Decisions," 123–24.

90. Perrine Simon-Nahum, "Émergence et spécificité d'une 'Science du Judaisme' française (1840–1890)," in Frank Alvarez-Pereyre and Jean Baumgartner, eds., *Les Études juives en France* (Paris: Éditions CNRS, 1990), 23.

91. Zeldin, *France, 1848–1945,* 274; Abitbol, *Les Deux terres promises,* 21.

92. Zeldin, *France, 1848–1945,* 274. Consider first how anti-Semitism made Jews draw together in common defense and identity. Édouard Drumont's *La France juive* was published in 1886. In the two remaining decades of the nineteenth century, the widely circulated organ of the Assumptionist order, *La Croix,* led an anti-Semitic attack with the constant theme of accusing Jews of the fantastic crimes of Christ-killing and Jewish ritual murder. See Pierre Sorlin, *"La Croix" et les Juifs* (Paris:

Grasset, 1967), 132, 141, 143. See also Wilson, *Ideology and Experience*, ch. 14.

93. Caron, *Between France and Germany*, ch. 9.

94. Maurice Liber, "L'Ésprit du Christianisme et du Judaisme," *Revue des études juives* 51 (1906): 192, 205.

95. Ibid., 14. It is a prophetic religion, a religion of community and a religion of "practices."

96. Ibid., 192.

97. Henri Prague, editor's reply to an anonymous letter, *Archives israélites* 61 (6 September 1900): 891.

98. See, for instance, the spiritualist trends of liberal Protestantism, also a feature of Zeldin's conception of Cartesianism in Zeldin, *France, 1848–1945*, 224f. For an archetypal example of liberal Protestant spiritualism, see Albert Réville, "Contemporaneous Materialism in Religion: The Sacred Heart," *Theological Review* 44 (January 1874): 138–56.

99. Henri Prague, "La caractéristique du nouvel israelite," *Archives israélites* 66 (28 September 1905): 306.

100. Henri Prague, "La caractéristique du nouvel israelite," *Archives israélites* 66 (21 September 1905): 297.

101. Caron, *Between France and Germany*, 8f.

102. Hyman, *From Dreyfus to Vichy*, 45f.

103. Aleksander Hertz, *The Jews in Polish Culture* (1961), trans. Richard Lourie, ed. Lucjan Dobroszycki (Evanston: Northwestern University Press, 1988), 28.

104. Hyman, *From Dreyfus to Vichy*, 33, 42–46.

105. Ibid., 42f.

106. See the discussion of the Wissenschaft des Judentums and its relation to its French incarnation, the Science du Judaïsme, in chapter 4.

107. Durkheim and Lavisse, *Lettres;* Émile Durkheim, *L'Allemagne au-dessus de tout: La Mentalité allemande et la guerre* (Paris: Armand Colin, 1915).

108. James Darmesteter, *Les Prophètes d'Israel* (Paris: Calmann Lévy, 1892), iii.

109. Marrus, *The Politics of Assimilation*, 100f., 108.

110. Ibid., 108.

111. Caron, *Between France and Germany*, 192f.

112. Salomon Reinach, "Pendant et après la guerre" (1922), *Cultes, mythes, et religions*, 1st ed., vol. 5, p. 382. Despite its significance at the time, we know that Reinach's Franco-Jewish universalism gradually became discredited as both anti-Semitism and Zionism grew in strength. See Abitbol, *Les Deux terres promises.*

113. Weber, *The Nationalist Revival in France.*

114. On the persistence of religiously tinged nationalist feelings, see Paul Sabatier, *France To-day*, trans. H. B. Binns (London: J. M. Dent, 1913), 43, ch. 4, and Weber, *The Nationalist Revival in France.*

115. Weber, *The Nationalist Revival in France*, 102; J. A. Gunn, *Modern French Philosophy* (New York: Dodd, Mead, 1922), 278.

116. Gunn, *Modern French Philosophy*, 278.

117. Paul Gerbod, "L'Ethique héroique en France (1870–1914)," *Revue historique* 268 (1982): 414.

118. Ibid., 414, 419.

119. Hyppolite Prague, *Archives israëlites* 76 (8 April 1915): 53 and (13 May 1915): 77.

120. Extreme Jewish liberals such as Salomon Reinach, who was still shaped by the individualism of the Napoleonic conception of 'religion,' were deeply distressed by nationalism—whether Jewish or not. A paradigmatic skeptical Cartesian, Reinach identified any nationalism as a mindless form of mass thinking, a herdlike stampede of chauvinism. The cosmopolitan internationalism of the Enlightenment, which Reinach labored to encourage as essential to Jewish identity, was sure to suffer.

121. Reinach, "Pendant et après la guerre," 382.

122. Note, for example, the growth of literature on the saints of France, especially the patriotic manuals of hero saints and martyrs such as Abbé Profillet's *Les Saintes militaires* (1886), discussed by Gerbod, "L'Ethique héroique en France," 414.

123. Daniel Robert, "Les intellectuels d'origine non-protestante dans le protestantisme des débuts de la Troisième République," in André Encrevé and Michel Robert, eds., *Actes du colloque: Les protestants dans les debuts de la Troisième République (1871–1885)* (Paris: Société de l'histoire du protestantisme français, 1979), 95.

124. Stuart R. Schram, *Protestantism and Politics in France* (Alençon: Corbière et Jugan, 1954), 58.

125. Ibid., 57.

126. Philippe Landau, " 'La Patrie en danger': D'une guerre à l'autre," in Pierre Birnbaum, ed., *Histoire politique des juifs de France* (Paris: Presses de la Fondation Nationale des sciences politiques, 1990), 74–91.

127. Hyppolite Prague, "Politique juive et patriotisme antisemite," *Archives israëlites* 27 (4 July 1895): 209.

128. On Jew as outsider and pollutant, see Shmuel Trigano, "From Individual to Collectivity: The Rebirth of the 'Jewish Nation' in France," in Malino and Wasserstrom, *The Jews in Modern France*, 245–81.

129. Caron, *Between France and Germany*, 18.

130. Simon Deploige, "Le Conflit de la morale et de la sociologie," *Revue néo-scolastique* 12 (1905): 405–17. Articles in *Revue néo-scolastique* follow with the same title in volume 13 (1906): 49–79, 135–63, 281–313, and volume 14 (1907): 329–54, 355–92. See also Jones and Kibbee, "Durkheim, Language, and History," 152–70.

131. Hyppolite Prague, "Kippour et l'ésprit du sacrifice," *Archives israëlites* 77 (5 October 1916): 157.

132. Hyppolite Prague, "Purim," *Archives israëlites* 77 (16 March 1916): 41.

133. *Archives israëlites* 76 (8 April 1915): 53.

134. Ibid. 76 (15 July 1915): 114.

135. Ibid. 76 (28 October 1915): 173.

136. Armand Bloch, "Le patriotisme juif," *Allocution prononcée à l'inauguration de la statue de Jeanne D'Arc, Nancy 28 June 1890* (Nancy: Imprimerie Nouvelle, 1890).

137. Jacques Henri Dreyfuss, "L'Esprit de sacrifice" (Sermon, 15 September 1890, Israelite Temple, Bruxelles), 4. See also Marrus, *The Politics of Assimilation*, 111f.

138. Dreyfuss, "L'Esprit de sacrifice," Bruxelles, 5.

139. Prague, "Kippour et l'ésprit du sacrifice," 157.

140. Ibid., 159.

141. André Spire, *Les Juifs et la guerre* (Paris: Payot, 1917), 158. On Spire, see Abitbol, *Les Deux terres promises*, 82, and Hyman, *From Dreyfus to Vichy*.

142. Spire, *Les Juifs et la guerre*, 32.

143. Salomon Reinach, "Zadok-Kahn" (1908), *Cultes, mythes, et religions*, 1st ed., vol. 5, pp. 433–45. Among Zadok Kahn's claims to fame were not only his scholarship on Maimonides and slavery in the Bible and Talmud but also his role in unmasking Esterhazy's authorship of the infamous *"bordereau,"* which had led to the conviction of Dreyfus, and his foundation of the Société des Études Juives and its journal, *Revue des études juives*.

144. Zadok Kahn, *Allocution prononcée à l'occasion du départ des seminaristes israelites pour l'armée* (Paris: Imprimerie Réunies, 1892), 21.

145. Ibid., 25.

146. Ibid., 25.

147. Ibid., 27.

148. Ibid., 26.

149. Quoted in S. Halff, "The Participation of the Jews of France in the Great War," *American Jewish Yearbook* 21 (1919–20): 85f.

150. Spire, *Les juifs et la guerre*, 18f.

151. Sabatier, *France To-day*, 55.

152. Alfred Loisy, *La Religion* (Paris: Nourry, 1917), 315.

153. Ibid., 290.

154. Ibid., 33.

155. Maude D. Petre, *Alfred Loisy: His Religious Significance* (Cambridge: Cambridge University Press, 1944), 117.

156. Hyppolite Prague, "Religion et Patrie," *Archives israélites* 75 (5 November 1914): 265.

157. Ibid.

158. Hubert Bourgin, *De Jaurès a Leon Blum* (Paris: Artheme Fayard, 1938), 484.

159. Moore, "David Emile Durkheim," 287–300.

160. Dom Besse, *Les Religions laïques: Un romanticisme religieux* (Paris: Nouvelle Librairie Nationale, 1913), 22.

161. Weber, *The Nationalist Revival in France.*

162. Besse, *Les Religions laïques,* 32.

163. Ibid., ch. 6.

THREE

1. Further, this vision of reality lurking beneath symbol even informed two other central interests of Durkheim's: in morality and education. In *Moral Education,* Durkheim charts the way forward toward "a complete recasting" of the educational technique required to undertake effective moral education. There he says:

> We must discover those moral forces that men, down to the present time, have conceived of only under the form of religious allegories. We must disengage them from their symbols, present them in their rational nakedness, . . . and find a way to make the child feel their reality without recourse to any mythological intermediary. . . .
>
> We must discover, in the old system, moral forces hidden in it, hidden under the forms that concealed their intrinsic nature. We must make their true reality appear.

Émile Durkheim, *Moral Education* (1925), trans. Everett K. Wilson and Herman Schnurer (New York: Free Press, 1961), 11.

2. Émile Durkheim, review of *L'Irreligion de l'avenir* (1887), by Jean-Marie Guyau, in W. S. F. Pickering, ed., *Durkheim on Religion* (London: Routledge and Kegan Paul, 1975), 27–28.

3. Émile Durkheim, *The Elementary Forms of the Religious Life,* trans. Joseph W. Swain (New York: Free Press, 1915), 14. See also 356, where Durkheim says that religious interests are symbolic forms of social interests.

4. Robert Alun Jones and Douglas A. Kibbee, "Durkheim, Language, and History: A Pragmatist Perspective," *Sociological Theory* 11 (1993): 167. This entire article, along with earlier presentations of

Jones's historicist approach to Durkheim, outlines an approach to which I owe obvious debts.

5. Brian J. Turner, "The Social Origins of Academic Sociology: Durkheim" (Ph.D. diss., Columbia University, 1977), 145. See as well John Skorupski, *Symbol and Theory* (Cambridge: Cambridge University Press, 1976), 22–23. Skorupski, however, misnames Durkheim's approach as "positivist."

6. Jean-Claude Filloux, "Il ne faut pas oublier que je suis fils de rabbin," *Revue française de sociologie* 17 (1976): 260ff.

7. Albert Houtin and Felix Sartiaux, *Alfred Loisy: Sa vie, son oeuvre* (Paris: Editions du CNRS, 1960), 286, quoting from Alfred Loisy, *Mémoires: Volume 2* (Paris: Nourry, 1930), 568.

8. Romain Rolland, *Jean-Christophe*, vol. 2, trans. Gilbert Cannan (New York: Henry Holt, 1915), 51. The character of Schertz is drawn from the real-life figure of Abbé Marcel Hébert, one of Alfred Loisy's modernist comrades-in-arms.

9. Roger Martin du Gard, *Jean Barois* (Paris: Gallimard, 1921), 37–65.

10. Ibid., 59.

11. I use the terms 'liberalism' and 'modernism' synonymously primarily to short-circuit current polemics in literary circles surrounding the terms 'modernism,' 'postmodernism,' and such. 'Modernism' in the religious sense was first applied by the Vatican authorities to categorize and thus more easily deal with the burgeoning liberal movements in the Roman church. It is nonetheless a useful term for naming a plurality of individuals who happened to agree on a certain approach to religion. See Lester R. Kurtz, *The Politics of Heresy: The Modernist Crisis in Roman Catholicism* (Berkeley: University of California Press, 1986.

12. Henri Hubert, review of *Die Opferanshauung des späteren Judentums und die Opferaussagen des Neunen Testaments*, by O. Schmitz, *L'Année sociologique* 12 (1913): 221.

13. Instead of joining religious modernists in an internal reform of the traditional religions, however, the Durkheimians usurped them. The Durkheimians, in their ambivalent and competitive approach to the clerical modernists, repeat their similarly nuanced attitude to the Marxists. See, in particular, the disappointed reaction of Sorel to Durkheim. Once seen, by Sorel, as Marxism's great hope in France, Durkheim again and again showed that he would be Marxism's competition. See J. R. Jennings, *Georges Sorel* (London: Macmillan, 1985), 56.

14. Only Samuel Preus considers a possible religious context of symbolist approaches to social and religious reality, even if Judaism nowhere figures in his inquiry. For Preus, Durkheim's talk of symbols recalls "the classic formula of biblical hermeneutics, that the letter kills." J. Samuel Preus, *Explaining Religion* (New Haven: Yale University Press,

1987), 163 (emphasis added). But see my review of Preus, "Religious Studies, Naturalism, and the Persistence of Astrology," *Religion* 19 (1989): 317–23.

15. Dominick LaCapra argued some time ago that the example of Balzac's "visionary realism" sensitized Durkheim to the role of myth and symbol in culture. Dominick LaCapra, *Emile Durkheim: Sociologist and Philosopher* (Ithaca: Cornell University Press, 1972), 197.

16. Roger Shattuck, *The Banquet Years* (New York: Vintage, 1967).

17. Edward Tiryakian, "L'École durkheimienne a la recherche de la société perdue: La Sociologie naissante et son milieu culturel," *Cahiers internationaux de sociologie* 66 (1979): 106.

18. Ibid., 97–114.

19. Ibid., 108.

20. Ibid. 106.

21. Agathon (Henri Massis), *L'Esprit de la nouvelle Sorbonne,* 3d ed. (Paris: Mercure de France, 1911).

22. This was written by the mysterious "Agathon"—the shared pseudonym for the Bergsonians, Henri Massis, and Alfred de Tarde. Quoted in Steven Lukes, *Emile Durkheim* (New York: Harper and Row, 1972), 373.

23. Mark Antliff, *Inventing Bergson: Cultural Politics and the Parisian Avant-Garde* (Princeton: Princeton University Press, 1993), 149. See Robert C. Grogin's characterization of symbolism in *The Bergsonian Controversy in France: 1900–1914* (Calgary: University of Calgary, 1988).

24. Antliff, *Inventing Bergson.*

25. Émile Durkheim, *Suicide* (1897), trans. John A. Spaulding and George Simpson (New York: Free Press, 1951), 370, quoted in Grogin, *The Bergsonian Controversy in France,* 38.

26. Durkheim, *Elementary Forms of the Religious Life,* 14.

27. Durkheim cited in Turner, "The Social Origins of Academic Sociology," 145.

28. Durkheim cited in ibid., 145, reported in *La Petite Gironde,* 24 May 1901.

29. W. S. F. Pickering, *Durkheim's Sociology of Religion: Themes and Theories* (London: Routledge and Kegan Paul, 1984), 277.

30. In *L'Année sociologique,* the arts fall under the rubric of "technology" or the "phenomenon of representation."

31. I thank M. Girard Hubert for his kindness in granting me access to his father's artwork.

32. Henri Hubert, review of *L'Art dans l'Afrique australe* (1911), by Fr. Christol, *L'Année sociologique* 12 (1913): 846. Later, however, in 1925, Hubert loosened up a bit in a review of what he called Paulcke's "moderniste" *Steinzeit Kunst und Moderne Kunst* (1923). There, he agreed that the comparison between paleolithic cave art and contemporary

primitivist art suggested some common "instinct" between the two sorts of artists who created the works. Henri Hubert, review of *Steinzeit Kunst und Moderne Kunst* (1923), by W. Paulcke, *L'Année sociologique*, n.s., 1 (1925): 961.

33. For the general connection between Bergson and symbolism, see Antliff, *Inventing Bergson*. Something of the same might also be said of the altogether conspicuous interests in the avant-garde art world by even leading Jewish rationalists of the time, like Salomon Reinach. See Salomon Reinach and Max Jacob, *Lettres à Liane de Pougy* (Paris: Plon, 1980).

34. Durkheim, review of *L'Irreligion de l'avenir*, 27–28.

35. Peter Brown, *Authority and the Sacred* (Cambridge: Cambridge University Press, 1995), 11.

36. Émile Durkheim, "Contribution to Discussion 'Religious Sentiment at the Present Time' " (1919), in Pickering, *Durkheim on Religion*, 181–89.

37. Ibid.

38. Donald A. Nielsen, "Auguste Sabatier and the Durkheimians on the Scientific Study of Religion," *Sociological Analysis* 47 (1987): 283–301.

39. Alfred Loisy, "Sociologie et religion," *Revue d'histoire et de littérature religieuses*, n.s., 4 (1913): 45–76; Pickering, *Durkheim's Sociology of Religion*, 143–44.

40. Martin du Gard, *Jean Barois*, 58.

41. Loisy, "Sociologie et religion," 69.

42. Marcel Hébert, *Revue d'histoire et de littérature religieuses*, n.s., 1 (1909): 71.

43. Paul Legay, *Revue d'histoire et de littérature religieuses* 7 (1902): 281 (emphasis added).

44. Jones refers to Durkheim's belief that scientific study was "morally edifying." Jones and Kibbee, "Durkheim, Language, and History," 165.

45. Louis M. Greenberg, "Bergson and Durkheim as Sons and Assimilators: The Early Years," *French Historical Studies* 9 (1976): 625.

46. Of course, we cannot talk of religious 'modernism' without speaking of religious 'liberalism.' Modernism is one species of liberalism. French Jewish modernism grew naturally out of the spirit of Jewish liberalism and traced its roots to such nineteenth-century figures as Michel Berr, Joseph Salvador, and James Darmesteter. See Salomon Reinach, "James Darmesteter," *Cultes, mythes, et religions*, 1st ed., vol. 5 (Paris: Ernest Leroux, 1923), 414–32.

47. See also Georges Sorel: "La Religion d'aujourd'hui," *Revue de metaphysique et de morale* 17 (1909): 422, 429, and "La Crise de la pensée catholique," *Revue de metaphysique et de morale* 10 (1902): 547.

48. Alfred Loisy, *My Duel with the Vatican* (1924; reprint, New York: Greenwood, 1968), 245.

49. Turner, "The Social Origins of Academic Sociology," 145.

50. Examples of this approach were Durkheim's devotion to concreteness and the notorious notion of 'things' in *The Rules*, which figured in Robert Alun Jones's treatment of Durkheimian societism in the previous chapter. See Jones and Kibbee, "Durkheim, Language, and History," 164. Jones's view comes close to Skorupski's in *Symbol and Theory*, 22–23.

51. Durkheim served on the board of examiners of Louis-Germain Lévy's thesis and, as one might imagine, was especially critical of Lévy's attempt to shield Judaism from the full force of comparison with 'primitive' religion. See Lukes, *Emile Durkheim*, 626–29.

52. Louis-Germain Lévy, *Une Religion rationelle et laïque: La Religion du XXe siecle* (Dijon: Barbier-Marillier, 1904); Dom Besse, *Les Religions laïques: Un romanticisme religieux* (Paris: Nouvelle Librairie Nationale, 1913), 113.

53. Louis-Germain Lévy, *La Famille dans l'antiquité Israëlite* (Paris: Alcan, 1905).

54. Houtin and Sartiaux, *Alfred Loisy*, 286, quoting from Loisy, *Mémoires: Volume 2*, 568.

55. Salomon Reinach, "Réponse aux 'Archives Isralites' sur le même question" (1900), *Cultes, mythes, et religions*, 1st ed., vol. 2, p. 16.

56. Besse, *Les Religions laïques*, 198.

57. The humanist Paul Doumer explicitly spoke of creating such a religion. See Eugen Weber, *The Nationalist Revival in France, 1905–1914* (Berkeley: University of California Press, 1959), 36.

58. Sorel, "La Religion d'aujourd'hui," 240–73, 413–47, and Georges Sorel, "Modernisme dans la religion et dans le socialisme," *Revue critique des idées et des livres* 2 (1908): 177–204. See also Besse, *Les Religions laïques*.

59. The link between modernism and symbolic interpretation is widely attested in the contemporary literature. See: Sorel, "La Religion d'aujourd'hui," 441, also 414, 442; Besse, *Les Religions laïques*, 54, 63f., 121; and Donald A. Nielsen, "Robert Hertz and the Sociological Study of Sin, Expiation, and Religion: A Neglected Chapter in the Durkheimian School," in Richard C. Monk, ed., *Structures of Knowing* (New York: University Press of America, 1986), 7–50.

60. Houtin and Sartiaux, *Alfred Loisy*, 286, quoting from Loisy, *Mémoires: Volume 2*, 568.

61. Martin du Gard, *Jean Barois*, 58.

62. Ibid., 59.

63. Isaac Benrubi, *Contemporary Thought in France*, trans. Ernest B. Dicker (London: Williams and Norgate, 1926), 202.

64. Phyllis Cohen Albert, "Nonorthodox Attitudes in Nineteenth Century French Judaism," in Frances Malino and Phyllis Cohen Albert, eds., *Essays in Modern Jewish History* (Rutherford, N.J.: Fairleigh Dickinson University Press, 1982), 123. The year 1907 marks the foundation of the first reformed Jewish synagogue in Paris by the Union Libérale Israëlite.

65. Jean-Marc Chouraqui, "Judaisme traditionnel, science et rationalisme: L'Exemple des rabbins français au XIXe siècle," in Frank Alvarez-Pereyre and Jean Baumgartner, eds., *Les études juives en France* (Paris: Éditions CNRS, 1990), 44.

66. Returning to a theme from the previous chapter, we can see that conservatives reacted to the fact of Jewry's 'becoming a religion' by accepting the limitations placed on Jewish peoplehood. They concluded that being Jewish was best served by drawing the community further into itself in terms of disciplined legal and ritual observance. Although deprived of peoplehood, the conservatives maintained a degree of religious 'embodiment' in the form of extensive and ramified ritual life, extending into all aspects of daily life. I fully realize that this line of argument seems to accept typically uncomplimentary descriptions of Judaism as 'carnal' or 'materialistic.' But today, we perhaps find their attitudes more sympathetic. Our sensibilities have changed, so that we view ourselves and our world in a more robust way. To call a religion only 'spiritual' or to characterize it as '*dis*embodied' is becoming the new pejorative. For better or for ill, we look on the body and materiality as aspects of a fuller reality. To us, speaking of a purely spiritual religion is to speak of a desiccated, sterile, and ineffectual religion. So if Judaism feels religion should be embodied, then we might say that today religious sensibility has in this way caught up with the Jews. The same might also be said about the implications of embodiment in religion for the larger question of the relation of religion and politics, especially nationalism. The metaphor of embodiment is also being increasingly used in literature on French Jews. See Paul Morris, "The Embodied Text: Covenant and Torah," *Religion* 20 (1990): 77–87. Michael A. Meyer interprets the movement in Jewish historiography from idealism to a greater sociological or material orientation as a leading trend of the nineteenth century. Of the great nineteenth-century Jewish historian Heinrich Graetz, Meyer says that in proposing a plan for Jewish historiography, Graetz did not give his attention "to the idea apart from the people that embodied it." Michael A. Meyer, *Ideas of Jewish History* (New York: Behrman, 1974), 28.

67. Albert, "Nonorthodox Attitudes in Nineteenth Century French Judaism," 124. Albert explains that the Menhagim are customs that the orthodox consider "binding."

68. On Salvador, see ibid., 126f. Also see Michael R. Marrus, *The*

Politics of Assimilation: A Study of the French Jewish Community at the Time of the Dreyfus Affair (Oxford: Oxford University Press, 1971).

69. For Durkheim's arguments with Louis-Germain Lévy, see Lukes, *Emile Durkheim*, 626–29, in which Durkheim takes Lévy to task as examiner of the latter's 1905 doctoral dissertation. Reflecting perhaps Munk's influence, Durkheim, for example, noted, "Sometimes Lévy allows himself to think that the Jewish people was a people apart" (627). By this Durkheim meant in part that Lévy gave no place to totemism in understanding the nature and growth of Jewish institutions. He, for example, had insisted that the ancient Jewish family had not evolved in the same way as families in totemic societies (628). These arguments also appeared in Lévy's 1904 article "Du totemisme chez les Hébreux," *Revue des études juives* 49 (1904): 13–26. Salomon Reinach, "L'Émancipation intérieure du Judaïsme" (1900), *Cultes, mythes, et religions*, 3d ed., vol. 2 (Paris: Ernest Leroux, 1928), 420.

70. Reinach, "L'Émancipation intérieure du Judaïsme," 419.

71. Ibid.

72. Reinach, "James Darmesteter," 414–32.

73. Durkheim, *Elementary Forms of the Religious Life*, 97–102.

74. Son of a poor bookbinder of Lorraine, James Darmesteter was reared in an orthodox Jewish home, where he received a classic Jewish education in texts and Jewish cultural lore. In 1852, the family migrated to Paris, where James's father believed that his children would be better positioned for careers in the professions. Thanks to both his traditional education in Hebrew and Talmud, James was well prepared to work in the field of Oriental philology, in which he eventually made for himself a great career. He soon became the greatest Avestan and Zoroastrian scholar of his generation. After Renan's death, some even called him the most distinguished scholar in France.

But Darmesteter was more than a philologist. A poet, a folklorist, a devotee of English literature, and a man of broad personal cultivation, he is best remembered as an Orientalist. He composed and published several articles and books of verse in English, the most remarkable of which was a volume of verses celebrating the higher meaning of Jesus. While in Persia and India, he found time to collect Afghanistani popular songs, partly for his own amusement and partly because he felt they showed traces of the Zend-Avestan language. He also published an important essay on Afghan life based on these songs. Late in life he served as chief editor of the illustrious literary and political magazine *La Revue de Paris*. See Morris Jastrow Jr., "Editor's Preface," in James Darmesteter, *Selected Essays of James Darmesteter*, trans. Helen B. Jastrow, ed. Morris Jastrow Jr. (Boston: Houghton and Mifflin, 1895), v–xv.

Darmesteter was closely linked with the main figures in the broader field of the study of religion, men of the generation bordering on the rise of the Durkheimians. Devoted throughout his life to his teacher Ernest Renan, Darmesteter was known affectionately in the liberal Jewish press as "un Renan Juif" and was the subject of an article entitled "Un Renan Juif: James Darmesteter (1849–1894)." See Jean Muzlak-May, *L'Univers Israëlite* 90/10 (29 November 1935): 151–52. This article began a series of seven, which ran in *L'Univers Israëlite* from 90 (29 November 1935) through 91/11–12, 91/16–19.

75. Two pieces especially should be noted: James Darmesteter, *Les Prophètes d'Israel* (Paris: Calmann Lévy, 1892), and James Darmesteter, "The Religions of the Future," *Selected Essays*, 1–15.

76. James Darmesteter, "La guerre et la paix intérieures (1871 à 1893)," *Critique et politique* (Paris: Calmann Lévy, 1895), 261.

77. Darmesteter, *Les Prophètes d'Israel*, vi.

78. Ibid., 12–14.

79. Ibid., 12.

80. See Jean Réville's review of *Les Prophètes d'Israel*, by Darmesteter, *Revue d'histoire des religions* 25 (1892): 253–56.

81. Lévy, *Une Religion rationelle et laïque*, 65.

82. Ibid.

83. Ibid., 65.

84. James Darmesteter, "Essay on the History of Judaism" (1880), *Selected Essays*, 261.

85. Lévy, *Une Religion rationelle et laïque*, 61.

86. Ibid., 26.

87. Ibid., epigram, citing Darmesteter, *Les Prophètes d'Israel*.

88. Lévy, *Une Religion rationelle et laïque*, 41.

89. Sorel, "Modernisme dans la religion et dans le socialisme," 200. We know that movements of religious modernism, featuring their symbolic approaches to dogmas, were significant in the cultural and religious worlds of the day. Romain Rolland's *Jean-Christophe* speaks of the "clerical symbolists . . . who reproduced the ideas of Kant in allegorical pictures." Romain Rolland, *Jean-Christophe*, vol. 2, trans. Gilbert Cannan (New York: Henry Holt, 1915), 51.

90. Houtin and Sartiaux, *Alfred Loisy*, 286, quoting from Loisy, *Mémoires: Volume 2*, 251.

91. Ibid., 252f.

92. Reinach and Jacob, *Lettres à Liane de Pougy*. See as well Reinach's reviews of Loisy's works in Reinach, *Cultes, mythes, et religions*, 3d ed., vol. 1, pp. 410–14, and Salomon Reinach, "De Bello Orphico," *Cultes, mythes, et religions*, 1st ed., vol. 5, pp. 438–85.

93. Salomon Reinach, "L'Evolution en théologie," *L'Anthropologie* (1903), reprinted in Reinach, *Cultes, mythes, et religions*, 3d ed., vol. 1, p. 414.

94. In this sense, pace Tiryakian, it is Reinach, not Durkheim, who

should show us "structural ambivalence." Ambivalence seems utterly lacking in Durkheim's identity as Jewish—he simply discounted it. Salomon Reinach, on the other hand, is full of unresolved tensions in being Jewish, especially after the Dreyfus Affair, when the bases of his liberalism began to erode.

95. Salomon's father, Baron Jacques Reinach, was an unhappy party to the scandal surrounding the Panama investment fraud of the late 1880s.

96. Michel Abitbol, *Les Deux terres promises: Les Juifs de France et le sionisme* (Paris: Olivier Orban, 1989), 86.

97. Henri Hubert, review of *Orpheus,* by Salomon Reinach, *L'Anthropologie* 20 (1909): 594 and *L'Année sociologique* 11 (1910): 72–73. In addition to Reinach's ambitions in popular letters, he was also a classical archaeologist and curator of the Musée des Antiquités Nationales at St. Germain-en-Laye. Henri Hubert served for some years as Reinach's assistant before finally succeeding him.

98. See Salomon Reinach's correspondence with Liane de Pougy, a sought-after woman of his day; these letters were published together in a volume of correspondence also including letters exchanged between her and Max Jacob. Reinach and Jacob, *Lettres à Liane de Pougy.* For his views on the relation of sex and marriage, see Salomon Reinach, "Une Mystique au XXe siècle, Antoinette Bourignon" (1894), *Cultes, mythes, et religions,* 3d ed., vol. 1, ch. 35.

99. Henri Hubert, review of *Cultes, mythes, et religions,* vol. 5, by Salomon Reinach, *L'Année sociologique* 9 (1906): 174.

100. Salomon Reinach, "The Growth of Mythological Study," *Quarterly Review* 215 (1911): 438.

101. See, for example, the first number of *L'Année sociologique* (1898), containing many reviews on subjects such as incest, totemism, and magic.

102. Durkheim, "Contribution to Discussion," 181–89.

103. Reinach, "Réponse aux 'Archives Israélites,' " 16.

104. Durkheim, "Contribution to Discussion," 181–89.

105. Reinach, "L'Émancipation intérieure du Judaïsme," 436. Also see his confession of faith, "Pourquoi je suis juif," *L'Univers israélite,* 13 April 1928, 135. We do, however, find Henri Hubert waxing poetic about *religion,* using the same metaphor of the tree.

> In the midst of social life, religion has sprung up. It has burst into blossoms of prayer, sacrifice, mythology, morality, metaphysics, and even extravagant growths of magic. This tree has but a single trunk and its main branches are mighty. But so weighty are they that they bend to the ground. There, having taken root like the banyan, new branches spring up and hide the central

trunk. As seasons pass and perspectives shift, the original shape of this tree changes so that one is hardly able to recognize it. Philosophers and historians mistake the tree for a forest—their error repeats the mistake of the early naturalists who defined beings in terms of external traits. But now we must clear way the branches and penetrate their sultry shade in order to catch a glimpse of the trunk.

Henri Hubert, "Introduction à la traduction française," in D. Chantepie de la Saussaye, *Manuel d'histoire des religions*, trans. Henri Hubert and Isidore Lévy (Paris: Colin, 1904), xlviii.

106. The case of Salomon Reinach thus confirms Phyllis Albert's thesis of the noteworthy degree of communal identification with Jewishness displayed even by some of those most committed to the values of the Enlightenment emancipation. See Phyllis C. Albert, "Ethnicity and Jewish Solidarity in the Nineteenth Century," in J. Reinharz and D. Swetschinski, eds., *Mystics, Philosophers, and Politicians* (Durham: Duke University Press, 1982).

107. Seymour De Ricci, "Salomon Reinach," *Revue des études juives* 94 (1933): 6.

108. This distaste for the hygienic habits of the new Jews was, for Reinach, literally true. He made a special point of attacking the lack of hygiene among the new Jewish immigrants to France, whereas these same pious folk went to scrupulous lengths to ensure ritual cleanliness. See Reinach, *Cultes, mythes, et religions*, 1st ed., vol. 2, pp. 426, 429. See also similar expressions of Reinach's disgust for Tunisian Jews in Michel Abitbol's account of Reinach's February 1884 report to the Alliance: "The Encounter between French Jewry and the Jews of North Africa: Analysis of a Discourse (1830–1914)," in Frances Malino and Bernard Wasserstrom, eds., *The Jews in Modern France* (Hanover, N.H.: University Press of New England, 1985), 48f.

109. Salomon Reinach, *Orpheus*, trans. Florence Simmonds (New York: Liveright, 1930), 224.

110. Salomon Reinach, "La pretendue race juive" (1903), *Cultes, mythes, et religions*, 1st ed., vol. 3, pp. 470–71.

111. Marrus, *The Politics of Assimilation*, 161–62.

112. Paula Hyman, "French Jewish Historiography since 1870," in Malino and Wasserstrom, *The Jews in Modern France*, 335.

113. Paula Hyman, *From Dreyfus to Vichy* (New York: Columbia University Press, 1979), 23–28.

114. Hubert, review of *Orpheus* (in *L'Anthropologie*), 594.

115. Henri Hubert, review of *Cultes, mythes, et religions*, vol. 2, by Salomon Reinach, *L'Année sociologique* 10 (1907): 219.

116. Hubert, review of *Orpheus* (in *L'Anthropologie*), 595.

117. Hubert, review of *Orpheus* (in *L'Année sociologique*), 73.

118. Salomon Reinach, review of *The Elementary Forms of the Religious Life*, by Émile Durkheim, in *Cultes, mythes, et religions*, 1st ed., vol. 4, pp. ii–v.

119. Émile Durkheim, "Concerning the Definition of Religious Phenomena," (1899), in Pickering, *Durkheim on Religion*, 74–99.

120. Reinach, review of *The Elementary Forms of the Religious Life*, iv.

121. Hubert, review of *Orpheus* (in *L'Anthropologie*), 594.

122. Reinach, review of *The Elementary Forms of the Religious Life*, iv.

123. Hubert, review of *Orpheus* (in *L'Anthropologie*), 594.

124. Ibid., 596.

125. Henri Hubert, review of *Cultes, mythes, et religions*, vol. 4, by Salomon Reinach, *L'Année sociologique* 12 (1913): 80.

126. Or as Pickering puts it, the "sacred-profane" (Pickering, *Durkheim's Sociology of Religion*, chs. 7–9).

127. Henri Hubert and Marcel Mauss, "Introduction à l'analyse de quelques phénomènes religieux" (1906), *Marcel Mauss: Oeuvres*, vol. 1, *Les Fonctions sociales du sacré*, ed. Victor Karady (Paris: Minuit, 1968), 16.

128. Ibid., 17.

129. Hubert and Mauss, in fact, rather than Durkheim himself, engineered this conceptual shift. In 1906, they attacked Reinach's negative definition of religion and replaced it with their positive definition of religion in terms of the sacred (ibid., 3–6).

130. Ibid., 16.

131. Hubert, review of *Orpheus* (in *L'Anthropologie*), 594.

132. Victor Karady, "The Durkheimians in Academe: A Reconsideration," in Philippe Besnard, ed., *The Sociological Domain* (Cambridge: Cambridge University Press, 1983), 71–89.

133. Ibid.

134. See, for example, the diplomacy toward the Church in Henri Hubert, review of *L'Evangile et l'Église*, by Alfred Loisy, *L'Année sociologique* 8 (1905): 290–92.

135. Émile Durkheim, "Pragmatism and Sociology" (1914), in Kurt H. Wolff, ed., *Essays on Sociology and Philosophy by Emile Durkheim et al.* (New York: Harper, 1960), 396.

136. See Hubert's diplomatic review of *L'Evangile et l'Église*, 290–92.

137. Loisy, *Mémoires: Volume 2*, 29–34.

138. Letter of Henri Hubert to Marcel Mauss, n.d., 1898, Mauss Archives, Collège de France. I thank Marcel Fournier for this citation. See also Marcel Fournier and Christine De Langle, "Autour du sacrifice: Lettres d'Emile Durkheim, J. G. Frazer, M. Mauss, et E. B. Tylor," *Études durkheimiennes/Durkheim Studies* 3 (1991): 2–9.

FOUR

1. Edward Tiryakian, "Emile Durkheim," in Tom Bottomore and Robert Nisbet, eds., *A History of Sociological Analysis* (New York: Basic Books, 1978), 233 n. 106. See also Edward Tiryakian, "L'École durkheimienne a la recherche de la société perdue: La Sociologie naissante et son milieu culturel," *Cahiers internationaux de sociologie* 66 (1979): 112.

2. Tiryakian, "L'École durkheimienne," 97–114, esp. 112.

3. Ibid., 97–114, and Tiryakian, "Emile Durkheim," 187–236. Note in particular Robert Alun Jones's citation of Tiryakian in "Robertson Smith, Durkheim, and Sacrifice: An Historical Context for *The Elementary Forms of the Religious Life*," *Journal for the History of the Behavioral Sciences* 17 (1981): 197.

4. Robert Alun Jones and Douglas A. Kibbee, "Durkheim, Language, and History: A Pragmatist Perspective," *Sociological Theory* 11 (1993): 152–70.

5. Ivan Strenski, *Religion in Relation: Theory, Application, and Moral Location* (London: Macmillan, 1993), 186–89.

6. Salomon Reinach notes sarcastically how often he had been accused of anti-Semtisim in his "L'Émancipation intérieure du Judaïsme" (1900), *Cultes, mythes, et religions*, 3d ed., vol. 2 (Paris: Ernest Leroux, 1928), 433. For Wellhausen, see Leon Poliakov, *The Aryan Myth* (New York: New American Library, 1971), 310, and on Lagarde, see Fritz Stern, *The Politics of Cultural Despair* (Berkeley: University of California Press, 1961), chs. 1–6. Their student William Robertson Smith shared this prevailing liberal view of degenerate Talmudic Judaism and pristine primitive Hebrew religion.

7. Alexandre Derczansky, "Note sur la Judéité de Durkheim," *Archives des sciences sociales des religions* 35/69 (1990): 157–60; Jean-Claude Filloux, "Il ne faut pas oublier que je suis fils de rabbin," *Revue française de sociologie* 17 (1976): 259–66; Louis M. Greenberg, "Bergson and Durkheim as Sons and Assimilators: The Early Years," *French Historical Studies* 9 (1976): 619–34; Eugen Schoenfeld and Stjepan Meštrović, "Durkheim's Concept of Justice and Its Relationship to Social Solidarity," *Sociological Analysis* 50 (1989): 111–27.

8. Schoenfeld and Meštrović, "Durkheim's Concept of Justice," 113; Derczansky, "Note sur la Judéité de Durkheim," 158.

9. Derczansky, "Note sur la Judéité de Durkheim," 158.

10. See especially the "hymns to society" in Émile Durkheim, *Moral Education* (1925), trans. Everett K. Wilson and Herman Schnurer (New York: Free Press, 1961), 69–79, 88–91. See also Émile Durkheim, *The Elementary Forms of the Religious Life,* trans. Joseph W. Swain (New York:

Free Press, 1915), 236–45, and Filloux, "Il ne faut pas oublier que je suis fils de rabbin," 260–62.

11. Durkheim, *Moral Education,* 217. Indeed, if we believe Wallwork, Durkheim held that "love" or "altruism" was the "ultimate justification of moral standards." See Ernest Wallwork, "Sentiment and Structure: A Durkheimian Critique of Kohlberg's Moral Theory," *Journal of Moral Education* 14 (1985): 91.

12. Rather than citing Charles Renouvier or Octave Hamelin in connection with Durkheim's moral philosophy, Schoenfeld and Meštrović, "Durkheim's Concept of Justice," raise the example of Tönnies as "expressing the dominant sentiment of the age" (118).

13. J. A. Gunn, *Modern French Philosophy* (New York: Dodd, Mead, 1922), 236.

14. Octave Hamelin, *Le Système de Renouvier* (Paris: Alcan, 1927), 382–83.

15. Ibid., 382.

16. Gunn, *Modern French Philosophy,* 239.

17. Émile Durkheim, "The Dualism of Human Nature and Its Social Conditions" (1914), in K. Wolff, ed., *Emile Durkheim: Essays on Sociology and Philosophy* (New York: Harper and Row, 1964), 329.

18. Ibid., 328.

19. Ivan Strenski, "Durkheim, Hamelin, and the 'French Hegel,' " *Historical Reflections/Refléxions historiques* 16 (1989): 153–55.

20. Derczansky, "Note sur la Judéité de Durkheim," 158.

21. Greenberg, "Bergson and Durkheim," 625.

22. The social arm of the *Revue des études juives,* the Société des Études Juives, listed some fellows of Durkheim's *équipe,* such as Lucien Lévy-Bruhl and Isidore Lévy (one of Hubert's students and coworkers); but Durkheim and Mauss are not to be found in the membership lists. Isidore Lévy was also a member of the editorial boards of both *L'Année sociologique* and *Revue des études juives.*

23. Perrine Simon-Nahum, "Émergence et spécificité d'une 'Science du Judaisme' française (1840–1890)," in Frank Alvarez-Pereyre and Jean Baumgartner, eds., *Les Études juives en France* (Paris: Éditions CNRS, 1990), 32.

24. Immanuel Wolf, "On the Concept of a Science of Judaism" (1822), in Paul Mendes-Flohr and Jehuda Reiharz, eds., *The Jew in the Modern World,* (Oxford: Oxford University Press, 1980), 194.

25. "Wissenschaft des Judentums," *Encyclopedia Judaica,* vol. 16 (New York: Macmillan, 1971), 576.

26. Phyllis C. Albert, *The Modernization of French Jewry: Consistory and Community in the Nineteenth Century* (Hanover, N.H.: Brandeis University Press, 1977), 246. Acceptance of Geiger's proposal would in effect have

given Judaism official recognition in the Reich and, with it, recognition of (at least some) Jewish authority in the modern world over the study and interpretation of Judaism.

27. Ibid., 251.

28. *Encyclopedia Judaica* gives 1838 as the year Geiger organized the group that was to become known under the banner of the Wissenschaft des Judentums (vol. 16, p. 577).

29. Albert, *The Modernization of French Jewry*, 250.

30. Although Hartwig's father, Joseph Derenbourg, taught the material included in Israël Lévi's commission from at least the 1870s, this was under the aegis of the philological section of the École Pratique des Hautes Études. Such an institutional location did not, apparently, limit Derenbourg's scope to matters of strict philology—even if the creation of Israël Lévi's chair in the religious sciences section represents a formal recognition of the dignity of Talmudic subject matter.

31. There is evidence that government approval of the new *séminaire* was influenced by the belief that such an institution would be more 'enlightened' than the old Talmudic school in Metz—even when transferred to the secular setting of Paris. See Albert, *The Modernization of French Jewry*, 249.

32. Ibid., 252.

33. In 1849, the French national assembly rejected the idea of a Jewish theological school in Paris under governmental administration—here ignoring the precedents of the Roman Catholic and Protestant *facultés*, which already existed in the capital. Nonetheless, the government continued to support the Talmudic school in Metz. Thus, in 1859, the idea of such a theological school in Paris was finally abandoned by its Jewish proponents. See ibid., 246f.

34. Ibid., 251.

35. Ibid., 252.

36. Israël Lévi, *Rapport moral et financier sur le séminaire israëlite et le Talmud-Thora, précédé d'une histoire des Juifs de France* (Paris: Imprimerie Ed. Lyon, 1903), 34–39.

37. Albert, *The Modernization of French Jewry*, 251. Durkheim's father seems to have completed his education far too early for the new influences from Germany to have formed him. See Steven Lukes, *Emile Durkheim* (New York: Harper and Row, 1972), 39.

38. Phyllis Cohen Albert, "Nonorthodox Attitudes in Nineteenth Century French Judaism," in Frances Malino and Phyllis Cohen Albert, eds., *Essays in Modern Jewish History* (Rutherford, N.J.: Fairleigh Dickinson University Press, 1982), 128.

39. Ibid., 135.

40. Maurice Level, "Sylvain Lévi," *L'Univers Israëlite* 91/7 (8 Novem-

ber 1935): 97. As a young man, Lévi taught first at the Séminaire. Zadok Kahn was reported to have asked Sylvain Lévi to be the religious tutor to his own children (97).

41. Jacob Neusner, *Take Judaism for Example: Studies toward the Comparison of Religions* (Chicago: University of Chicago Press, 1983).

42. Simon-Nahum, "Émergence et spécificité d'une 'Science du Judaisme' française," 26.

43. This fact was celebrated by the editors of the *Monatschrift* on the occasion of the inaugural publication of the *Revue*. See *Monatschrift für Geschichte und Wissenschaft des Judentums* 30 (1881): 459–70. Throughout the years, the *Monatschrift* noted the publications of its French counterpart, especially the Derenbourgs. However, nothing of the publications of the Durkheimians was noted in the *Monatschrift*.

44. The Editors, "A Nos lecteurs," *Revue des études juives* 1 (1880): vii.

45. Ibid., viii.

46. Ibid., vii.

47. *Encyclopedia Judaica*, vol. 14, p. 134.

48. The Editors, "A Nos lecteurs," vi.

49. Ibid., v.

50. Ibid., vii.

51. Louis-Germain Lévy, "Du totemism chez les Hébreux," *Revue des études juives* 45 (1902): 13–26.

52. Salomon Reinach, "L'Origine des prières pour les morts," *Cultes, mythes, et religions*, 3d ed., vol. 1, pp. 316–31; Salomon Reinach, "L'Inquisition et le Juifs," *Cultes, mythes, et religions*, 3d ed., vol. 2, pp. 401–17; Salomon Reinach, "La Prétendue race juive," *Cultes, mythes, et religions*, 3d ed., vol. 3, pp. 457–71; Salomon Reinach, "L'Accusation du meurtre rituel en 1892," *Cultes, mythes, et religions*, 1st ed., vol. 5 (Paris: Ernest Leroux, 1923), 451–74.

53. Israël Lévi, "Le sacrifice d'Isaac et la mort de Jésus," *Revue des études juives* 64 (1912): 161–84. Sylvain Lévi published his comparative inquiries of Judaism and Hinduism there. See Sylvain Lévi, "Problèmes indo-hébraïques," *Revue des études juives* 82 (1926): 49–54.

54. Paula Hyman, *From Dreyfus to Vichy* (New York: Columbia University Press, 1979), 22, quoting Romain Rolland.

55. Sylvain Lévi, "Allocution to the General Assembly of the Société des Études Juives, séance of 24 January 1904," *Revue des études juives* 66 (1913): ii.

56. Ibid.

57. Salomon Reinach, "Zadok-Kahn" (1908), *Cultes, mythes, et religions*, 1st ed., vol. 5, p. 443.

58. James Darmesteter, *Les Prophètes d'Israel* (Paris: Calmann Lévy, 1892), 4.

59. James Darmesteter, "The Prophets of Israel," *Selected Essays of*

James Darmesteter, trans. Helen B. Jastrow, ed. Morris Jastrow Jr. (Boston: Houghton and Mifflin, 1895), 20.

60. Edouard Gans, "A Society to Further Jewish Integration" (1822), translation of "Halbjahriger Bericht im Verein für Cultur und Wissenschaft des Juden," in Mendes-Flohr and Reiharz, *The Jew in the Modern World*, 193. See also Salomon Reinach's tribute to Zadok Kahn, the founder of the Société des Études Juives and the *Revue des études juives* in "Zadok-Kahn," 442–43.

61. Leopold Zunz, "On Talmudic Literature" (1818), translation of "Etwas über rabbinische Literatur," in Mendes-Flohr and Reiharz, *The Jew in the Modern World*, 198.

62. George Mosse, *The Crisis of German Ideology* (New York: Grosset and Dunlap, 1964), 31–39; Poliakov, *The Aryan Myth*, 307–10. Lagarde's political orientations were well-known by his contemporaries in France. See the notice of his death in the *Revue d'histoire des religions* 25 (1892): 135.

63. Stern, *The Politics of Cultural Despair*, part 1, esp. 27–53; Poliakov, *The Aryan Myth*, 307–9.

64. Stern, *The Politics of Cultural Despair*, 41.

65. Recall that Darmesteter saw a religious compromise at the heart of the history of Israel. Ezekiel's time represented a compromise between prophetic Israel and its sacerdotal and ritualist religiosity: "A sacred nation cannot be created by the State; it requires a ritual. Sacerdotal development was the necessary consequence of political annihilation" (Darmesteter, "The Prophets of Israel," 86).

66. Henri Hubert, review of *Prolegomena zur Geschichte Israels* (1899), by Julius Wellhausen, *L'Année sociologique* 4 (1901): 218.

67. "Wellhausen, Julius," *Jewish Encyclopedia*, vol. 12 (New York: KTAV, 1960), 501.

68. See also Jean Réville, review of *Les Prophètes d'Israel*, by James Darmesteter, *Revue d'histoire des religions* 25 (1892): 256.

69. Ernest Renan, "History of the People of Israel," *Studies in Religious History*, 2d series, trans. W. M. Thompson (London: Mathieson, 1857), 94–95.

70. Salomon Reinach, "La flagellation rituele" (1904), *Cultes, mythes, et religions*, 1st ed., vol. 1, p. 173.

71. Robert Ackerman, *J. G. Frazer: His Life and Work* (Cambridge: Cambridge University Press, 1987), 81.

72. Ivan Strenski, "Henri Hubert, Racial Science, and Political Myth," *Journal of the History of the Behavioral Sciences* 23 (1987): 353–67.

73. In this vein, it should be remembered that Mannhardt and Frazer argued a version of the so-called Aryanist thesis. See Stern, *The Politics of Cultural Despair*, 40–41, and Poliakov, *The Aryan Myth*, 308–10.

74. These attempts to isolate Jews from the West doubtless stimulated Salomon Munk in particular to articulate his distinctive plans of research for the Science du Judaïsme. In precise opposition to the ideological thrust of the Aryanist desire to separate Jew and Gentile, Munk labored to show how much Judaism contributed to building the French spirit. See The Editors, "A Nos lecteurs," vii.

75. Ackerman, *J. G. Frazer*, 82.

76. Poliakov, *The Aryan Myth*, 247.

77. Louis-Gemain Lévi wrote his doctoral thesis on the family in ancient Israel. See Lukes's report of Durkheim's comments as examiner, in Lukes, *Emile Durkheim*, 626–29.

78. Israël Lévi, review of the French edition of *Rameau d'Or*, by Sir James Frazer, *Revue des études juives* 66 (1913): 141–56. Besides his piece on Frazer, Lévi wrote articles on ancient Hebrew sacrifice and ritual fasting. See Lévi, "Le Sacrifice d'Isaac et la morte de Jesus," 161–84, and Israël Lévi, "Notes sur les jêunes chez les Juifs," *Revue des études juives* 47 (1903): 161–71.

79. See the excellent discussion in Robert Ackerman, "J. G. Frazer and the Jews," *Religion* 22 (1992): 135–50.

80. Lévi, review of the French edition of *Rameau d'Or*, 141–56, esp. 156. For a thorough review of Frazer's anti-Semitism and his friendship with Solomon Schechter, see Ackerman, "J. G. Frazer and the Jews," 135–50.

81. Israël Lévi, review of the French translation of *The Golden Bough*, by Sir James Frazer, *Revue des études juives* 66 (1913): 156.

82. Richard Dorson, *The British Folklorists* (Chicago: University of Chicago Press, 1968), 285–86.

83. Marcel Mauss, "Critique interne de la 'légende d'Abraham' " (1926), *Marcel Mauss: Oeuvres*, vol. 2, *Les Fonctions sociales du sacré*, ed. Victor Karady (Paris: Minuit, 1968), 527–36.

84. Strenski, "Henri Hubert, Racial Science, and Political Myth," 353–67.

85. Émile Durkheim, contribution to H. Dagan, *Enquête sur l'antisémitisme* (Paris: Stock, 1899), 59–63.

86. Renan, "History of the People of Israel," 85.

87. Ibid., 92.

88. Ibid., 85–86. Even a scholar with the impeccable credentials of Jean Réville was apt to call Talmudic Judaism *"stérile."* See Jean Réville, review of *Die Religion des Judentums im neutestamentlichen Zeitalter*, by Wilhelm Bousset, *Revue d'histoire des religions* 48 (1903): 244.

89. Édouard Drumont, *La France juive*, 19th ed., vol. 1 (Paris: C. Marpon et E. Flammarion, 1886), 20.

90. See the exchange between Salomon Reinach and H. Prague in the pages of the conservative-leaning *Archives israëlites*. Reinach's letter

appears in 61 (1900): 389 and is answered by Prague in an emotional feature article, "Pour la foi, pour la Loi de nos pères!" *Archives israélites* 61 (1900): 393–96. The word 'ritualisme' seems to occur first in Reinach's letter to *Archives israélites*, 6 December 1900, 389, reprinted as "Réponse aux 'Archives israélites' sur le même sujet," *Cultes, mythes, et religions*, 3d ed., vol. 2, pp. 16–17, and in letters written in the same year to *L'Univers israélite* (1900), reprinted in collated form as "L'Émancipation intérieure du Judaïsme," 419.

91. Nelly Wilson, *Bernard-Lazare* (Cambridge: Cambridge University Press, 1978), 74–78.

92. Ibid., 90–92.

93. Reinach, *Cultes, mythes, et religions*, 3d ed., vol. 2, p. 420.

94. Terry N. Clark, *Prophets and Patrons* (Cambridge: Harvard University Press, 1973).

95. Lévi, "Le sacrifice d'Isaac et la mort de Jésus," 171.

96. Israël Lévi's precise place in the 're-orthodoxing' of French Judaism is not clear to me, even though his central place in the leadership of the community would seem to indicate at least a moderate position between ideological extremes. See Jean-Marc Chouraqui, "Judaisme traditionnel, science et rationalisme: L'Exemple des rabbins français au XIXe siècle," in Alvarez-Pereyre and Baumgartner, *Les études juives en France*, 44.

97. See Maurice Liber's critique of Adolf von Harnack's interpretation of Talmudic Judaism, as well as Liber's defense of it: "L'Ésprit du Christianisme et du Judaïsme," *Revue des études juives* 51 (1906): 191–216, 52 (1906): 1–23.

98. Ibid., 51:191.

99. Ibid., 52:4–7.

100. Ibid., 52:11f.

101. Ibid., 51:205.

102. Mauss, "Critique interne de la 'légende d'Abraham,'" 527–36.

103. Ibid., 530 (emphasis added).

104. Mauss, *Oeuvres*, vol. 2, p. 382.

105. Marcel Mauss, review of *Jewish Religious Movements at the Time of Jesus* (1908), by Moriz Friedländer, *Oeuvres*, vol. 2, p. 588. Mauss also cites Jacob Loeb, the founder of the *Revue des études juives*, for showing the synagogue in its best light or as a prototype of the egalitarian socialist community. See *Marcel Mauss: Oeuvres*, vol. 3, *Cohesion sociale et divisions de la sociologie*, ed. Victor Karady (Paris: Éditions de Minuit, 1969), 589, 555f.

106. Mauss, review of *Jewish Religious Movements*, 589.

107. Isidore Lévy, review of *Geschichte des Jüdischen Volkes im Zeitalter Jesu Christi*, by Emil Schürer, *L'Année sociologique* 7 (1904): 250.

108. Ibid., 253.

109. Marcel Mauss, review of *Das Gebet in altesten Christenheit* (1901), by E. Von Goltz, *L'Année sociologique* 6 (1903): 216, in *Oeuvres*, vol. 1, p. 482.

110. Ibid.

111. Ibid.

112. Extract from a letter by Durkheim and Waltz to the periodical *Le Nouvelliste* (February 1898) denying accusations that they had advised their students to take to the streets in support of Dreyfus (Dossier Emile Durkheim, Faculté de Letters, University of Bordeaux, p. 8).

113. The Durkheimians were, however, critical of some aspects of the historicism that typified the scholarship of the Science du Judaïsme.

114. Henri Dagan, "Enquête sur l'antisemitisme," in V. Karady, ed., *Émile Durkheim, Textes: religion, morale, anomie*, vol. 2 (Paris: Éditions de Minuit, 1975), 252.

115. Émile Durkheim in ibid., 253.

116. See the remarkable testament of the classicist Pierre Vidal-Naquet to this effect in *The Jews: History, Memory, and the Present* (New York: Columbia University Press, 1996), 241–42.

117. Hyman, *From Dreyfus to Vichy*, 58.

118. Hubert Bourgin, *De Jaurès à Léon Blum* (Paris: Arthème Fayard, 1938), 484.

119. Durkheim, "Report on the Situation of Russians in France in 1916," 183.

FIVE

1. Georges Condominas, "Marcel Mauss, père d'ethnographie française," *Critique* 297 (1970): 130f.

2. Jules Bloch, "Le Savant," *L'Univers Israëlite* 91 / 7 (29 November 1935): 99. This influence is especially marked in Henri Hubert and Marcel Mauss, *Sacrifice: Its Nature and Functions* (1899), trans W. D. Halls (Chicago: University of Chicago Press, 1964).

3. Sylvain Lévi, "La science des religions et les religions de l'Inde" (1892), in Jacques Bacot, ed., *Mémorial Sylvain Lévi* (Paris: Paul Hartmann, 1937), 16.

4. Marcel Mauss, review of *La Doctrine du sacrifice dans les Brâhmanas*, by Sylvain Lévi, *L'Année sociologique* 3 (1900): 293–95. The review was republished in *Marcel Mauss: Oeuvres*, vol. 1, *Les Fonctions sociales du sacré*, ed. Victor Karady (Paris: Minuit, 1968), 352.

5. Maurice Level, "Sylvain Lévi," *L'Univers Israëlite* 91 / 7 (8 November 1935): 97–98.

6. Major sources for the life and works of Sylvain Lévi are Marcel Mauss, "Sylvain Lévi" (1935), *Marcel Mauss: Oeuvres*, vol. 3, *Cohesion*

sociale et divisions de la sociologie, ed. Victor Karady (Paris: Éditions de Minuit, 1969), 535–47, and Bacot, *Mémorial Sylvain Lévi.* See also the *nécrologie* by Isidore Lévy, "Sylvain Lévi (1863–1935)," *Revue des études juives* 100 (1935): 1–3.

7. Mauss, "Sylvain Lévi," 537.

8. Ibid., 539.

9. See the records of the debate within the Fifth Section over Hubert's election. Leading those pressing Hubert's case was Sylvain Lévi. *Proces Verbaux. Ecole Pratique des Hautes Etudes, Fifth Section,* 9 June 1901, 26off.

10. Level, "Sylvain Lévi," 97.

11. Leon Poliakov, *The Aryan Myth* (New York: New American Library, 1971), ch. 9.

12. In his *L'Avenir religieux des sociétés modernes* (1860), Renan said, "The Semites have nothing further to do that is essential" (quoted in Poliakov, *The Aryan Myth,* 207).

13. Jean Filliozat, "Diversité d'oeuvre de Sylvain Lévi," in Luciano Petech, ed., *Hommage à Sylvain Lévi: Pour le centenaire de sa naissance (1963)* (Paris: Bocard, 1964), 53.

14. Mauss, "Sylvain Lévi," 542.

15. In citing the Science du Judaïsme, I am also tipping my hat at least halfway toward Robert Alun Jones's claims as to the *ultimate* importance of German thought in the Durkheimian circle, even if not quite as he conceives it. The original Jewish Wissenschaft des Judentums was born, after all, from a German ancestor. As a Jewish adaptation of the text-critical historical methods of early-nineteenth-century German history, it owed much to non-Jewish sources. But having established the ultimate (and by the beginning of the twentieth century) the remote origins of Mauss's historicist concern with 'things,' its immediate lineage is clearly both Jewish and French. Hubert, on the other hand, was trained in essentially the same (ultimately German) historiography, but in its Catholic modernist incarnation, at the hands of the great Catholic church historian Monseigneur Louis Duchesne, by way of Renan—and thus of course by the same German traditions of historical criticism of the Bible. The story of Mauss's becoming a historian in the spirit of the Science du Judaïsme is a real conversion story and is worth telling for insight into how significant his move was from Cartesian idealism to historicist concern with 'things.'

16. Perrine Simon-Nahum, "Émergence et spécificité d'une 'Science du Judaisme' française (1840–1890)," in Frank Alvarez-Pereyre and Jean Baumgartner, eds., *Les Études juives en France* (Paris: Éditions CNRS, 1990), 26.

17. Sylvain Lévi, "Problèmes indo-hébraïques," *Revue des études juives* 82 (1926): 49–54.

18. Simon-Nahum, "Émergence et spécificité d'une 'Science du Judaisme' française," 26.

19. Sylvain Lévi was, along with Durkheim, Mauss, Lucien Herr, and about five hundred others, a member of the "gauchiste" association, the "Ligue républicaine d'Alsace et de Lorraine." See Charles Andler, *Vie de Lucien Herr* (Paris: Rieder, 1932), 261. For biographical details, see also Level, "Sylvain Lévi," 97–98. Durkheim himself also worked to aid Russian Jewish immigrants at the same time.

20. Level, "Sylvain Lévi," 97.

21. Émile Durkheim, "Individualism and the Intellectuals" (1898), in W. S. F. Pickering, ed., *Durkheim on Religion* (London: Routledge and Kegan Paul, 1975), ch. 4.

22. See the many articles, especially in the conservative *Archives israëlites*, advocating renewal of ritual life among the members of the French Jewish community. In *Archives israëlites* 61 (1900) alone, note "Rituel du Judaisme" (62), "La Régéneration Religieuse" and a practical guide to religious practice (181), and the recurrent headline "Études de culte" (870–71).

23. Level, "Sylvain Lévi," 97.

24. Ibid., 97.

25. Sylvain Lévi, "Rituel du Judaisme," *Archives israëlites* 61 (1900): 62, and "La Régéneration Religieuse," *Archives israëlites* 61 (1900): 181.

26. See chapter 4 of this work, "How Durkheim Read the Talmud."

27. Phyllis Cohen Albert, "Nonorthodox Attitudes in Nineteenth Century French Judaism," in Frances Malino and Phyllis Cohen Albert, eds., *Essays in Modern Jewish History* (Rutherford, N.J.: Fairleigh Dickinson University Press, 1982), 135.

28. Mauss, "Sylvain Lévi," 541.

29. Ibid. *(necrologie)*, 543.

30. In conversation, both Georges Dumézil and Girard Hubert, the younger son of Henri Hubert, claimed that at least in the 1940s, Mauss observed certain Jewish holidays—but apparently only those reserved for the home.

31. Mauss, "Sylvain Lévi," 542.

32. Marcel Mauss, "Critique interne de la 'légende d'Abraham'" (1926), originally in "Mélanges offerts à M. Israël Lévi," *Revue des études juives* 82 (1926), reprinted in *Oeuvres*, vol. 2, p. 530 (emphasis added).

33. Poliakov, *The Aryan Myth*, 183–88; on Renan as Aryanist, see 206–9.

34. Ernest Renan, "Discours d'ouverture au Collège de France" (1862), cited in Poliakov, *The Aryan Myth*, 207. Later, as a member of the Société des Études Juives, Renan changed his tune, but by then his anti-Semitic opinions had already spread abroad. See Poliakov, *The*

Aryan Myth, 206. See also Renan's *Le Judaisme comme race et comme religion* (Paris: Calmann Lévy, 1883).

35. An example of how this was true for the study of the ancient Aryan religions can be found in Poliakov, *The Aryan Myth*, and as undertaken by the Durkheimians in Ivan Strenski, "Henri Hubert, Racial Science, and Political Myth," *Journal of the History of the Behavioral Sciences* 23 (1987): 353–67.

36. Poliakov, *The Aryan Myth*.

37. Lévi, "Problèmes indo-hébraïques," 49–54; Sylvain Lévi, "Allocution to the General Assembly of the Sociéte des Études Juives, séance of 24 January 1904," *Revue des études juives* 66 (1913); Sylvain Lévi, "Eastern Humanism" (1922), *L'Inde et le monde* (Paris: Honoré Champion, 1926); Sylvain Lévi, "Religions universelles et religions particulières" (1928), in Bacot, *Mémorial Sylvain Lévi;* Sylvain Lévi, *Pré-aryen et pré-dravidien dans L'Inde* (Paris: Imprimerie Nationale, 1923).

38. In this sense as well, Mauss's student Louis Dumont operates by the same logic of posing India as a kind of mirror image of ourselves. See Louis Dumont, *La Civilisation indienne et nous* (Paris: Armand Colin, 1964).

39. Readers familiar with the work of historian John Dunn will recognize my own version of his view that intellectual history ought to be seen as "the history of an activity" (87). Here the "activity" in question is a pitched intellectual battle against scholarly anti-Semitism. John Dunn, "The Identity of the History of Ideas," *Philosophy* 43 (1968): 85–104.

40. The use that German scholars made of such symbols was well understood in the 1930s. See "Dans le troisième Reich," *L'Univers Israélite* 91/7 (29 November 1935): 103. There the author cites the German interior minister, Dr. Frick, as saying that German cultural sciences generally wanted sharply to demarcate Germans from other peoples.

41. Lévi, *Pré-aryen et pré-dravidien dans L'Inde*, 52.

42. The cultural significance of Buddhism in France at this time should be noted. Although surely a great exaggeration, contemporary sources have claimed that there were "300,000 practicing French Buddhists in the early 1890's." Richard D. Sonn, *Anarchism and Cultural Politics in Fin de Siécle France* (Lincoln: University of Nebraska Press, 1989), 277, citing Emile Cère, "Le Bréviare du Boudhhiste," *Les Entretiens Politiques et Littéraires* 7 (10 August 1893): 113.

43. Paul Mus claims that Marcel Mauss brought out this conclusion from Sylvain Lévi's work, but I can find no trace of this view attributed to Mauss in his review of *La Doctrine du sacrifice*, 293–95. See Paul Mus, "La Mythologie primitive et la pensée de l'Inde," *Bulletin de la Societé Française de Philosophie* 37 (1937): 111.

44. Note in particular Sylvain Lévi's arguments about the role of

Indian Buddhist sea merchants in spreading Indian civilization or the evidence of Jewish settlements on the subcontinent. See, respectively, Sylvain Lévi, "Les 'marchands de mer' et leur rôle dans le bouddhisme primitif" (1929), in Bacot, *Mémorial Sylvain Lévi*, 133–44, and Lévi, "Problemes Indo-hebraiques," 49–54.

45. Strenski, "Henri Hubert, Racial Science, and Political Myth," 353–67.

46. In this way, the Aryanists seemed to fulfil Schopenhauer's vision of a renovated Christianity achieved by replacing its Jewish foundation with Hinduism. See Poliakov, *The Aryan Myth*, 247.

47. The Assumptionist fathers who edited *La Croix* likewise held Talmudic Judaism in contempt, viewing it as a form of anti-Christianism created in opposition to the new teachings of Jesus. See Pierre Sorlin, *"La Croix" et les Juifs* (Paris: Grasset, 1967), 138.

48. Louis Renou, "Sylvain Lévi et son oeuvre scientifique," in Bacot, *Mémorial Sylvain Lévi*, xxii.

49. Sylvain Lévi, *Une Renaissance juive en Judée*, Ligue des Amis du Sionisme, Tract No. 5 (Paris: Driay-Cahen, 1918).

50. Ibid., 22; James Darmesteter, *Les Prophètes d'Israel* (Paris: Calmann Lévy, 1892).

51. Lévi, *Une Renaissance juive en Judée*, 22.

52. Ibid., 13.

53. Ibid., 22.

54. Ibid., 22.

55. Strenski, "Henri Hubert, Racial Science, and Political Myth," 353–67.

56. Louis Dumont, "Marcel Mauss: A Science in Becoming," *Essays on Individualism* (Chicago: University of Chicago Press, 1986), 185.

57. Albert Réville, "Contemporaneous Materialism in Religion: The Sacred Heart," *Theological Review* 44 (January 1874): 154.

58. Mauss, review of *La Doctrine du sacrifice*, 353.

59. François-A. Isambert, "At the Frontier of Folklore and Sociology: Hubert, Hertz, and Czarnowski, Founders of a Sociology of Folk Religion," in Philippe Besnard, ed., *The Sociological Domain* (Cambridge: Cambridge University Press, 1983), 189.

60. Émile Durkheim, "Contribution to Discussion 'Religious Sentiment at the Present Time' " (1919), in Pickering, *Durkheim on Religion*, 182.

61. See David N. Myers, *Re-Inventing the Jewish Past: European Jewish Intellectuals and the Zionist Return to History* (New York: Oxford University Press, 1995), 31, for a discussion of the parallel trends among German Jewish thinkers for seeing Judaism as requiring a "materialization."

62. Maurice Liber, "L'Ésprit du Christianisme et du Judaisme," *Revue des études juives* 51 (1906): 192.

63. Henri Prague, editor's reply to an anonymous letter, *Archives israélites* 61 (6 September 1900): 891.

64. Lévi, "Eastern Humanism," 158–59.

65. Ibid., 168.

66. Ibid., 168, 170.

67. Ibid., 169.

68. Sylvain Lévi, "Civilisation brahmanique," *L'Inde et le monde*, 90.

69. Sylvain Lévi, *La Doctrine du sacrifice dans les Brâhmanas* (Paris: Leroux, 1898), 10–11.

70. Lévi, "Civilisation brahmanique," 88. Note that the role of sacrifice in preserving Hindu culture was picked up in Albrecht Barth's review of *La Doctrine du sacrifice dans les Brâhmanas*, by Sylvain Lévi, *Revue d'histoire des religions* 39 (1899): 90.

71. In this vein, one cannot in all likelihood separate Lévi's horror at the Islamic conquest of India from the present-day danger that was posed by a renascent, militant, and thus socially incarnate Islam against the virtually disembodied Jews living in Muslim lands. Jews were virtually defenseless without an appropriately 'muscular' social body to preserve them from an embodied Islam. Lévi doubtless saw in the perceived Muslim threat to contemporary Jews in the Near East the potential for a historical replay of Muslim intolerance toward Buddhists and Hindus during the Mughal invasion of India. He felt that the brutal destruction of so much of Indian civilization during the invasion could be laid at the door of Muslim "fanatics." See Sylvain Lévi, "Abel Bergaigne et l'Indianisme" (1890), in Bacot, *Mémorial Sylvain Lévi*, 13.

Compounding Lévi's concern was the fact that reactionary anti-Semitic Catholics in the France of his day were, like the Muslims, notorious for their desire to see religion and state fused into a seamless (of course, Roman Catholic) unity. Making matters worse, intransigent Catholic propaganda routinely proclaimed the virtues of Islam in making the case for Catholic renewal. Given the fundamental fusion of politics and religion by Muslims and intransigent Catholics, and the relative vulnerability of Jews in the Muslim lands and (at least after Dreyfus) perhaps also in France, Lévi contemplated some very disturbing symbolic equivalences. See Richard Griffiths, *The Reactionary Revolution: The Catholic Revival in French Literature, 1870–1914* (London: Constable, 1966), 244ff.

72. Lévi, *L'Inde et le monde*, 161, 168.

73. Lévi, "Civilisation brahmanique," 91.

74. Sylvain Lévi, "Civilisation bouddhique," *L'Inde et le monde*, 123.

75. Ibid., 118.

76. Ibid., 119.

77. Ibid., 125.

78. Ibid., 123.

79. Ibid., 119.

80. Michel Abitbol, *Les Deux terres promises: Les Juifs de France et le sionisme* (Paris: Olivier Orban, 1989), 37f., 68–88.

81. Ibid., 69.

82. Ibid., 71.

83. Ibid., 69.

84. Ibid., 71–80.

85. Ibid., 78f.

86. Ibid., 38.

87. Ibid., 38f.

88. Lévi, *Une Renaissance juive en Judée,* 14. Lévi reportedly asked that he be sent on this mission by the French foreign ministry (Level, "Sylvain Lévi," 98).

89. Lévi, *Une Renaissance juive en Judée,* 18.

90. Ibid., 11–12.

91. Ibid., 20.

92. Ibid., 21.

93. Level, "Sylvain Lévi," 98.

94. Ibid., 97. Level reports that Lévi was "shaken" by the Dreyfus decision.

95. Myers, *Re-Inventing the Jewish Past,* 31.

96. Thus, the German historicist origins of the methodology of the Wissenschaft des Judentums reinforces Jones's claim about the importance of German thought for the Durkheimian conviction of the need to study 'things.'

97. Hubert and Mauss, *Sacrifice,* was little more than a Durkheimian theology of sacrifice, "a kind of *philosophy* of sacrificial ritual"—*Revue d'histoire et de littérature religieuses* 7 (1902): 281 (emphasis added). It pretended to be "*the* theory of sacrifice" but was only "*one* of the theories which explain certain aspects of sacrifices in certain circumstances of time and place." Marcel Hébert, *Revue d'histoire et de littérature religieuses,* n.s. 1 (1909): 71.

98. Dumont, "Marcel Mauss," 184.

99. Ibid., 183–201.

100. Robert Alun Jones and Douglas A. Kibbee, "Durkheim, Language, and History: A Pragmatist Perspective," *Sociological Theory* 11 (1993): 152–70.

101. Ivan Strenski, "Émile Durkheim, Henri Hubert, et le discours des modernistes religieux sur le symbolisme," *L'Ethnographie* 91/117 (1995): 33–52.

102. Mauss, "Sylvain Lévi," 535.

103. Ibid., 537.

104. Hartwig Derenbourg, "La Science des religions et l'Islamisme," *Revue de l'histoire des religions* 13 (1886): 302.

105. See chapter 7 of my manuscript in preparation, "Positivism, Sacrifice, and a New History of Religions: The Durkheimians and Roman Catholic Liberalism."

106. Dumont, "Marcel Mauss," ch. 7.

107. Ivan Strenski, "Durkheim, Hamelin, and the 'French Hegel,' " *Historical Reflections/Réfléxions historiques* 16 (1989): 135–70.

108. Mauss, "Sylvain Lévi," 537.

109. Sylvain Lévi, letter to Marcel Mauss, Katmandu, 19 February 1898, Mauss Archives, Collège de France. I thank Marcel Fournier for this citation.

110. Mauss, "Sylvain Lévi," 537.

111. Lévi, *La Doctrine.*

112. Mauss, "Sylvain Lévi," 539.

113. Dumont, "Marcel Mauss," 183f.

114. Griffiths, *The Reactionary Revolution;* Réville, "Contemporaneous Materialism in Religion," 138–56.

115. This priority of performance over text became for Sylvain Lévi part of the polemics he and Abel Bergaigne waged against the German Aryan nationalists and even Max Müller (Renou, "Sylvain Lévi et son oeuvre scientifique," xiv); the other seems to have been Bergaigne's reading of Andrew Lang's ritualist criticism of Müller. Further, along with his teacher Bergaigne, Sylvain Lévi had a strong feeling for the arts, especially theater. Under Bergaigne, he wrote his groundbreaking doctorate on the history of Indian theater (1890). Renou locates the work within the context of a longer French tradition of interest in ancient Indian dramatic texts but credits Lévi with being the first to master the entire range of Indian dramatic texts *and* performances, from popular to classic forms. Lévi went so far as to suggest general priority of various theatrical performances to the poetry attending them.

116. Renou, "Sylvain Lévi et son oeuvre scientifique," xv.

117. Mus, "La Mythologie primitive," 119. See also Hubert and Mauss's connection of James Darmesteter to Bergaigne and Sylvain Lévi on Vedic texts in Hubert and Mauss, *Sacrifice,* 64 and n. 370.

118. Salomon Reinach, "The Growth of Mythological Study," *Quarterly Review* 215 (1911): 437.

119. Gabriel Monod, "James Darmesteter," *Portraits et souvenirs* (Paris: Calmann Lévy, 1897), 162f. Also see Darmesteter on the need for religion to be embodied in rituals: "The Prophets of Israel," *Selected Essays of James Darmesteter,* trans. Helen B. Jastrow, ed. Morris Jastrow Jr. (Boston: Houghton and Mifflin, 1895), 59.

120. Mus, "La Mythologie primitive," 119. See also Lévi, "Abel Ber-

gaigne et l'Indianisme," 7–9. Although he was more concerned about Max Müller's solarist interpretation of myths than his mythological reading of the Vedas, Salomon Reinach identifies our ritualists as the first critics of solarism—"Max Müllerism" as he calls it—as "Barth, Bergaigne and Darmesteter" (Reinach, "The Growth of Mythological Study," 437).

121. Abel Bergaigne, *Abel Bergaigne's "Vedic Religion,"* vol. 3 (1878–83), trans. V. G. Paranjoti (Delhi: Motilal Banarsidass, 1978), 283.

122. Ibid.

123. Mauss, "Sylvain Lévi," 537.

124. Robert Alun Jones, "Robertson Smith, Durkheim, and Sacrifice: An Historical Context for *The Elementary Forms of the Religious Life,*" *Journal of the History of the Behavioral Sciences* 17 (1981): 184–205. But see Durkheim's citations to Bergaigne in Émile Durkheim, *The Elementary Forms of the Religious Life,* trans. Joseph W. Swain (New York: Free Press, 1915), 49–50.

125. Mauss, "Sylvain Lévi," 538.

126. But also note that Sylvain Lévi allows a role for the spoken word: "Sacrifice is a learned and complicated combination of ritual acts and sacred speech, or rather it is the impalpable and irresistible power which is released from their reconciliation, like electricity is born from elements put into contact" (Lévi, *La Doctrine,* 77).

127. This is confirmed by Louis Renou, who says that for Lévi, "ritual dominates mythology" (Renou, "Sylvain Lévi et son oeuvre scientifique," xxiii).

128. Lévi, *La Doctrine,* ch. 2. This is noted as well by Mauss in his review of *La Doctrine du sacrifice,* 353.

129. Ibid.

130. Lévi, *La Doctrine,* 27. See also p. 38, where sacrifice is identified as the life source of the gods; p. 54, where it is said to save the gods; and p. 76, where the superiority of sacrifice to the gods—in particular, Indra—is asserted.

131. Louis Renou, preface to *La Doctrine du sacrifice dans les brâhmanas,* by Sylvain Lévi, 2d ed. (Paris: Presses Universitaires de France, 1966), viii. Renou refers specifically to sacrificial ritual.

132. Mauss, review of *La Doctrine du sacrifice,* 353.

133. Marcel Mauss, "An Intellectual Self-Portrait," in Besnard, *The Sociological Domain,* 148.

134. Lévi, *La Doctrine,* 77.

135. Ibid.

136. Henri Hubert and Marcel Mauss, "Introduction à l'analyse de quelques phénomènes religieux" (1906), *Oeuvres,* vol. 1, p. 17.

137. Lévi, *La Doctrine,* 10–11. Renou even notes that *La Doctrine du*

sacrifice serves as a "counterpart" for Abel Bergaigne's *Vedic Religion* (Renou, "Sylvain Lévi et son oeuvre scientifique," xxiii).

138. Durkheim, however, does not explicitly refer here to the authority of Sylvain Lévi but to Abel Bergaigne (Lévi's own teacher), Eugene Burnouf, and Hermann Oldenberg. See Durkheim, *Elementary Forms of the Religious Life*, 45–50.

139. Lévi, *La Doctrine*, 9. Unlike Max Müller and the German *volkish* thinkers, Lévi held that the later Brâhmanas are even more ritualistic, indeed more 'primitive' and brutal than the Vedas. Interestingly Sylvain Lévi's claim that the Brahmins practiced a violent rite conflicts with early German romantic views—for example, those of Herder—that the Brahmins were actually remarkably gentle. See Poliakov, *The Aryan Myth*, 186. Barth is critical of Lévi, saying he paints a "blacker" picture of the Brahmins than the reality, indeed perhaps even painting a "caricature" (Barth, review of *La Doctrine du sacrifice*, 91).

140. Lévi, *La Doctrine*, 9.

141. Ibid., 10.

142. Fritz Stern, *The Politics of Cultural Despair* (Berkeley: University of California Press, 1961), ch. 1.

143. Émile Durkheim, review of *L'Irreligion de l'avenir* (1887), by Jean-Marie Guyau, in Pickering, *Durkheim on Religion*, 26. Also cited in W. S. F. Pickering, *Durkheim's Sociology of Religion: Themes and Theories* (London: Routledge and Kegan Paul, 1984), 326.

144. Sylvain Lévi had maintained very close personal relations with Marcel Mauss from at least the last years of the nineteenth century until his own death in 1935.

SIX

1. Richard B. Straus, "Avraham Burg: Seizing the Moment to Transform Israel into a Peaceful, Modern Nation" (interview), *Los Angeles Times*, 31 March 1996, M3.

2. Émile Durkheim, *The Elementary Forms of the Religious Life*, trans. Joseph W. Swain (New York: Free Press, 1915), 13.

3. Ibid.

4. See, for instance, Émile Durkheim and Ernest Lavisse, *Lettres à tous les français* (1916), ed. Michel Maffesoli (Paris: Armand Colin, 1992), and Émile Durkheim, *L'Allemagne au-dessus de tout: La Mentalité allemande et la guerre* (Paris: Armand Colin, 1915).

5. Durkheim, *L'Allemagne*.

6. Ibid., 23 (emphasis in original).

7. On Protestant views of the war, see Daniel Robert, "Les Protestants français et la guerre de 1914–1918," *Francia* 2 (1974): 415–30.

8. Durkheim, *Elementary Forms of the Religious Life*, 381–85.

9. Ibid., 384–85.

10. Robert Alun Jones and Douglas A. Kibbee, "Durkheim, Language, and History: A Pragmatist Perspective," *Sociological Theory* 11 (1993): 152–70.

11. Émile Durkheim, "Course in Social Science: Inaugural Lecture" (1887), translated with an introduction by Neville Layne, in "Émile Durkheim's Inaugural Lecture at Bordeaux," *Sociological Inquiry* 44 (1974): 197.

12. Marc Bloch, *The Royal Touch: Monarchy and Miracles in France and England*, trans. J. E. Anderson (1923; reprint, New York: Dorset Press, 1961).

13. Marc Bloch, *Feudal Society: The Growth of Ties of Dependence*, vol. 1, trans. L. A. Manyon (Chicago: University of Chicago Press, 1961), 81–87.

14. Talcott Parsons, *The Structure of Social Action* (New York: Free Press, 1937), 29, 476f., referring to Alfred North Whitehead's *Science and the Modern World* (New York: MacMillan, 1925), 75f. On these points, see as well Jeffrey Alexander, *Theoretical Logic in Sociology*, vol. 2, *The Antinomies of Classical Thought: Marx and Durkheim* (Berkeley: University of California Press, 1982), 79f.

INDEX